Caribbean Theology

Research in Religion and Family
Black Perspectives

Noel Leo Erskine
General Editor

Vol. 2

PETER LANG
New York • Washington, DC/Baltimore • San Francisco
Bern • Frankfurt am Main • Berlin • Vienna • Paris

Lewin Williams

Caribbean Theology

PETER LANG
New York • Washington, DC/Baltimore • San Francisco
Bern • Frankfurt am Main • Berlin • Vienna • Paris

Library of Congress Cataloging-in-Publication Data

Williams, Lewin Lascelles.
   Caribbean theology / Lewin Lascelles Williams.
      p.   cm. — (Research in religion and family; vol. 2)
   Includes bibliographical references.
      1. Theology, Doctrinal—Caribbean Area. 2. Christianity and culture.
   I. Title. II. Series.
   BT30.C27.W55   1994   230'.09729—dc20   93-16707
   ISBN 0-8204-1859-5 (hardcover)   CIP
   ISBN 0-8204-6709-X (paperback)
   ISSN 1055-1158

Die Deutsche Bibliothek-CIP-Einheitsaufnahme

Williams, Lewin L.:
Caribbean theology / Lewin L. Williams. - New York; Bern; Berlin;
Frankfurt/M.; Paris; Wien: Lang, 1994
   (Research in religion and family; Vol. 2)
   ISBN 0-8204-1859-5
NE: GT

Cover design by James F. Brisson

The paper in this book meets the guidelines for permanence and durability of
the Committee on Production Guidelines for Book Longevity of the
Council on Library Resources.

Table of Contents

Acknowledgements... vii

Prologue ix

Introduction.. 1

Part One   **Factors Giving Rise to Indigenization** 5
Chapter One   Geo-Political Expansion and
                Evangelization... 9
Chapter Two   Missionary Theology As Theology of
                Domination 31

Part Two   **Essential Characteristics of Caribbean**
                Theology... 55
Chapter Three Interpretive Tools... 59
Chapter Four   Sources and Method for Caribbean
                Theology.. 93
Chapter Five   Issues in Caribbean Theology 123

Part Three   **A Critical Evaluation**..................................... 175
Chapter Six   The Theological Consensus........................ 177
Chapter Seven The Validity of Indigenization.................... 193

Epilogue 215

Bibliography... 219

Acknowledgements

There are several persons whose contributions in one way or another have helped to make this project possible. I will be eternally grateful to Professor Christopher Morse whose persistent demand for clarity has been of enormous help in shaping it. In fact I consider myself fortunate to have had the support of persons such as Professors Tom Driver, James Washington and Noel Erskine whose guidance has meant much for my personal growth. Special thanks to Professor Erskine for introducing me to the publishers.

As for the library and research help, I now know what a pest I must have been to Betty Bolden in the Union Theological Seminary library. I owe a debt of gratitude to the Rev. Allan Kirton, General Secretary of the Caribbean Conference of Churches for the use of the C.C.C.'s research center, and especially to Ms. Lisbeth Bessil-Watson for her enormous help with research material. I extend my sincere thanks to the United Theological College of the West Indies for the totally unrestricted use of the library, and to the past librarian Ms. Carol Gregory for her personal assistance. I am grateful to Winnifred Reynolds who not only overburdened her library privileges on my account but actually visited libraries to collect material on my behalf. My sincere gratitude goes to Piere DePass, without whose computer expertise this document could have been lost more times than it was.

Finally, I come to Joyce Williams. I here mention the fact that she typed and retyped this work, only because it is a physically draining experience to spend sleepless nights trying to meet deadlines. However Joyce's involvement in this project goes beyond the typing. I cannot even imagine having the courage to tackle this project without her constant emotional support and intellectual stimulation. When I add to that her personal concern for my health and welfare, and yet her spurring me to keep pace with requirements and deadlines, I can only conclude that for this project, as for any other, Joyce is "the wind beneath my wing." To Joyce I owe an undying debt of gratitude.

Prologue

Professor Lewin Williams has placed us in his debt in giving us this excellent treatment of *Caribbean Theology*. Because there are some seven hundred Islands bathed by the Caribbean sea representing many cultures and languages few persons have undertaken this large task of relating theology to this region. The decade of the eighties is in some regard a lost decade as the church and its theologians in the Caribbean have been very quiet. But Dr. Williams has broken the silence and has sought to allow us to listen in on the conversation among these various cultures in the region as they relate God-talk to their own situation. Williams helps us make the connection between the divine and the worldly, faith and life, Jesus and the times. This joining of faith and life Jesus and the times, forces the church to talk about its mission from the concreteness of everyday life. The central issue that confronts the church in this region has to do with its understanding of its mission. How may the church understand its mission?

Journey Inward and Outward

How may the church in the Caribbean understand its mission? Is it by preserving and maintaining its identity or is it by becoming relevant in relation to its context? How may the church make a difference in the Caribbean? For some churches the first tendency is to attempt to protect and preserve their own distinctiveness. This often means *the journey inward,* to protect and preserve faith. Many churches seem to find their identity focused around their internal experience as congregations in worship and fellowship. The church's fear of losing its faith makes it protective and defensive. This fear threatens the freedom of faith and makes Caribbean Christians afraid to venture into the world witnessing to the gospel.

This fear also makes the church withdraw from the world in the hope of preserving its identity. A consequence of this withdrawal is that the church becomes preoccupied with itself and thereby becomes irrelevant in its context. This is sometimes seen in a local church's preoccupation with survival. Its budgets are for buildings and maintenance, very little if anything is for mission to those who die from poverty and neglect.

Professor Williams reminds us that in the Caribbean a great number of the expressions of faith result in an accommodation to culture. The Christ witnessed to in the church is often the "Christ of culture" rather than the "Christ who transforms culture". A great deal of the preaching presents a Christ who comforts the comfortable rather than a Christ who disturbs the complacent. The worship is often not in dialogue with the world but rather represents a withdrawal from the world. This means that the idols that the world worships are the very ones that are worshipped in the church; the idols of class, race, success, prestige and power.

This journey inward fails to come to grips with issues of economic justice and inequality in Caribbean society. The journey inward often leads the church into a compromise with the status quo's attempt to keep the poor in their place, and thereby ignores their struggle for meaning in the world.

It is precisely at this point that Colonial theology emphasizes the saving of souls while the unjust conditions in which victims live are ignored. Needless to say this gospel is individualistic and private, neglecting the needs of the community and the circumstances that keep the community in bondage. This approach to the church's mission in the Caribbean fails to make a connection between evangelization and humanization. This is illustrated in the old forms of missiology in which the churches in North America and Europe would send missionaries to the Caribbean to save the souls of the "natives" while the structures of oppression remain unchanged. Missionary theology does not see the task of the church as improving the quality of life for Caribbean people in terms of health care, better housing, education and the destruction of poverty that crushes the souls of our people. Missionary theology has been content to preach to the soul while it neglects the environment in which the soul seeks to make meaning.

Breaking the Chains

As the Caribbean Church begins to perceive its mission as the breaking of the chains that bind the poor and oppress the weak and deliver them from inner apathy and indifference, this church begins to learn that in Jesus Christ evangelization and humanization are joined. For the church to ask for a changed person and not changed circumstance in which the person lives is for the church to refuse to ask for a changed life. Also, to ask for changed circumstance without a changed person is an exercise in futility.

The gospel of our Lord makes it clear that situations in which there is no freedom are contexts that must be broken through for Christ. As the church grounds its identity in Jesus Christ it cannot any longer be content to co-exist side by side with any form of economic and social oppression. The Christian faith must address issues and problems of politics, which for economic and social reason oppress and make impossible the life of faith.

As the church articulates its mission, it must announce that God sets people free from all prisons. The prisoners must be freed. The weak must be strengthened. The empty must be filled. And all humanity must come to see the salvation of our God.

Christian mission must be informed by two warrants at once. Personal salvation must mean at the same time a commitment for structural social change. The believer who has discovered God's will for his or her life cannot any longer be a detached observer of history but must seek to discover what God is up to in the world and join God.

The Caribbean church must affirm that commitment to the transformation of the world and the individual is the church's primary task. In a profound sense then the changing of the individual and the transformation of the world are not two separate events but two aspects of the same event. It is rather similar to justification and sanctification. In justification God's will for our lives and our world is made plain. In sanctification we respond in obedience to Jesus Christ and discover that not merely our private islands are transformed but also our world.

As the Caribbean church takes its mission seriously it must call attention to the corporate nature of sin. The church must assert that sin is not merely a private and individualistic transgression which will be cured by an individual act of repentance, which leaves unchallenged the social order. Rather, the church must begin to view sin as a social, historical fact that manifests itself in oppressive structures, in human exploitations and domination of peoples, races, and classes.

St. Paul hints at this when he speaks of evil as "principalities and powers." Sin builds up corporate structures of alienation and oppression which a person cannot overcome by an act of repentance; salvation from corporate evil may mean for the church to participate in political processes that seek to destroy poverty and injustice. The Caribbean church must assert that action in the name of justice and participation in the changing of unjust structures are integral to its mission.

The Good News Is For The Poor

This approach to the mission of the church will ensure that the poor are not excluded. The good news is for the poor. This approach to mission will also ensure that the Caribbean church will not be able to sit on the fence of indifference and ineffectively wash its hands as Pilate did in an attempt to be uninvolved. Mission will mean risking with those whom the world count as nothing. Faith becomes activity with and on behalf of those who are weak and heavy laden. Authentic mission will mean solidarity with the poor and oppressed. As the church lives out its mission it is called to become the body of Christ in the world (Luke 10:25-37). As our Lord took our infirmities and diseases upon himself (Matthew 8:17) so ought we to risk ourselves for others.

The theme of a God who is made known through suffering is one that runs through scripture and the Christian tradition. Philippians 2:5 indicates that the form Christ takes in the world is that of servant. In 2 Corinthians 8:9 Paul reminds his congregation, that though Christ was rich yet for their sakes he became poor, so that through his poverty they may become rich. In 2 Corinthians 4:10 Paul states that he carries around in his own body the death of Jesus, so that the life of Jesus may also be manifested in our bodies... So death is work in us, but life in you.

This sharing in the death and sufferings of Jesus is what it means to be a church in mission (John 20:21). It is as the church enters into solidarity with the victims of oppression that it becomes the focus of divine activity in the world. To know God's will is to be united with Christ and to be homeless as Jesus was homeless. The church's mission is to risk itself in obedience to Christ. It is to take up the cross daily and follow Jesus.

Noel Leo Erskine

To Joyce

Introduction

In November 1971, (5 years before the celebrated meeting of EATWOT in Dar-es-Salaam) church representatives from various parts of the Caribbean met in Trinidad for the Caribbean Ecumenical Consultation for Development. Here the social, political and economic issues were addressed on an unprecedented scale, by the church in the region.[1] This conference has been recognized as the birth of the indigenizing process of theology in the area.[2] The working consensus was an established desire to disengage with the missionary theology of Europe and North America and formulate a new theology which would address problems of the Caribbean context. The papers presented at two follow-up conferences in 1973 are a testimony to that consensus.[3]

Subsequent to these conferences has been an outpouring of theological reflection which is not only determined by the Caribbean context, but also addresses it directly, utilizing a forum comprising books, periodicals, sermons and newspapers. The arguments range from the failure of missionary theology to address Caribbean self-development, to how theology ought to be shaped to address contextual problems.

The task of this work is to:

1. Compile the data into a continuum, submitted to a process of interpretation.

2. Examine some of the issues raised in the new process of indigenization and attempt to clarify them into a system of thought.

3. Evaluate the prospect for its success in dealing with the contextual issues pertinent to self-actualization of the Caribbean people.

4. One of the questions posed in the region is whether it should be considered a unit, or should each territory stand on its own individual merit. Some are inclined to conclude that neither history nor sociology will allow any meaningful separations. Yet it is the hope of this investigative effort that indigenous theology will speak for the corporate self-awareness which will foster unity of purpose if not uniformity.

Columbus, who arrived with the banner of State and Church, made his first landing in the Bahamas 1492 and within 11 years the region was colonized by the Spanish, through the combined agencies of the Bible and the sword. However, the British, French, and Dutch who never did accept the Spanish declaration of dominance, intervened in the colonizing and evangelizing process.[4] As a result of Britain's becoming subsequently the dominant power in the region, most of the territories are English speaking. Numerically, however, more people speak Spanish than English because some of the Spanish territories (Cuba and the Dominican Republic) have the largest populations. The other languages are French (Martinique, Guadelope and Haiti) and Dutch (Curacao, Aruba, and the Dutch Leeward Islands). In the case of Surinam, although Dutch is the official language there is no common language among the ethnic groups which make up the population. For example, the Moravian Church employs as many as six dialects with which to conduct its mission.[5] All the rest except for Puerto Rico (which is Spanish) speak English. On the mainland English is the language of both Belize and Guyana.

Whatever the language in which each territory has been colonized, the experience has been similar. Not only has the region endured one of the longest periods of colonialism in modern history, but at the end of its colonial period it has been made subject to neo-colonialism. Furthermore the missionary church has given comfort to both colonialism and neo-colonialism. The similarity of experience in the different territories is the most insistent factor in the creation of a Caribbean unit.

This project therefore defines "Caribbean" as the territories within and in close proximity to the Caribbean Sea, which are characterized by their experience with slavery, colonialism and neo-colonialism, and are struggling for self-actualization. It defines "neo-colonialism" as economic, social and political control by outside forces, yet often through the agency of inside privileged classes. In recognition of the historical and sociological relationships of the region, the region is treated as a unit.

The geographical definition used sets its boundaries by the "crescent" of islands from Cuba to Trinidad. It includes portions of the mainland, Belize, Guyana and Surinam. Because of its unique revolutionary experience, Cuba receives separate treatment for that period. It is seen as a liberated entity, and therefore a reference for the other territories.

Notes

1 Taylor, Burchell K. "Caribbean Theology," in *Caribbean Journal of Religious Studies*, Volume 3. Number 2. September 1980. p.13.

2 Ibid.

3 These papers were later published in book form under Hamid, Edris, ed., *Troubling of the Waters*, Trinidad, W.I. Rahaman Printery Limited, 1973, p.26.

4 Mitchell, David I. *New Mission For A New People*. U.S.A., Friendship Press, 1977. p.12.

5 Mitchell, David I., *New Mission for A New People*, U.S.A., Friendship Press, 1977. p.12.

PART ONE

FACTORS GIVING RISE TO INDIGENIZATION

The notion of indigenization is not as clear as it sometimes appears at face value. It comes with its own complications. For example, the question of influence is unavoidable. With communication as developed as it has become, there is scarcely any significant portion of the world that is not influenced by some other portion of it. As a result, the world by national and international interaction has indeed become smaller than it was in the not too distant past. That reality by itself requires that the distinction be made between influence on the level of partners of communication on the one hand and influence as an imposition on the other, void of all reciprocity between groups, especially in the colonial patterns. There is a sense in which influence can be healthy, that is, when it is a sharing experience. However, when it becomes imposed to the detriment of the cultural and religious authenticity of the people upon whom the imposition is made, it is by no means benign.

In the case of the European evangelization of the Caribbean, the process was not always healthy. It was unhealthy because of the presumptions the Europeans made in regard to the people whom they sought to evangelize. For example, it was a feeling of cultural superiority that led the Rev. J.G. Pearson, an English Anglican clergy person in Guyana, to make the following remark about the people to whom he came to bear Christian witness:

> ...We owe it to the Negro to think for him, to help him by placing over him trustworthy men, armed with almost feudal authority to enforce such social duties as devolve upon him, and so save him from him-

self...We legislate as men for men; and so far as men are concerned all is well, but the Negro is a child.[1]

The inevitable result of such attitudes is institutional classism, not to speak of racism.

On the other hand however, processes such as the European evangelization of the Caribbean usually create their own "backlash." In this particular case, the backlash is indigenization itself. People who have had their authenticity denied and their dignity trampled will eventually react in rejection of the process which degrades them. Of course there is the question of the great length of time that the "backlash" took to come to recognizable maturity in the Caribbean. The answer to such a question is related to the thesis under consideration. That thesis is that European evangelization has been inextricably bound to European geo-political expansionism. Eugene F. Rice, Jr., a "First World" historian, confirms that it was so from the very outset:

> In 1492, shortly before the Portuguese, having thrust south and east, entered the Indian Ocean, the Spaniards were sailing westward across the Atlantic. The motives of the two were identical: to acquire wealth and save souls...Christopher Columbus (1451-1506), like Henry the Navigator, was touched by the fact that "many people believing in idolatries were lost by receiving doctrine of perdition." He left Spain prepared to smite the heathen, and he did, in fact convert them in droves to the true European faith. He also wanted to get rich.[2]

Colonialism and the missionary program, united as in matrimony, created mutually the socio-economic, political and religious conditions which in turn delayed the "indigenous backlash." Specifically, the union controlled the Caribbean body and soul in political and religious imperialism.

However, no matter how strong the desire of one group to control, manipulate and exploit another under the guise that the controlled people are like children, some things change. Children grow up, perceived needs do change, and therefore the means of meeting those needs must change also. When the evangelizing process to the Caribbean failed to change its own premise, means of communicating and style of practice, it became obsolete and incompatible with the reality of change.

Consequently part of the process of indigenization is organized against its stagnant and stagnating effects.

The process of indigenization has begun; which is not the same as saying that it is complete, because the roots of the missio-colonial control are not dead. The very reluctance of Caribbean thinkers to admit to the local authentication of the emerging process suggests that there may be some lingering need for European blessing on the process.

Notes

1 Williams, Geoffrey B., S.J. "Classicism and the Caribbean Church," ed. Idris Hamid, *Out of the Depths,* Trinidad W.I. St. Andrews Theological College, 1977, pp 53-54, citing *History of the Lutherans in Guyana* pp. 84-85.

2 Rice, Eugene F. Jr. *Foundations of Early Modern Europe, 1460-1559,* New York, W. W. Norton and Company Inc. 1970 p. 32.

Chapter One

Geo-Political Expansion and Evangelization

Various arguments suggest that missiology is its true self only when it is transported and that the missionary church has only done its duty when it has exported its faith. A Caribbean scholar, William Watty, former president of the United Theological College of the West Indies, makes the point that since communication is of the essence of theology, theology by its very nature is exported and imported. As a result there is a "built in" futility in the quest for a purely indigenous theology.[1] The point is well taken, especially when one of Watty's emphases is that the indigenization of theology is not as easily achieved as the notion is expressed. Yet it is at the very point where theology is transportable that the need for indigenization is most crucial for the Caribbean. This is so for two reasons: (1) The companion with which the European missionary theology was transported was intrinsically detrimental to the Caribbean region, and (2) its transportation lacked the reciprocity that makes communication healthy.

Missionary Influence in the Roots of Colonialism

Even if the only motive behind Columbus' voyage in search of India was to find less expensive trade routes for Spain, the venture would not have been without church influence. A prominent commodity basic to that era's trade was spices, many of which were used in the manufacture of substances for religious observances.[2] However, the cooperation between church and state in these ventures was far more intricate. Watty's research shows that while Columbus planned his second voyage it was advertised as a *missionary* journey, however when he set sail only 6 of the 1200 persons on board were clergy.[3] Watty's point is that the fewness of the missionary personnel is ample evidence that the expedition had stronger motives. Furthermore, the European evangelization process tended to venture only into areas where there was material reward. It is by no means accidental then, that the Caribbean territories first settled by the Spanish expeditions were those that had mineral resources. In fact the deposits of gold and silver found in the Caribbean and on the Mainland promptly inspired colonialism for the sole benefit of economic expansion for Europe while it brought death and destruction to the "natives." An example of how bad it was for the natives is the fact that of over one million Indians who lived in Hispaniola when Columbus landed, there were only a hundred thousand by 1510.[4] The rest had been slaughtered by the over work of slavery, imported diseases and plain Spanish cruelty. Colonial power had begun its work of destruction, and despite all the plunder and death prompted by colonial greed, the church did not disclaim its partnership with the state. Later when, because of the demise of the Indians, the decision was taken to import Africans to the New World to take up where the Indians had left off in mining and the new and permanent field of agriculture, the missionary church gave more than its sanction. Quite apart from Christianizing the Caribbean the missionary church from the outset had motives that were not Christian. Indeed by those motives the church can be said to have compromised the Christian faith as it supported and was supported by the colonial structures. The papal permission of 1503 for the enslavement of Africans and plunder of the New World is a good example of such compromise.

> Being as they are hardened in their habits of idolatry and cannibalism, it is agreed that I should issue this decree...I hereby give license and permission...to capture them...paying us the share that belongs to us and to sell them and utilize their services without incurring any penalty thereby, because if the Christians bring them to these lands and make use of their services they will be more easily converted and attracted to our Holy Faith.[5]

On the other hand, the fact that hindsight is clearer than foresight and insight has to be taken into consideration here. In all fairness one must admit that it is quite easy to view the past as an almost abstract reality with faceless groups, labeled according to various emphases one may wish to make in favor of one's position. In this case the "colonizer" and the "colonized" may be handy terms in the creation of that useful split. Hence it may be admitted that though they serve well to make the case for indigenization in the Caribbean, there are intricate factors that ought to be considered, if those labels may be understood in space and time. For example, it may be argued that the charge of compromise between missiology and colonialism as one of complicity and confusion between present day church and state, must take into consideration that "state" in 1492 was a far more complicated word than it is today. As for its separation from church, the matter requires far more than the casual glance. Garrett Mattingly makes the point that the word "state" in the middle ages was used to depict a condition instead of a political system.[6] The word lacked that meaning because the period lacked the actual political structure. He writes:

> The actual political structure they knew was a crazy quilt of overlapping jurisdictions, feudal, ecclesiastical, dynastic, corporate.[7]

In which case it is the word "estate" that was important. As Mattingly further states:

> The king kept his state in his palace, but also the baron kept his state in his hall, the abbot in his monastery and the merchant in his counting house. In more abstract discourse, men in medieval times talked not about "states" but "about estates", the ordered ranks of society which combined, usually three or more of them together, to make up particular realms, and the totality of which composed the mystic body of Christendom.[8]

In these data it can be observed, not only that "state" did not have a single clear cut jurisdiction, but also that in the strange amalgam that comprised the political system, the church could not be considered separate and distinct from secular leadership. Whether the church in such a situation could maintain its independence so to be critical of the rest of society is another pertinent question. In any case there are other factors which may have forced the church to be more conciliatory to secular powers than usual.

If, for example, the Renaissance were dated 1300 to 1600 as some scholars tend to do, its significance would include the church's dwindling power under the humanistic impact of the Renaissance itself. Noting the struggles between the popes and princes in the period, it would not be implausible to think that in 1492 when Columbus sailed for the New World the Church would probably not have been excessively eager to cross swords with the princely powers on the "simple matter" of the plunder of the New World. In fact, with the intricate network of "Church" and "state", as delicate as that might have become, the church stood to gain influence by supporting the secular expansionism in progress instead of opposing it. Furthermore the Spanish Peninsula by itself was a special case in terms of cooperation from Rome. It is said that Machiavelle, once when asked what he thought of Ferdinand, King of Spain, responded that Ferdinand was not even a "statesman," he was just a lucky person.[9]   Of course Machiavelle, an Italian, was probably thinking of Ferdinand's role in the Italian conflict, but Ferdinand was not just lucky, he was an astute Christian and as Christian he had the full and unqualified support of Rome in the consolidation of Spain under Christendom. As Christian he had succeeded leadership in a long war against the Moslems who populated a good portion of the Spanish Peninsula. In fact it was in 1492, the same year Columbus sailed to the New World, that the Christians finally conquered the Kingdom of Granada,[10] the last stronghold of the Moslems. Ferdinand's astute moves, including his marriage to Isabella, though designed to add more property and wealth to the family name could easily be subsumed under the portfolio of the process of Christianizing the Spanish Peninsula.

Indeed, as soon as he and Isabella had brought the kingdoms of Navare, Aragon, Castile and Granada together, Spain, which heretofore had not featured too greatly in the development of Europe, became a power to be reckoned with.[11]   The desire for more and more power drove them to even wider expansions. Hence when the Caribbean became part of the New World prize it also became a part of the incentive and prize for power plays between Spain and other parts of Europe. It did not matter that the Caribbean people had no say with regards to their own destiny. Yet even as that program of expansion into the New World began, the church perhaps saw no exploitation of other human beings, only the opportunity to bolster a tottering Christendom. The cruelty and indignity that the Indians suffered at the hands of the early colonizers were probably considered only normal expressions of the zealous character of the Castilian people whose flag Columbus had planted in the New World in 1492. As in the wars between Christians and Moslems both for faith and territory, the Castilians had become as violent as they were orthodox, their rampage through the New World with the sword in the right hand and the Bible in the left was permitted. By the time Spain's control of the Caribbean was shared by other European countries, the pattern was already set. Colonizing governments, no matter what their character, could not be separated from the colonizing church. The very structure of church and state made it impossible to extricate one from the other. Thus, despite the definition of Church and State for the time, the union itself, as well as its consequences, forces an important question for debate: how right is it for church and state to be so utterly confused that the church loses its prophetic voice as far as the government is concerned?

Some people may contend that the confusion of church and state in the Middle Ages was not a legacy of the Early Church. If they support a sacred/secular split they may conclude that Jesus himself had no illusions as to the difference between the secular power and divine power, as is evidenced by his statement, "Give to Caesar that which is Caesar's, and unto God that which is God's."(Matt 22:21) On the other hand it may be argued that he seemed to have understood that the divine power can be exercised through the state. In his encounter with Pilate just before the crucifixion, it may be suggested that his retort to Pilate, "You have no power over me except that which is given to you from above," (John 19:10) bears witness to such an understanding. Further, some observe that within the Early Church both Peter and Paul supported the idea of divine power exercised through state action. However, as John L. McKenzie points out, power in such respect as Peter and Paul understood it was morally neutral. Though it could not be possessed unless by divine generosity, it was the exercise of power that made the difference. In the exercise of power a state could become either good or evil.[12]   Hence, despite the general acceptance by its subjects (including the early Christian community) of the enormous power of Rome, for example, the Apocalypse could see it for the monster it could become. The very language the Apocalypse uses in its message signals both the fear and the contempt the community had for Rome.[13]   Rome had acted both ways. It had given the *religio lecita* to Christianity as a sect of Judaism, but of course Rome had also from time to time used its enormous power against the people of God.[14] Therefore even if Paul had seen this use of power as a distinct possibility of divine punishment for waywardness on the part of Christians, the Apocalypse saw Rome as the "beast" which had surpassed its authority and even while acting under the permissive will of God ultimately would be destroyed. But the Church has been sufficiently astute in keeping itself intact by accommodating itself to the use of power as the state may choose to demonstrate.[15]   One would hope that the church "intact" is not merely a physical structure but the structure with a prophetic eye and voice against evil. It is therefore the Caribbean charge that the missionary church compromised its prophetic position from the very inception of the European expansion into the New World, through the long colonial period endured and even into the neo-colonial period.

Neo-Colonialism and the Contemporary Church

In the neo-colonial period, the faces of some of the players changed but the play remains the same.

The nature of neo-colonialism in the Caribbean in its bi-dimensional composite makes the colonial pattern a little more subtle but just as devastating. This means that neo-colonialism has to be defined in two ways.

1. Even those Caribbean territories which are still colonies of Europe, boast of a certain amount of independence. They are all able to formulate their own regulations by which to partially govern themselves. There is not a physical invasion and occupation by the superpowers. However, with each territory having to relate to a global economy, they must operate within the international marketplace. Here is where real power differentiates itself from lip service to action, and because of the mere size of the economy of the major powers, small territories are over-whelmed in the struggle of that marketplace. As a result their economy is manipulated and controlled by the major powers to the extent that they might as well be colonized. Michael Manley, past Prime Minister of Jamaica, speaks of this as "structural dependence."[16] This is a reality made possible by the dominance of the major powers in the international marketplace where the Caribbean countries are forced both to sell and to purchase at prices set by the major powers. The result, according to Manley, is that these countries become merely an extension of "Western Capitalism."[17]

Holly Sklar, a "first world" person with first hand "Third World" experience is in agreement with this position. In her book *Trilateralism* she talks about the industrial nations which, through their global corporations, dominate the economy of the world:

> Trilateralism is the creed of an international ruling class whose locus of power is the global corporation. The owners and managers of global corporations view the entire world as their factory, farm, supermarket, and playground.[18]

They justify such behavior with the conclusion that somebody has to be the custodian of the world economy. As Sklar explains, the Trilateral Commission is a private entity determined to set public policy. Hence, because it is based upon principles of Western Capitalism, and also because of its desire to dominate world economy, the Commission comes into confrontation with the countries that would seek to resist its domination through other political and economic experiments including efforts at "nonalignment." Such countries are seen as anti-Western in their outlook and are therefore forced into the East/West dichotomy and conflict.

Major power countries have determined that non-alignment is never a viable option for small Third World countries such as those in the Caribbean. Historically, non-alignment has been grossly misunderstood. While it sees its primary task as being rid of all colonial domination, the dominant powers always see it as an attempt to switch loyalty from one dominant system to another.[19] This is exactly the reason a quest for liberation of the poor in a North/South economic situation can be read so easily by the Northern neighbors of the Caribbean as an ideological ferment of Marxist persuasion. It is also exactly the point at which the traditional church becomes involved.   Ashley Smith, past president of the United Theological College of the West Indies writes:

> One of the less desirable features of the institutionalized church is its ideological conservatism. Because of the human tendency of church men to become entrenched in the present, the church as a whole has been guilty of resisting any kind of structural or ideological change in society until the new forms become established. [20]

When the East/West ideological charge is made against the dominated country, the missionary church, in considering any switch to the "Eastern" value system, is inclined to take sides with the dominant country in an effort to secure the "stability" it has known. As a result the church is never in the forefront in the struggle to liberate the poor, if that struggle means the changing of ideological structures. In fact it is usually seen more in cooperation with the dominant than in a posture of willingness to dismantle old structures and create new ones.

2. Neo-colonialism is not only the economic and ideological dominance of the Caribbean by more powerful outside forces, but such forces operate through "natives" who have so internalized the ideology of the powerful that they are willing to take sides with them. It is not difficult for neo-colonialism to find such people who are willing to serve as the vehicle of domination within their own country. Denis Goulet has lived

within many Third World situations, particularly to study their struggle for freedom and development under economic colonialism. He comments on the "cruel choice" that some countries must make in accepting technical and economic aid from the very source of their domination, in futile efforts to dispense with that domination.[21] He points out however that certain classes of people within such dominated countries are not disturbed by the paradox of having dominant outsiders dictate the terms of liberation for the dominated. Goulet writes:

> These classes either felt or stimulated shame of their own culture. By shaping the values of the colonizers, they gained entry into the "respectable" world of those having money, power, and "culture." All these were of course defined ethnocentrically according to the dominant attitudes, whims, and styles of the occupiers.[22]

From the time of colonialism by occupation they received their grooming. However that grooming was often a part of the colonial machination for securing vehicles through which to dominate more efficiently. They have already been taught to respect the dominance of the imposing outsider as the inevitable controller of power. On the other hand, although they never become a real part of the power base, they enjoy the privileged ease in the classism of the rank consciousness for which Europeans are noted. They already knew how to be the privileged servants of the powerful. Therefore, when the new forms of colonialism arrived for imposition, their gullibility became an asset to the dominant. Whether it is true or not that in a situation of classism real power is not found in the center but in the outer rings of society, in neo-colonialism the power of the dominant outsider needs to be transmitted for its success. With the cooperation of the privileged class as the tool, and with the aid of the church as a vehicle, neo-colonialism is practiced with surprising ease in the Caribbean.

The conservative church is more easily deluded than the liberal when it comes to cooperation with the neo-colonial powers. Usually, the real conservative church is simply the satellite of the conservative groups in the major power countries. Their intricate strategy has not escaped the insightful assessment of Caribbean thinkers such as Ashley Smith, who remarks:

> It has been suggested that religion, both Christian and non-Christian, in the Caribbean is not merely a sign of "cultural lag" but an instrument used deliberately in "softening up" the dominated people of the region for economic exploitation, thus delaying their awakening to the realities of the interaction between the cultures. The divermissionary aspect of contemporary religious activity perpetuated especially by North American neo-pietistic groups, has...been confirmed by the proliferation of revivalist groups in Jamaica in the two years or so preceding the 1980 general elections. There was strong pro-capitalistic emphasis in the proclamation of many of these people, a tendency to downplay the importance of the sovereignty of nations (especially small nations like those of the Caribbean) an obviously heavy involvement of North American based big business in the financing of their activities.[23]

A strong conservative movement in the local church usually accompanies two opposing factors: (1) A strong conservative political thrust in North America and (2) the growth of radical politics on the local scene. The inevitable target is the local radical politics which is always sought to be destroyed by North American economic and political conservatism. Ernle P. Gordon, a Caribbean Anglican priest, reveals that the vicious cycle is that of big business and government in major power countries working through churches to destabilize countries, such as in the Caribbean. He writes:

> It is interesting to note that the Independent Evangelicals from the United States of North America have compiled a document for the U.S. State Department, which asked the political directorate to do something positive about the theology of liberation in the Caribbean, because it is preventing the spread of "productive capitalism."[24]

Missionary Culture as Colonial Christianity

Indigenization is itself a process of adaptation to the local culture. The process is only meaningful as those who do the adaptation do it for the benefit of their culture. In the case of the indigenization of theology in the Caribbean, the adaptation is in support of Caribbean self- authentication, self awareness, self development, self- actualization and self determination. The process includes a critique and transformation of the colonizers' theology which by its very presence in the region has been a foreign imposition on the Caribbean. A large portion of that foreign imposition is a result of the colonizers' use of the colonizing culture as a vehicle for its transportation. In fact the vehicle *became* the message, so that with Christianity the Caribbean received a large dose of European culture. Furthermore, the colonizing culture cannot avoid presenting itself as superior to the host culture. Colonization is the presumption of superiority.

Conversely, the critique demands care in its assessment because of the danger of contradictions. The very case for indigenization is one that can give comfort not only to the understanding of the gospel in the colonizers' culture but the use of that culture as a vehicle for its transportation. One argument against indigenization is that a missionary, as a product of her or his culture, moves with the right to carry that cultural baggage along. If Caribbean culture is authentic for the Caribbean people, the European culture is just as authentic for the European and inevitably the missionary's message is transported in and through his or her culture. The point here is that Caribbean theology in its critique of Euro-American perspectives must avoid the trap of becoming the norm for every other perspective.

The possibility of the Christian message being transported through the colonizing culture is readily admitted by most Caribbean thinkers. Geoffrey B. Williams who looks at the area in depth, can even think of a Biblical rationale for it: 1 Thess. 2:8, where Paul informs the Thessalonians "We were eager to hand over to you not only the Good News, but our lives as well."[25] The real problem, however, arises when the colonizing culture brings a message of superiority and inauthentication to bear upon the host culture. The Caribbean people have had their share of the particular problems of cultural stratification as imposed by the European colonizers.

Cultural Stratification

Recently Charles Darwin has come back into the limelight because of the hoopla over the principles of creationism versus evolutionism. Some conservative Christians in the Southern

United States, having seen evolutionism as a threat to the theological theory of direct divine intervention as a means of
creation, are charging Darwin anew with an atheism that the
world could well do without. Evolutionism is a direct development from Darwin's theory on the origin of the species.
After its encounter with the sophistication of "liberal arts,"the
missionary church would have to revert to childish naivete to
ignore the success of science in finding other answers to questions surrounding the origin of the earth and its life. Thus the
church usually takes three steps toward an understanding of
human origin. It glosses over the idea of human evolution
from some primate, but supports the broad theory of human
origin through "cause and effect," if in that theory there is
room for "first cause." This gives the evolution theory a
chance to arrive at the same conclusion as Genesis 1: "In the
beginning God..."

Yet there is a certain "denseness" in generalities and what
the missionary church supports here is no exception to that
rule. "In-the-beginning-God" is only a beginning and a general one at that. The "denseness" begins to clear only in the
process of understanding human origin, not so much in terms
of its scientific value (because even "scientific accounts contra-
dict themselves") but in its covenant significance.[26] Walbert
Buhlmann suggests that by the endorsement of life at its
beginning in all its goodness, God has offered a covenant in its
creation.[27] This creation covenant is based not only upon life
but upon a certain grace of equity and equality in humanity.
Of course, this equity is based on the concept that we are not
merely created, but created in God's image. Human beings
have the ability for awareness of these bases. However, somewhere along the way, some portions of humanity decided to
dismantle the covenant of creation based on equality, replac-
ing it with a concept of cultural stratification.

In the Caribbean, what Darwin needs to be criticized for is
not so much his theory on the origin of the species, as on his
theory of the "survival of the fittest" out of his work on the
natural selection principle. This theory has reinforced the
ideas of cultural stratification globally and put the creation
covenant out of commission. When Darwin arrived in the

regions of South America, he was astonished not only by the culture of the Amerindians but also by the color of their skin. He recorded his feelings, which were not complimentary to the Indians. To him their skin was of a dirty copper color, and their culture was so much lower than that of the "civilized" European that it warranted a worse verdict than in the comparison between the domestic animal and the wild one.[28]

Of course Darwin post dates the inception of the enslavement of the African, and Bartolome de Las Casas had published an eyewitness account of the slaughter of the Caribbean and mainland Indians way back in 1552. Hence Darwin cannot be made responsible for these atrocities. Yet while those atrocities have been charged in their time to religious ignorance and insatiable human greed, Social Darwinism even more than Darwin gave cultural stratification scientific sanctions. Social Darwinism suggests that just as in the wild where there are chains of predators and prey and only the "fittest" survive, so cultural stratification is at best a "natural selection." Furthermore, there was no doubt in the European mind that the cultures of Europe were at the apex of that stratification and those cultures that did not resemble the European's were considered not only inferior but, in the theory of the survival of the fittest, could be justifiably exploited.

The attitude of Reginald Heber is a prime example that the church was not unaffected by thoughts of cultural superiority. One must admit that when he wrote his famous missionary hymn, Darwin was only 10 years old and cannot therefore be held responsible for Heber's anthropology and sociology. However, the hymn helps to make the point that when cultures were stratified by even the church, the cultures of Europe formed the apex of the stratification:

From Greenland's Icy Mountains
From India's coral strand,
Where Afric's sunny fountains
Roll down their golden sand,
From many an ancient river,
From many a palmy plain
They call us to deliver
Their land from error's chain.

Can we, whose souls are lighted
With wisdom from on high,
Can we to men benighted
The lamp of life deny?

When the gospel came to the Caribbean it arrived not merely clothed in European culture but the European culture was consciously promoted as superior to all cultures. So strong was the feeling of superiority in the cultures of Europe, it would have been impossible for the church to avoid it. Again Geoffrey B. Williams in his research for his paper "Classicism and the Caribbean Church" cites Arthur de Gabineau who wrote in *The Inequality of Human Races*:

> Such is the lesson of history. It shows us that all civilization derives from the white race, that none can exist without its help and that a society is great and brilliant only in so far as it preserves the blood of the noble group that created it... There is no true civilization among the European peoples where the Aryan branch is not predominant. In the above list no negro race is seen as the initiator of civilization...Similarly, no spontaneous civilization is found among the yellow races; and when the Aryan blood is exhausted stagnation supervenes.[29]

Without having to evoke the historical significance of the civilizations of some of the Amerindians, which developed with tremendous sophistication without the inspiration of European blood and paternalism, when accounts such as those of Bartolome de Las Casas are investigated it is not difficult to decide who were more civilized: the Spanish colonizers or the colonized Indians. How can the barbarous butchery of innocent, defenseless people be listed as a mark of high civilization? Furthermore, it is clear that from the very inception of the colonizing process the church should take some responsibility for the perpetrating of the cultural and physical genocide upon the people of the Caribbean. Of course the social scientists are agreed that on the other hand, if the Spanish conquerors had no theology, they would have murdered the Indians for their gold. In either case, the cultural stratification has been present, in that the Indians would have been considered too inferior to keep their own heritage. The fact of the matter is that when the church intervened, the Indians were killed for an additional reason. Their death sentence was passed also because their culture did not contain the Christian faith, as did the culture which Europeans brought to the Caribbean. Again de Las Casas wrote:

> This wretch of a Governor thus gave such instructions...to attack and rob a settlement of Indians where he had heard there was a store of gold, telling them to go at night when the inhabitants were securely in their houses and that, when half a league away from the settlement, they should read in a loud voice his order: "Caciques and Indians of this land, hark ye! We notify you that there is but one God and one Pope and one King of Castile who is the Lord of these lands. Give heed and show obedience!...And if not, be warned that we will wage war against you and will slay you or take you into captivity"...Then, in the early dawn, then these innocents are asleep with their wives and children, the Spaniards attack and enter the town and set fire to the houses, which, being commonly made of straw, burn rapidly with all who are within them.[30]

De Las Casas also reported that these Indians were not even given credit for the ability to understand the gospel as preached and therefore come of their volition to embrace the Christian faith. They were simply "rounded up" and ordered to accept the unfamiliar faith or die. In fact, it was by "their blood and fire" that faith was imparted to them. So repulsive was the whole situation that indigenization probably began when an Indian in Cuba, while tied to be burned at the stake, was ordered to accept the faith so he could go to heaven, but he stated his preference for hell. He had been assured that in heaven he would be with the Franciscans and he, not wishing to be in the same place with them chose hell instead.[31]

We concur with history that as the centuries marched on the church became less inclined to take part in the slaughter of its would be converts. Yet the feeling of cultural superiority encountered no sudden death. In 1840 missionary Goldie, writing back to Scotland to report on his efforts to evangelize the Caribbean said, he "sought a location amidst a wild waste of heathenism."[32] Rev. George McNeill, recording the history of the activity of the Presbyterian witness in the Caribbean, as late as 1910 wrote of the newly freed slaves:

> The simplicity and directness of their speech were almost pathetic. An old man said he wanted to have his sins washed away even if it were only half of them.[33]

Curiously enough it is quite possible that any doctrine fostered by the Christian gospel preached within the cultural expressions of the Africans would have been grasped more readily by them. It did not dawn on the missionaries who had decided that their own language concepts were the norm, that had the concepts been expressed to them as non-Africans in some African language they would have had the same problems appropriating their meaning.

Culture and the New Missionary

Jimmy Carter, in his inauguration speech, made a statement to the world outside of the United States:

> I have chosen the occasion of my inauguration as president to speak not only to my countrymen — which is traditional — but also to you, citizens of the world who did not participate in our election but who will nevertheless be affected by my decisions.[34]

This statement is by no means an admission that the super powers were at war for influence over the rest of the world. Yet it is a statement made by one who was a member of the Trilateral Commission and who understands the ethics of multinational corporations and how through them and other means, major governments change cultural norms in efforts to control Third World politics and economics. Ernle P. Gordon in his paper on "Evangelization and Politics: A British Caribbean Perspective," reminds some and informs others that President Gerald Ford, who preceded Jimmy Carter, had not only admitted the C.I.A. involvement for economic and political reasons in Third World countries, but also that the C.I.A. has used missionaries to gather valuable information in these parts for the State Department.[35] The fact is that during Carter's presidency there were more C.I.A. agents in the Caribbean than ever before, and the onslaught of neo-pietistic evangelism reached its highest peak.

One need not agonize over the fact that missionaries of the Christian gospel could allow themselves to be so used by a force such as the C.I.A. Furthermore, when the question about the morality of their involvement is raised, missionaries from North America need not be viewed as indulgent cloak and dagger Christians who would sell out their poorer neighbors for the dollar. The situation has a deeper meaning. It is related not only to the view of cultural superiority but also to the charge that Ernle Gordon brings against the Independent Evangelicals from the United States who complain that liberation perspectives are preventing "the spread of productive capitalism."[36] Capitalism is a permanent part of North American culture and anything that does not look like it becomes a threat to church and state alike.

In North America not only is capitalism often confused with democracy, it is so steeped in the culture that capitalism has become one of the most important aspects of its religious value system. Not often does the need arise to disguise capitalism as anything else but capitalism when it presents itself as a religious perspective. Max Weber has seen to that, ever since his work on *The Protestant Ethic and the Spirit of Capitalism.* Some conclude that it is Karl Marx who is to blame. If he could narrow down Hegel's philosophy into the single aspect of materialism, Weber had the right not only to invert those theories for capitalism, but to couch the result in Protestant religiosity.[37] He made Reformation Theology say in effect that good Christians live by the capitalist ethic. Of course some Calvinists object to Max Weber's conclusions, but John Calvin did not help the situation when he insisted that wealth is a divine endowment.[38] Furthermore, while he also argued that that endowment may be shared with the poor, that sharing smacks of paternalism in a trickle down system, and with the idea of divine determinism already in place, there is no mechanism for the changing of structures for the sake of an equity that suggests that poverty should not exist. In any case since Calvin neglected to say whose gift poverty is, the idea gives the rich reason to feel that their endowment is their inalienable right, as if they had earned it. Conversely, poverty must then be by predestination, or the consequence of wrongdoing on the part of the poor.

Just as the old colonial church communicated the gospel with impositions of cultural superiority, so the Evangelicals as some of the new missionaries in the age of neo-colonialism bring the gospel in capitalistic garb. They set up their Caribbean satellites with state of the art equipment for broadcasting and transportation. In fact what is lavished upon the worship centers is in such stark contrast to the poverty that exists in the communities in which they launch their crusades, that it is obscene. They put the poor to shame deliberately to demonstrate what catering to the North American capitalist culture can produce for the "good" client.

While it is true that most of the Caribbean subscribes to capitalist structures there, it is also true that some have been desirous of experimenting with models that are more suitable to the area's needs. History will record and prove that Michael Manley's experiments in Jamaica could not pass even for "mongrelized" communism. Yet, without expropriating one root of sugar cane he was considered a threat to the "free enterprise system." That fact alone goes to prove that not only is the will of the North against radical alternatives to the capitalist culture, it is against anything that does not ape the North American capitalist culture. Ironically the same systems that damned Manley in the 70's are now praising his liberalization in the 90's because liberalization is the American recommendation. Yet common to the capitalist culture is the rugged individualism which promotes greed. It sets up competition where only those who already have may get more. This is a case which heightens the cardinal problem of "Third World" existence where the wealth and the means of it are in the ownership of a very few. Indeed while many people starve in Jamaica the banks may never be able to utilize their windfall profits out of liberalization. They have made just too much.

If it is true that in low economic times people become more religiously insular, there is a case for Evangelical missionary responsibility for the preparation of Third World people for rugged individualism. People who live in small communities such as the Caribbean territories, are usually not as individualistic as their Northern neighbors. Because they are not as urbanized as the people of the metropolitian centers, who lead nuclear lifestyles, Caribbean people maintain long lists of relationships. They create and foster close and supportive communities instead of the cut-throat competitiveness that European cultures have excused as mere aggressiveness. However, by the time the Evangelical missionaries have preached the gospel of "individual salvation," the people are ready for the more hardened political views of right-wing selfishness and greed which are as evident in some capitalist structures as in the corporate war among electronic evangelists. Even more important is the fact that while their leaders benefit from their "holy greed," the people are constantly fed a theological diet that transfers all redress to their present economic problems into the "great by and by." While other-worldly theology may serve as a temporary psychological relief for those who carry the heaviest burdens of the Third World reality, it does nothing to dismantle the structures that oppress. If anything, it postpones liberation thoughts and schemes while the threat of recolonization solidifies itself.

Notes

1 Watty, William "The De-Colonization of Theology" ed. Idris Hamid, *Troubling of the Waters*, Trinidad W. I. Rahaman Printery Limited, 1973. p. 53.

2 Rice, Eugene F. Jr. *Foundations of Early Europe, 1460-1559*, New York, W.W. Norton and Company Inc, 1970, p.31.

3 Watty, William, "The Decolonization of Theology," ed. Idris Hamid, *Troubling of the Waters*, Trinidad W.I. Rahaman Printery, 1973 p.59.

4 Rice, Eugene F. Jr. *Foundations of Early Europe, 1460-1559*, New York, W.W. Norton and Company Inc., 1970 p.31.

5 Carew, Jan, "The Origin of Racism in the Americas," ed. John Hearne, *Carifesta Forum: An Anthology of Twenty Caribbean Voices*. Jamaica W.I., Institute of Jamaica and Jamaica Journal, 1976, p. 77, Citing Richard Moore, 'Caribs, Cannibals and Human Relations." (Essay).

6 Mattingly, Garrett, "Changing Attitudes Towards the State During the Renaissance," eds. Wallace K. Ferguson et al, *Facets of the Renaissance*, New York, Harper and Row, Publishers Inc., 1963 p. 21.

7 Ibid.

8 Ibid. p. 21.

9 Harbison, Harris E. "Machiavelli's Prince and More's Utopia," eds Wallace K. Ferguson et al, *Facets of the Renaissance*, New York, Harper and Row Publishers Inc., 1963, p. 48.

10 Ferguson, Wallace K. ed. *A Survey of European Civilization Part I, 1660*, Boston, Houghton Mufflin Company, 1958, p.356.

11 Ibid. p.356.

12 McKenzie, John L. "The Christian and the State," ed Bennett D. Hill, *Church and State in the Middle Ages*, New York, John Wiley and Sons, Inc. 1970. p.12.

13 Ibid.,p. 9.

14 Ibid. p.8f.

15 Ibid. p. 8F

16 Manley, Michael, *Up The Down Escalator*, London, Andre Deutsch Limited, 1987, p. 81.

17 Ibid. p. 81.

18 Sklar, Holly, ed. *Trilateralism: Managing Dependence and Democracy*, Boston, South End Press, pp. 8-9

19 Manley, Michael, *Up The Down Escalator*, London, Andre Deutsch Limited, 1987 p.81.

20 Smith, Ashley, *Real Roots and Potted Plants*. Mandeville, Jamaica, W.I. Mandeville Publishers, 1984, p.78.

21 Goulet, Dennis, *The Cruel Choice*, New York, Antheneum, 1975 p. 45.

22 Ibid.

23 Smith, Ashley, *Real Roots and Potted Plants*, Mandeville, Jamaica, West Indies, Mandeville Publishers, 1984, pp. 10-11.

24 Gordon, Ernle P., "Evangelization and Politics: A British Caribbean Perspective," eds. Sergio Arce and Oden Marichal, *Evangelization and Politics*, New York, Circus Inc, 1982. pp. 88-99.

25 Williams, Geoffrey B., S.J. "Classicism And The Caribbean Church," ed. Idris Hamid, *Out of the Depths*, Trinidad, West Indies, St. Andrews Theological College, 1977, p. 49.

26 Buhlmann, Walbert, *God's Chosen People*, Maryknoll, New York, Obis 1982, p.15.

27 Ibid. p. 15.

28 Darwin, Charles, *Journal of Researches into the Natural History and Geology of the Countries Visited During the Voyage of H.M.S. Beagle, Round the World Under the Command of Capt. Fitzroy, R.N.*, New York, D. Appleton and Co, 1898, p. 205.

29 Williams, Geoffrey B., S.J., "Classicism And The Caribbean Church," ed. Idris Hamid, *Out of The Depths*, Trinidad, West Indies, St. Andrew's Theological College, 1977 p. 53, Citing Arthur de Gabineau in "The Inequality of Human Races" 1854.

30 De Las Casas, Bartolome, *The Devastation of the Indians: A Brief Account*, Trans., Herma Briffault, New York, Seabury Press, 1974 pp.59-60.

31 Ibid., p. 58-59.

32 McNeill, George, *The Story of Our Mission In the West Indies*, Edinburgh, Scotland, The Foreign Mission Committee of the Free Church of Scotland, 1911, p. 33.

33 Ibid.

34 Sklar, Holly, ed. *Trilateralism: Managing Dependence and Democracy*, Boston, South End Press, 1980, p. 1.

35 Gordon, Ernle P., "Evangelization and Politics: A British Caribbean Perspective," eds. Sergio Arce and Oden, Marichal, *Evangelization and Politics*, New York, Circus Inc., 1982, p. 100.

36 Ibid. p. 99

37 Lowith, Karl, *From Hegel Nietzsche*, Trans. David E. Green, Garden City, New York, Doubleday and Company Inc. 1976, p. 94.

38 Calvin, John, *Institutes, Book Three*, Chapt. VII, Article 9.

Chapter Two

Missionary Theology as Theology of Domination

Ashley Smith sums up the unrelatedness of missiology to the Caribbean social reality by saying:

> Caribbean historians, political scientists, sociologists and economists are all agreed that what they refer to as "missionary" Christianity has been a major factor in the reinforcement and perpetuation of the domination of the non-European Caribbean man by his brother from the European continent, Great Britain and North America.[1]

For the missionary church to be able to support the colonial structures as completely as it has done, it has to have ignored some of the socio-economic realities of the Caribbean situation. Its gospel emphasis therefore has failed to address these socio-economic realities in ways that would suggest that God is ever interested in changing the social structures that oppress. As a result, sin has been assessed only in personal and private terms. As long as one was concerned only about one's personal salvation, sin in its institutional form was never a problem. Hence the corporate need and thrusts for socio-economic liberation and self-actualization have never been a priority for missionary Christianity. As Smith puts it again:

> To Caribbean persons who have been merely churched "belonging to Christendom" has little to do with the business of bringing home bread, having shelter over one's head or experiencing life as satisfying, fulfilling or meaningful. Christianity means little more than not to be "pagan", heathen" or "uncivilized". It has nothing to do with their perspective on what is human, what constitutes the good life or the viable and affirmative community.[2]

Theological Denial of Self Actualization

To fail in self-actualization is to sin. Even if sin were to be held strictly to its personal and privatized significance, there is enough evidence to show that one of the basic tenets in the concept of sin is its demand for improvement on the part of the sinner. The word most often used in the New Testament for sin is "Hamartia" which in its most important sense means failing to reach one's highest potential. When this meaning is taken seriously it is easily understood how self-actualization is not merely a psychological concept but a theological one as well. Even so the real sinner has to be the one who prevents self-actualization among a people whose situation demands it most. Self-actualization as a process, says Abraham H. Maslow,

> refers to man's desire for self-actualization, namely, to the tendency for him to become actualized in what he is potentially. This tendency might be phrased as a desire to become everything that one is capable of becoming.[3]

While it is true that Maslow is describing individual personality at this point the profundity of the idea is not lost or even reduced when it is applied to the corporate personality. Since, according to Maslow, self-actualization is related to basic needs of safety, love, and esteem,[4] what is good for the one is also good for the group. In fact, when he extends the concept of self-actualization to group personalities he relates the concept to "self-decision, self government... deciding agents rather than pawns".[5] He then concludes that in the case of the unfree there is a detrimental denial of responsibility:

> What this nonresponsibility means for self-choice politics and economics is of course obvious; it is catastrophic. Democratic self-choice society must have self-movers, self-deciders, self-choosers who make up their own minds, free agents, freewillers.[6]

If the propensity toward self-actualization is truly innate, those who believe in the divine creativity that involves humanity must conclude that God has made it so. In every human being there is a divinely instituted will against colonization, slavery and oppression or anything else that may stand in the way of self-determination. Freedom from colonization and oppression, to self-determination in the Caribbean is analogous to the basic understanding of human freedom anywhere.   Yet although every Euro-American missionary could understand such a concept and apply it at home base successfully, when it comes to the colonized and neo-colonized Caribbean their gospel has been found devoid of the capacity to support freedom for the territories. Something has always been wrong with that evangelization method, and therefore with the interpretation of the gospel. If a missionary believes in freedom for the home people under God but not the same freedom for the colonized under God, then missionary theology has to be a misrepresentation of Christian theology, to accommodate the contradiction.

God as Foreign Dictator

Bartolome De Las Casas, relating the cruel atrocities of the Spanish colonizers against the Amerindians, wrote of how they were introduced to the gospel:

> ...they are told they must embrace the Christian faith immediately, without hearing any sermon preached and without any indoctrination. They are told to subject themselves to a King they have never heard nor seen and are told this by the King's messengers who are such despicable and cruel tyrants that deprive them of their liberty, their possessions, their wives and children.[7]

The inference here is that the Indians were bound to equate the tyranny with which they were devastated with the power of the God of the perpetrators. If the conquistadors were exercising the will of their God in such absolute cruelty then their God must be one who was absolutely cruel. Of course, since the cruelty was directed only toward the native they had to conclude this "foreign" God was a cruel dictator who was against them. No wonder the Cuban Indian chose to go to hell so as not to meet the Spanish bearers of Christianity in heaven.

Clement Gayle, professor emeritus of the United Theological College of the West Indies, in an examination of the history of the Church's attitude to the concept of freedom in the Caribbean, discovers that although the Moravians were the first to send missionaries directly for the evangelization of the African slaves in the Caribbean they made very few converts.[8] Gayle argues that this sparsity of African converts among the Moravian flock was due primarily to the fact that the missionaries acquired property, bought slaves, used them to carve out their livelihood and treated them no differently from the way the other slave owners treated theirs. They were whipped when their masters felt it necessary. As a result the slaves found it difficult to differentiate between the missionary and the colonizer. However, because the missionaries came as the representatives of God, this European God had to be viewed with suspicion.[9] Gayle further points out that Zinzendorf, the father of Moravianism, in his doctrine prepared for the Caribbean, suggested to the slaves that slavery was divine punishment upon the earth's first negroes and Christianity had come to the Caribbean to set negroes free. However, that freedom was not from slavery and their master's control, but from their wicked thoughts and deeds and anything which would make them malcontents in their predestined condition of slavery.[10]

If the publisher's note is an adequate summary of Ashley Smith's meaning in *Real Roots and Potted Plants*, the reason for such a conclusion by Smith is crystal clear. The note summarizes Smith to say:

> Christianity has never really taken root in the Caribbean but has remained a potted plant which has managed to survive in the little container in which it was brought from the nurseries.[11]

This does not mean that even in contemporary situations evangelism from the Euro-American fronts could dare to overtly try to convince the Caribbean that economic, social, and political oppression is a divine mandate to the oppressors because of their color. Yet the fact that the missionary church's "Thus saith the Lord" is scarcely directed toward Third World despotism, is enough to warrant the conclusion that the missionary church has never come with a God who is interested in the Caribbean plight for its own sake.

Even if the church's lack of interest in the socio-economic and political problems were due strictly to the controversy between empiricism and rationalism, it does not answer the deep questions of its silence on the matter of justice. One does understand that the question of the sacred and the secular is still an unsettled one, whether the arguments are imported or not. However, the concept of justice is itself an answer that transcends the division, contrived or real. Hence a God who keeps silent on issues concerning justice has to be prepared to be seen as one who does not care that there is injustice. In fact such a God may even be seen as dictating the injustices since those who are most closely related to their perpetration are not only their beneficiaries but are also the bearers of the brand of gospel that embraces them. On the other hand the fact that the missionary church has always had a tendency to take sides with the powerful,[12] and also because God has been portrayed in unconcerned omnipotence, the missionary church has been adept at killing the impetus toward liberation struggle.

No Caribbean person would dare ask for a God who is not omnipotent. No Caribbean person would want to deal with a God who did not in some way transcend the human condition. The problem, however, is not so simple, because it arises out of the suggestion that God can be so easily portrayed as totally transcendent that transcendence becomes uncaring. As a result God becomes so powerful and at the same time so far removed from the human struggle for justice that the weak encounters this doctrine with the consequences of even weaker nature.

If the Judeo-Christian continuum offers to the world anything portentous it is not the "God principle." That preceded both Judaism and Christianity. However, Judaism made a unique contribution to Christianity and the world in the idea of a "moral God." By the time the eighth century prophets had dealt with the word "Qodesh" it described more than the otherness of God. It described also the inner nature of God which is that God is righteous.[13] This is not so descriptive of a God who takes pleasure in peeping through key holes, as it is of a God who takes sides against oppression and powerlessness.

Furthermore it must be understood here that the Jewish God does not merely object with cool passivity to the exploitation of the poor. The wrath of this God is kindled against those powerful who exploit the powerless, to upset radically the structures of oppression.[14] It is the same eighth century prophetic development that sees that the "tsedeq" (righteousness) that God demands of human persons is more than some ethical treatment. "Tsedeq" had come to be a divine demand for justice among the people. Norman Snaith admits that:

> Tsedeq certainly stands for the establishment of justice in the land. We would not detract to any degree from the importance of that, but important as it is, it is but half the truth. It is incidental that tsedeq actually stands for the establishment of God's will in the land, and secondarily for justice because that in part is God's will. It is in part, because God's will is wider than justice. He has particular regard for the helpless ones of the earth to rescue them from the clutches of those that are stronger than they.[15]

When it comes to the gospel message that came to the Caribbean, not only without this understanding but in support of those who performed the injustices, it certainly is not representative of Biblical truth. The skewing of the theology of justice to justify the colonial thrust placed God outside of the reach of the powerless. Hence the doctrine of the work of Christ results in similar unconcern.

Christ As Inaccessible Infiltrator

In West Indian folklore there is a story about a slave master who had a glass eye, and who on seasonal departure would place the eye where the slaves could see it. They, being quite familiar with perspectives of mediation such as "absomism" of the Ashantis,[16] obeyed the master by the presence of the eye. The eye was highly representative of the master's presence. This illustrates the point that in a certain sense Jesus, despite certain views concerning socio-economic and political detachment, is in fact present in the Caribbean condition. As such Jesus offers a personality with a limited degree of accessibility since he is only God's glass eye, so to speak. Barry Chevannes, in his article "Some Notes on African Religious Survivals in the Caribbean," differentiates between the perceived immanence of God and Jesus:

> God is thought of as Creator, living in or beyond the sky, but at any rate removed from the world of man. His relationship to the world is similar to the relationship which the owner of the estate had with his property—a relationship mediated by the overseer and bookkeeper. Hence his name 'Massa God' (in Surinam Massa Gadu). Thus while his ultimate responsibility is acknowledged, he has little or no direct links with man...
>
> On the other hand, it is Jesus and the Holy Spirit who are regarded as interveners in the affairs of the world—a factor no doubt reinforced by Christian teachings about their mediating role, particularly that of Jesus.[17]

As true as that assessment is, it does not deal with all the complications that further facts on the subject supply. For example, it does not explain why, by Chevannes' own admission, some persons who ostentatiously support the rituals of missionary Christianity, secretly deny its ability to provide effective healing ministry, by turning to "bush" doctors or the "obeahman"[18] in illness. Neither does it explain why some of the same people from time to time refer to Jesus as "Massa Jesus" and furthermore address his soteriological capabilities only in terms of the Parousia. The problem may receive some light, however, as it is seen that Jesus is recognized as an intermediary between the people and God but only for the purpose of dealing with individual sin and maintaining a divinely ordered vigil against it. Jesus is therefore just as strongly associated with the powerful as is "Massa God," and liberation is limited to getting one's name in the "Lamb's book of life." Of course that "life" is not here and now, but in the great by and by, a concept which only detracts attention from the socio-economic and political defalcation of the present and postpones its rectification. This critique raises to a larger degree the philosophical question alluded to earlier, which is whether the weak can be adequately liberated when the power which comes to liberate overwhelms the effort of the weak. Bevis Byfield touches base with this question when he remarks that:

...the church must help people to understand that freedom is not something that is donated nor does it come through theological speculation. People who are oppressed must assume a posture of freedom.[19]

This is not to say that Byfield has laid out the intricate details of the arguments which respond to this question. Yet the statement is related to such arguments.

It must be admitted here that the arguments foster such a subtle position and one that can so easily be misinterpreted by even those for whom it speaks, that it warrants much elaboration. The position is based upon soteriology from the point of view of liberation theology which declares that God through Christ provides for the subjugated the freedom necessary for their own fight for liberation. This is supported at least tangentially by even Paul whose preoccupation with justification by faith is so complete that it borders on the "helplessness" of faith. Yet he is able to suggest to the Phillipians that they "work out their own salvation" even if it is "with fear and trembling" (Philippians 2:12). When this point comes in contact with some aspects of a "substitution theory of atonement" in which divine power becomes the total substitute for human effort, the human being by virtue of his or her helplessness becomes totally obscured. Thus the powerless are rendered even more powerless by the very reality which should empower them. Admittedly, "Massa God" and "Massa Jesus" are appellations of slaves and descendants of slaves and not the missionary church. Yet the missionary church by virtue of doctrinal interpretation is quite responsible for the gap it places between God and the weak.

The Christ that comes to the post-colonial and contemporary neo-colonial setting with a "massaness" that privatizes sin and therefore does not call into question the systemic and structural damage done and being done to the powerless, is not on the side of the powerless. In fact such a Christ is detrimental to the powerless. Of course calling for a Caribbean Christ is calling for more than some liturgical awareness. It is calling for a Christology which, while recognizing that "Jesus Christ is Lord" never forgets that Jesus

Christ is also the oppressed one who, by the resurrection liberates the oppressed ones.

Defective Praxis in Missionary Christianity

It is now obvious that one of the main reasons that the Caribbean resisted liberation theology for as long as it did is the perennial struggle to appropriate the relationship of the "sacred" to the "secular." Of course the problem has been the legacy of European perspectives and is not unique to the Caribbean process. Liberation theology everywhere has had to fight adverse definitions such as anthropology or sociology and the like. Furthermore it is no secret that those adverse definitions come as a result of liberation theology's concern for the socio-economic and political. On the other hand liberation pioneers such as James Cone have never said that the spiritual is of no value in the theological enterprise. What they have said is that the gospel has traditionally been spiritualized out of all proportion to its socio-economic and political value. In such a case the spiritualization is placed in the category of "theory", to the exclusion of the socio-economic and political consciousness in the area of "praxis" where the action really is. Certainly praxis has to be defined, not so much in its general sense, but within its particular context. Because praxis bears reference to definite action, praxis must carry with it a certain particularity. It may very well be that the praxis for one situation is to "go sell all your possessions and give to the poor" (Luke 12:33). However, if you are already the poor and you have no possessions your praxis is another story. By the time reason for your poverty is established you will have discovered that your praxis will have to match the context of your poverty, assuming that you intend to do something about it. It is true to say, then, that praxis for the Caribbean situation has to bear relevance to its own context. It is also true to say that if the praxis suitable for the Caribbean context bears reference to self-actualization on the part of the Caribbean people, the praxis of the missionary theology fell woefully short.

Praxis in Caribbean Theology

It has been established that even when placed in juxtaposition
with "theory," "praxis" means more than the mere action that
ordinary "practice" implies. Richard Bernstein has made this
quite an issue in his thesis of the same title *Praxis and
Action* — in which he points out that "praxis and action" is not a
phrase of redundancy.[20] Bernstein traces the etymology of the
word "praxis" to the philosophy of Aristotle where the delicate
distinction between "practice" and praxis is established. "Practice" refers to execution of the myriad mundane activities
which need no more than common sense to perform[21]
whereas Aristotle's "praxis" has to do with those activities
which issue from intellectual and artistic concepts and those
that relate to one's ethical and political life.[22]

Aristotle also contrasted "theoria" (theory) with praxis, and
when that is done the concept which liberation would support
begins to take shape. Theoria is knowledge, and this knowledge may cover any number of important disciplines such as
the sciences. Obviously the acquiring of such knowledge
entails some activity on the part of the person acquiring the
knowledge. However theoria differs radically from praxis in
that theoria is related to knowledge sought for its own sake.[23]
Praxis on the other hand is concerned with knowledge that
seeks to cause change. Bernstein also points out that all perspectives on "praxis" were given birth by Aristotle's approach
to the concept. Actually when liberation theologians develop
perspectives on praxis, many of them are influenced by Marx
who himself was influenced, in a way, by Hegel.[24]

Marx gave praxis its fullest treatment because it is central to
his philosophy and crucial to the understanding of socio-economic and political chronology in history.[25] In his *Eleven Theses on Feuerbach*, Marx suggested that human thought in search
of objective truth is not a theoretical exercise but a practical
one. The rationale here is that as long as the search is objective it involves not merely the assorting of ideas but the conscious "active" effort of proving the truth. In this sense
thinking that is isolated from practice is merely an academic
exercise. Furthermore, this actual objective proving of truth

presumes change. In fact the concept of change is inherent in the process itself, since the seeker (even the educator) becomes the educated. This fact constitutes not merely a change in academic position but a change in circumstance.

Marx then takes the argument in its logical sequence and applies it to the doctrine of materialism wherein the objective search becomes revolutionary political action, which is "praxis." However it is precisely at this point that many people become diffident and therefore avoid the conclusions. They are afraid because (1) Revolutionary praxis in the Western value systems, always precipitates the conjuring up of thoughts of violence, bloodshed and massacre. (2) "Materialism" is skillfully made to seem a non-Western godlessness which would be a dangerous imposition upon the Judeo-Christian consciousness. (3) There is a Western conditioning that confuses democracy with capitalism and capitalism with Christianity. Hence any criticism of capitalism that may suggest radical changes in its structure is regarded as sacrilege. Yet it is here that Caribbean theology finds its own praxis.

The idea of change is not foreign to the Christian community. In fact change is a prerequisite to becoming Christian. John the Baptist, heralding the mission of Jesus preached: "Repent for the Kingdom of heaven is at hand" (Matthew 3:2). When Jesus began that mission he preached also: "Repent, for the Kingdom of heaven is at hand" (Matthew 4:17). Repentance is change. Furthermore, repentance suggests change that resembles the concept of "praxis." The Greek word for repentance is *metanoia* which literally means "changing one's mind." But changing one's mind in this sense is more than changing one's abstract thoughts. It means that having been convinced that a course is wrong, one changes course. One changes course by changing the value system under which one operated previously. The obvious question then has to be, is it possible for Christians to live in a world where their value system is not informed and influenced by the socio-economic and political realities of that world? And if the answer to that question is in the negative, the inescapable conclusion here is that *metanoia* entails changing those socio-economic and political realities which exist out of a faulty value system. That change in itself constitutes praxis.

Prior mention has been made of the fact that basic Caribbean resistance to liberation theology is the age old dualism between the sacred and secular. However, any understanding of the problem that suggests that liberation theology is interested only in the social is simplistic, to say the least. When liberation theology charges that traditional theology tends to spiritualize the gospel out of all proportion to its socio-economic and political value, it does not mean that with the liberation perspectives all spiritual content is irrelevant to theological discourse. Nor does it mean that the social question is a non-issue with traditional perspectives. Rather, the charge means broadly that liberation from socio-economic and political oppression has not been the central focus of the traditional perspectives. It is just as well that liberation theology should mean this because the missionary societies can be expected to send some food for some hungry people, and the missionary church has never failed in its interest in education and public health. The problem with colonial education and public health however is that the colonized are not educated for freedom, and public health is not geared toward the changing of oppressive structures.

Rev. Atherton Didier of Dominica once preached a sermon entitled "What is the Mission of the Church?"[26] The topic is timely, mainly because Rev. Atherton Didier is a Caribbean person and the Caribbean church is in the process of redefining its mission. The preacher took to task the General Secretary of the Caribbean Conference of Churches for wishing that the New Year would bring the region "closer to the day when all people will be able to thank God for a share in the national cake".[27] Didier contended that this was a bald statement, devoid of any spiritual significance for a Christian people.[28] He does not object to the church's interest in a so-called secular ministry but warns that if the soul is not taken care of first, all other changes are futile.[29] In fact he warns the church that Marxism as observed in the Soviet Union is likely to be the result of merely changing structures in the Caribbean. Didier's case shows clearly that even some Caribbean persons perceive a kind of "secularization" in the liberation thrust of the Caribbean Conference of Churches. The discourse will return to Didier to examine whether he is justified in his conclusions. Suffice it to say now that the question concerning secularization is one that liberation theology has looked at as it faces its own strategy for praxis. If Marx, Hegel, and Aristotle are right in suggesting that the rationality of theory is present in the activity of praxis, then liberation theology must decide whether it is ever possible to begin with the so called concrete situation, for even the concrete cannot be successfully appropriated without a philosophy. This is a question which will be dealt with later under the consideration of philosophy as an interpretation tool. It shall only be noted here that philosophy without the concrete leaves credibility gaps in a theology, if it is meant to deal with liberation. Jesus' own mandate for mission is bringing the good news to the poor, proclaiming release to the captives, recovering of sight to the blind, bringing liberation to the oppressed and proclaiming the divinely ordered redress for the powerless (Luke 4:18-19). If the church takes this mandate seriously it must have something to say about the church's agenda, as the mandate informs its praxis.

It is important to note that the sacred-secular split is avoided in this mandate. The gospel addresses the socio-economic and political situation uninhibitedly. Yet, the reason there is any concern at all for the socio-economic and political is that the Spirit of the Lord dictates it. So then Didier is right. But he is right only as far as the principle goes. His timing is awfully off. The split existed long before the Caribbean Conference of Churches, and as a matter of fact, with its liberation perspective the Caribbean Conference of Churches is making a somewhat late effort to close its consequential gap.

Our Latin American neighbor, Gustavo Gutierrez has thought through the problem of the sacred-secular split and has placed the responsibility for the "secularization" side of the split squarely on the shoulders of the church[30] (and for the Caribbean situation, the missionary church). Among the reasons for this conclusion are two factors:

1. The church has always felt the need to be in total control of human life and destiny.[31] The strategy it has employed to maintain that control is to point humanity away from the benefits of participation in this world, to some "other worldly" situation.[32]

2. As a result of the lack of efficacy in this other worldly escapade, humanity is finding answers to its destiny in other ways.[33] And the liberation perspective is largely responsible for that process. Gutierrez writes:

> Secularization is, above all, the result of transformation of the
> self-understanding of man. From a cosmological vision, due
> especially to scientific developments, man perceives himself as a
> creative subject. Moreover, man becomes aware as we have noted
> above—that he is an agent of history, responsible for his own
> destiny. His mind discovers not only the laws of nature, but also
> penetrates those of society, history, and psychology. This new
> self-understanding of man necessarily brings in its wake a
> different way of conceiving his relationship with God.[34]

Here then, secularization is not a dirty word after all, because it contributes to human self-understanding which encourages a holistic approach to the role of the human person as co-creator of history with God. In which case, given the present situation in the Caribbean, an over-emphasis on the spiritual simply intensifies the sacred-secular split.

Another serious problem with an over-emphasis on the spiritual in the sacred-secular split is that it frequently works to the detriment of the poor and powerless. Geoffrey B. Williams of Guyana researched from the Lutheran history of Guyana the following quote from instructions and advice given in 1816 by the British Missionary Society to missionaries working among slaves in Guyana:

> Not a word must escape you in public or private which might render
> the slaves displeased with their station. You are not sent to relieve
> them of their servile condition, but afford them the consolations of reli-
> gion and to enforce upon them the necessity of being subject 'not only
> for wrath but for conscience sake' (Romans 13:5 and II Peter 2:19). The
> Holy Gospel which you preach will render the slaves who receive it the
> more diligent, faithful, patient and useful servants, will render severe
> discipline unnecessary, and make them more valuable slaves on estates,

and thus you will recommend yourself and your ministry even to those gentlemen who have been adverse to the religious instruction to the Negroes.[35]

In contemporary times the affinity between right wing politics and the conservative church is highly suggestive of perfect grasp of the idea in the rough and tumble of the political arena. As long as humanity can be successfully steered toward the portals of heaven it becomes so preoccupied with the heavenly demands that it looks away from the human condition of here and now. When that happens it is not the poor who benefit. Didier quotes from Colin Morris to prove the importance of the spiritual in the lives of Caribbean Christians:

> One of the striking things about the history of the church is that those Christians who have done most for this earth are those whose eyes have been firmly fixed on heaven...And it was 18th century evangelicals who seemed so pious and ethereal they might vapourize at any moment, who were instrumental in abolishing slavery and child labour.[36]

Without even mentioning the significant fact that Colin Morris is being quoted as the President of the British Methodist Conference, there are some things that need to be stated in regard to this statement:

1. Since the abolitionists were few and far between in the colonial church, championing the cause of the siaves, by that church, was more the exception than the rule.

2. One of the more important contributory factors in the process of the abolition of slavery in the Caribbean was the rebelliousness of the slaves themselves. Completely against the popular teachings of the church they refused to lose the consciousness that freedom belonged to all of humanity.

3. Colonialism existed in the Caribbean for more than a century after emancipation, proving that it takes more than the anti-slavery conscience to support equality, not to mention equity.

4. If it is true that the atrocities of child labor were a factor
   in his desire to reconstruct a society void of greed and
   exploitation, Marx, who claimed no allegiance to the
   Christian church, was more horrified by child labor in
   Britain than many leaders of the church were.

What all this means is that the church's praxis needs to entail
the truth of the equality of all peoples, by virtue of the *imago
dei* as the rationality of its action. As a result it will join in the
effort toward the changing of infrastructures as well as super-
structures in which there is no reason for the existence of
powerlessness. Instead of emphasizing the sacred/secular split,
the church would be more interested in a faith that works.

Faith and Justice

Dr. Horace Russell raises a pertinent issue when he says:

> In general terms, theology takes its point of departure from one of
> three points (a) God (Theos), (b) Man (Anthropos) and (c) The World
> (Cosmos). It would appear that except for some notable exceptions,
> theology has been concerned primarily with God and Man, with some
> passing and scant regard for the world. The result has been that by and
> large, theological constructions have either been primarily 'theocentric'
> or 'anthropocentric.'[37]

Russell is understood here to be addressing the question as to
how valid and acceptable Caribbean theology is in a Caribbean
context. As a result his contribution will be examined more
closely when the discourse comes to deal with the particularity
of the Caribbean context and the significance of contextualization in the process of indigenization. For now it is enough to
deal with the question in its general sense and support the legitimacy of Russell's inference that whether one begins with it
or not, it is the "cosmological" condition to which theology
relates that concretizes the theological position. In time the
examination will have to particularize that position so that
each situation in a world of different needs, hopes and aspirations may provide the particular situation in life for its own
case. But this much suggests that faith has to address
"worldly" situations if it must have any validity in this world.

However, if the concept of the Kingdom of God being rooted in history must avoid any charge of mere ideological and mental gymnastics the biblical endorsement must be sought.

Another neighbor, George Pixley, (once professor of Old Testament at the Seminario Bautista in Mexico, and now teaching in Nicaragua,) has done a monumental work on the subject entitled *God's Kingdom*. For Pixley, the Galilean movement under the leadership of Jesus began with the understanding that the Reign of God was a historical project[38] where justice is done in favor of the poor and powerless.[39] That movement, seeing the Temple as the base from which emanated the classism that left the poor bearing the brunt of a system of oppression and exploitation, declared itself the champion for the cause of the poor.[40] As such it saw itself as the usher of the Reign and on that basis it attacked the seat of power, the Temple,[41] by word:

> And as he came out of the temple, one of the disciples said to him, "Look, Teacher, what wonderful stories and what wonderful buildings!" And Jesus said to him, Do you see these great buildings? There will not be left here one stone upon another, that will not be thrown down." (Mark 13:1-2)

And by deed:

> And he entered the temple and began to drive out those who sold, saying to them, "It is written, 'my house shall be called a house of prayer, but you have made it a den of robbers'" (Luke 19:45-46)

This self-declared mandate existed for some time in the Palestinian base of this movement, if at a less intense measure, even after the assassination of the leader, Jesus. It is no accident that the community attempted to set up an egalitarian lifestyle. The concept of the Reign as a historical project was still at work, and for the moment the principle of the Reign was speaking eloquently against private ownership of property, which led to insatiable greed:

> Now the company of those who believed were of one heart and soul, and no one said that any of the things which he possessed was his own, but they had everything in common. And with great power the apostles gave their testimony to the resurrection of the Lord Jesus, and

great grace was upon them all. There was not a needy person among them, for as many as were possessors of lands or houses sold them, and brought the proceeds of what was sold and laid it at the apostles' feet; and distribution was made to each as any had need. (Acts 4:32-35)

With the nature of the Kingdom thus established as a just society, it is not difficult to see how faith would relate to justice here. Faith would be total commitment to the just cause. If the demands of Jesus, as the narrative sees them, have anything to do with this movement, then faith is that consuming passion to see justice take place in the situation where justice does not exist.[42] Hence the leader declares his own position:

And his mother and his brothers came; and standing outside they sent to him and called him. And a crowd was sitting about him; and they said to him, "Your mother and your brothers are outside asking for you". And he replied, "Who are my mother and my brothers?" And looking around on those who sat about him, he said, "Here are my mother and my brothers! Whoever does the will of God is my brother, and sister, and mother." (Mark 3:31-35)

And in turn the leader declares what the position of the members of the movement ought to be:

He who loves father or mother more than me is not worthy of me; and he who loves son or daughter more than me is not worthy of me; and he who does not take up his cross and follow me is not worthy of me. He who finds his life will lose it, and he who loses his life for my sake will find it. (Matthew 10:37-39)

Special care must be taken to note that Pixley sees the reference to the resurrection idea, whether in the case of Jesus' own or the larger principle of finding life after losing it, as reference to the appropriation of the historical Reign. Ever since the Maccabean period as evidenced in 2 Maccabees 7, resurrection has been associated with the Reign of God.[43]

It was only when St. Paul entered the scene that the resurrection was no longer considered a symbol of participation in the Reign but as assurance of the preservation of the soul.[44] The Reign was made to give up its historical orientation for a spiritual one, a localized interpretation for a universal one. Pixley understands that it is only outside of Palestine that this change becomes necessary. After the death of Jesus:

The Palestinian Jesus movement lived in the hope that Jesus their Messiah would return soon to Galilee to establish God's Kingdom. It was a movement of the oppressed classes of Palestine, which focused their hope for their historical liberation. As such, the destruction of the independence movement during the war against Rome also meant the end of their project. For those who listened to the story of Jesus outside of Palestine, the destruction of the temple and the independence movement in Palestine meant instead the removal of the Jews from importance and the internalization of the gospel. The gospel of God could no longer be taken as a Jewish Messianic hope, but now appeared in a more spiritual form of heavenly hope.[45]

The emphasis of the gospel message itself became privatized because it focused upon the redemption of the individual soul, instead of upon a social liberation containing historical redress. Hence when Paul preached:

The person to whom Paul addresses his message is no longer "the poor" but rather "the sinner." And because sin is universal human condition since the sin of Adam, the gospel is actually addressed without distinction to all humankind, to every person. All have sinned and are liable to the judgment of God. For that reason Christ died in order to free humankind from the anger that God will direct at his chosen moment against sin.[46]

Now this privatized gospel with generalized principles is the gospel that the Caribbean has known. This is the gospel that it received from Europe and is being reinforced by the evangelical concentration. This is the gospel that is most handy for both the colonizing and neo-colonizing processes. Just as Paul saw no necessity for the slave Onesimus in Philemon 8-20 to get his physical freedom (since he had already received liberty of the soul through Christ),[47] the European gospel has never seen social justice as the primary concern of faith. Just as Paul made sure to interpret the Reign of God in ahistorical terms, so European Christianity sought to evangelize by placing the Reign in heavenly reaches. The real problem is that this gospel has been so thoroughly internalized by the Caribbean that ideas of radical change often become an affront to some of the Caribbean people themselves. The Rev. Burchell K. Taylor, reflecting on the factors of opposition to a Caribbean theology says:

Again, this reaction from within should not be wholly unexpected. Knowing the theological diet we have been brought up on, and the taste patterns are quite naturally acquired, there would be those who would resent being presented with a new theological diet and making the required, necessary adjustment in the taste pattern, even though — or especially if — the fare is home grown.[48]

And Rev. William Watty's comment on the subject identifies the area as a source of conflict in the indigenization process:

But the Pelau society has not yet produced its own theologian, inspite of the fact that Caribbean societies are saturated with religion and that Caribbean churchmen have won academic distinctions for themselves in the institutions of Europe and America. The reason is simple: Caribbean churches are committed to foreign theologies. These are imported by missionaries or imbibed by Caribbean people abroad, while missionaries, for reasons best known to themselves are dedicated to frustrating the emergence of a Caribbean theology.[49]

Yet despite all the obstacles in the way of indigenization, the ethics which will confront the colonial legacy and neo-colonial onslaught in the Caribbean awaits its creation in and through indigenous theology. Caribbean indigenization must find the will to reinterpret its faith so that it may rectify the lack of historicity in the reality of the Reign of God and the problems of justice which arise in it.

Notes

1 Smith, Ashley, *Real Roots And Potted Plants*, Mandeville, Jamaica, West Indies, Mandeville Publishers, 1984, p. 10.

2 Ibid. p. 9.

3 Maslow, Abraham H., *Motivation and Personality*, New York, Harper and Row Publishers, 1970, p. 46.

4 Ibid. p. 47

5 Ibid. p. 161.

6 Ibid. p. 161.

7 De Las Casas, Bartolome, *The Devastation of the Indians*, trans., Herma Briffault, New York, The Seabury Press, 1974, p. 59.

8 Gayle, Clement H.L., "The Church in The West Indies-Bondage and Freedom, "*Caribbean Journal of Religious Studies*, Vol. III, no. 1, April, 1980, p. 21.

9 Ibid.

10 Ibid. p. 22.

11 See Cover, Smith, Ashley, *Real Roots and Potted Plants*, Mandeville, Jamaica, West Indies, Mandeville Publishers, 1984.

12 Rocourt, Alain, "The Challenge of Development in Haiti," *With Eyes Wide Open*, ed. David I. Mitchell, Jamaica, West Indies, Christian Action for Development In the Caribbean (CADEC), 1973, p. 75.

13 Snaith, Norman H., *The Distinctive Ideas of the Old Testament*, London. The Epworth Press, 1962, pp. 51-52.

14 Ward, Barbara, *Nationalism and Ideology*, New York, W. W. Norton and Company, 1966, pp. 42-43.

15 Snaith, Norman H. *The Distinctive Ideas of the Old Testament*, London, The Epworth Press, 1962, pp. 69-70.

16   Absomism is an African belief in the spanning of vast space through spirit intermediaries. See Mbiti, John S., *African Religion and Philosophy*, Garden City, New York, Doubleday and Company, Inc., 1970, p. 98.

17   Chevannes, Barry, "Some Notes on African Religious Survivals In the Caribbean, *Caribbean Journal of Religious Studies*, Vol.V, No.II, September, 1983, pp. 21-22.

18   Ibid. p. 18-19

19   Byfield, Bevis, "Transformation and the Jamaican Society," *Caribbean Journal of Religious Studies*, Volume V, Nov. 1, April 1983, p. 37.

20   Bernstein, Richard J, *Praxis and Action*, Philadelphia, University of Pennsylvania Press 1971, p. IX.

21   Ibid. p. PX.

22   Ibid. p. IX.

23   Ibid. p. IX.

24   Ibid. p. XI.

25   Ibid. p. 13.

26   Didier, Atherton, "What is the Mission of the Church." *The Caribbean Pulpit*, eds. C.H. Gayle, W.W. Watty, Kingston, Jamaica, 1983, pp. 29-33.

27   Ibid. pp. 29-33.

28   Ibid. p. 30.

29   Ibid. p. 30

30   Gutierrez, Gustavo, *A Theology of Liberation*, trans., Sister Caridad Inda and John Eagleson, New York, Maryknoll, New York, 1973 p. 66.

31   Ibid. p. 66.

32   Ibid. p. 67.

33   Ibid. p. 67.

34   Ibid. p. 67.

35   Williams, Geoffrey B., "Classicism And The Caribbean Church, "*Out of the Depths*, ed. Idris Hamid, Trinidad, West Indies, St. Andrew's Theological Seminary 1977, p. 59.

36 Didier, Atherton, "What Is the Mission of the Church," *The Caribbean Pulpit*, eds. C.H.L. Gayle and W.W. Watty, Kingston, Jamaica 1983, p. 30 citing Colin Morris, President British Methodist Conference.

37 Russell, Horace, "The Challenge of Theological Reflection in the Caribbean Today," *Troubling of the Waters*, ed. Idris Hamid, Trinidad, W.I. Rahaman Printery Limited, 1973. p. 26.

38 Pixley, George V., *God's Kingdom*, Trans. Donald D. Walsh, Maryknoll, New York, Orbis, 1977. p. 72.

39 Ibid. p. 77.

40 Ibid. p. 72.

41 Ibid. p. 75

42 Ibid. p. 72.

43 Ibid. p. 95.

44 Ibid. p. 96.

45 Ibid. p. 72.

46 Ibid. p. 91.

47 Ibid. p. 93.

48 Taylor, Burchell K. "Caribbean Theology", *Caribbean Journal of Religious Studies*, Vol.4, No.1. April 1982, p. 14.

49 Watty, William, "Struggling to Be," ed. David I. Mitchell, *New Mission for a New People*, Friendship Press, 1977, p. 108.

PART TWO

ESSENTIAL CHARACTERISTICS
OF CARIBBEAN THEOLOGY

Dr. Horace Russell, past president of the United Theological College of the West Indies, takes traditional theology to task. He points out, as already has been mentioned in chapter two, that in its anxiety to present itself as God talk, traditional theology, while showing much interest in God and humanity has demonstrated little regard for the "Cosmos."[1] He concludes that this is a situation which ought to be avoided in the search for a Caribbean theology:

> ...theology of the Caribbean must take 'cosmos' seriously. But because 'cosmos' is a composite idea, i.e. creative event and 'process of creation; then history and geography have to be taken seriously. This might be illustrated by the fact that the word 'Caribbean' is both a geographical as well as an historical term. Geography links together not only the physical island chain, but its inhabitants into a scheme of Caribbean unity, while history attempts to systematize varied island experiences into a common theme.[2]

Here Russell has identified two basic areas to which theology in the Caribbean must relate. One is history and the other is geography. Both are inseparable. Of course when application is examined carefully, "geography" means more than distance and proximity. It describes the sociology of a people within a certain hemisphere, as that sociology which is shaped by historical events. Hence Russell has suggested two realities as tools for doing Caribbean theology, history and sociology.

The choice of the third tool is made on its introduction by spokespersons such as Dr. Burchell K. Taylor, senior pastor of Bethel Baptist Church in Kingston and part time lecturer at the United Theological College of the West Indies. This tool is "philosophy." Taylor, of course, registers a certain ambivalence with this tool, inasmuch as he, on the one hand, does not trust its abstractness, while on the other wonders whether we can actually do without it when it comes to the systematization of theology.[3] In any case if Caribbean perspectives have to be systematized there has to be some interpretive factor serving as an agent of cohesion. It would seem therefore that philosophy is unavoidable. Here then are the three areas which will function as interpretive tools: history, sociology and philosophy. Along with the interpretive tools must be included some other very important ingredients in the theological process. These are the sources and the over all method in the development of the enterprise.

Ultimately, when a theological perspective is developed, it is done basically for the faith of the people on whose experience the reflection is being done. Here perhaps the Caribbean perspective may determine that theology is not rewritten merely for "each succeeding generation" but several times within a single generation. Like theological perspectives in any other Third World peripheral context,

> It must constantly reformulate its views at each concrete historical moment, for it must serve faith as it is lived by people in the concrete circumstance of history.[4]

It is this very process that produces the content of the Caribbean perspective. In the case of the Caribbean, the concrete circumstances of history have to do with the imposition of the will of some upon others for the longest span of time in modern history. The theological perspective, therefore, is worked out in the tension of that imposition. If a philosophy is possible at all in that tension, the analysis of the situation, the reflection on the ethical perspectives in the tension within the situation, and the plan of action to change the situation are all factors in the method employed in Caribbean indigenization.

Notes

1 Russell, Horace, "The Challenge of Theological Reflection in the Caribbean," ed. Idris Hamid, *Troubling of the Waters*, Trinidad W.I. Rahaman Printery Limited. 1973, p.26.

2 Ibid. p. 27.

3 Taylor, Burchell, "Caribbean Theology, *"Caribbean Journal of Religious Studies*, Vol.3, No.2, September 198, p.21.

4 Vidales, Raul, "Methodological Issues in Liberation Theology," ed. Rosino Givellini, *Frontiers of Theology in Latin America*, Maryknoll, New York, Orbis, 1979, p. 37.

Chapter Three

Interpretive Tools

History

It may do well to note here that the discussion at this point will not focus so much on history as the accumulation of data, nor even as reflection on historical data. It will be primarily focused as reflection upon the *use* of history in the Caribbean process; its legitimacy and practicality as an interpretive tool. History is not merely an accumulation and dating of facts relating to events, because facts about events are a record of experience. As a result, when it comes to authenticity a lot depends on who is the recorder and reporter of events, because interpretation is of vital importance. For example, when the history of slavery is reported from a Caribbean perspective, the monstrosity of the crime against humanity is the crucial point of view. In many cases when the same history is reported from the British perspective, it is the rigors of the sympathizers of emancipation which become the focal reference. With this thought in mind one may judge that it is probably just as well that the colonial educational system in the West Indies took its time to sanction West Indian history as anything more than a tangential requirement for "proper" education. West Indian history, written from a European perspective at its best, can only create a warped consciousness for West Indian learners. Compare a David Mitchell approach in writing about Haiti with that of Basil Cracknell on the same subject. Cracknell writes:

> Ever since Haiti became the first Caribbean country to achieve its independence in 1804, the other countries of the region have been striving for independence and for political maturity as self-governing

nations.　Probably Haiti achieved its independence too early for its own good and it has since paid a high price in terms of economic and political stagnanation.[1]

With one casual and sweeping sentence on the independence gained by Haiti in 1804, Cracknell makes it seem as if Haiti had merely established some frivolous fad that ultimately became fashionable with the rest of the Caribbean who became "copy cats."[2] In the very next sentence he manages to insinuate that Haiti might have been better off without its independence, that coming into it as early as it did, it has always been unable to manage its internal affairs, politically and economically.[3] David Mitchell, on the other hand, writes:

> Haiti is called "the Pearl of the Antilles." It was the second country in the Americas, after the United States, to win independence, and the first Negro state in the modern world.　During the Haitian revolution, however, the factories and irrigation systems of the hated French-owned plantations were destroyed, precipitating a long erosion of Haitian agriculture, and the nation was divided between black ex-slaves in the north and a mulatto "free elite"in the south.[4]

Mitchell does not gloss over the economic and political realities of Haiti, but he takes time to be cognizant of the inner workings of the Haitian system, examining the causes, for example, of how much easier it is to gain physical independence than it is to gain psychological independence.　It is quite evident that Mitchell's approach sees Haitian independence as more than a fad.　Its being the first Negro state anywhere in the New World has been an absolutely brilliant source of inspiration to the rest of the Caribbean.[5]　So while both reporters bring out the facts, it is the one who has everything at stake in the Caribbean who interprets more meaningfully. It is at this point where interpretation becomes crucial for the reporting of history, that the importance of history itself as a theological tool is highlighted.　Flippancy will bypass the heart of the problems in the region.　Self-indulgence may kill the impetus to struggle.　Avoiding the harsh realities of the truth will impede the development of an eschatology for liberation.

History and Value System

The Rev. Roy Neehall, in his paper "Christian Witness and Mission in the Caribbean Development" quotes from William Demas:

> The critical area in which change is required is that of values. Only a change of values would hold out hope for a solution of the unemployment problem and for a transformation of agriculture and rural society. Only a change of values would enable the people to accept a revised definition of development itself and reject the Madison Avenue definition of the "Good Life." Only a change of values could contain the revolution of rising expectations for material improvement. Only a change of values could give the people the motivation to build from below.[6]

There is no question that this statement comes out of a milieu or at least an understanding that a tremendous struggle exists within the Caribbean. It is a struggle for self-development as achieved through a process of self-actualization. That fact comes as a sobering reminder after hearing the optimism in Neehall's opening statement:

> We the people of the Caribbean, are emerging from the long night of dependence and imitation as we assert our selfhood and identity. We are developing because we are searching for new ways to deal with the realities of today, because we are building community on values that are our own, and because we are changing the designs for living that were imposed upon us. Our development can never be a gift from others. It is our own struggle and we know that means hard work, continuous cooperation and personal sacrifice.[7]

It is the idea of the Caribbean building community on values that are its own that warrants some scrutiny. One recalls the Caenwood Union Theological Seminary's dining room as a place where students were judged for civilized exposure and cultural appropriation, by the demonstration of European dexterity with the cutlery. But with the desire for change in the sixties, some students in rebellion against Europeanization violated most "barbarously" a European taboo by taking the fork in the right hand. The problem is that this "radicalism" was simply the prelude to the exchange between European colonialism and North American neo-colonialism. The question for Roy Neehall then is, whose value system is the Caribbean calling its own?

Yet this critique is not to say that a Caribbean value system is impossible. On the contrary it is saying that if it does exist, whatever it is, it must be extracted from the milieu with diligence so that it may be judged as truly Caribbean. It is saying that if the students had even demonstrated some innovation by discarding the cutlery and using their fingers it would not have meant that the Caribbean value system was identified. On the other hand, when history reminds us that using the fingers has been in African, Indian and European cultures, history becomes an important tool in the search for an indigenous value system because Africa, India and Europe are part of Caribbean history. But since the Caribbean is not Africa, is not India, is not Europe, a diligent study of Caribbean history then becomes crucial because what the Caribbean has been, gives a vivid prospectus on at least what it ought to be.

History as Common Denominator

The Rev. William Watty describes the Caribbean reality as the Trinidadian "Pelau."[8] The word "Pelau," used in relation to the Caribbean situation is an essay in itself, because Pelau is a meal of simple culinary artistry where all the leftovers of the week are skillfully made into a tasty dish.[9] Watty explains that it is the unity among the ingredients that makes Pelau a tasty meal and it is the same principle that makes for the viability of the Caribbean as a people. He writes:

> Caribbean peoples are like a Pelau. As long as they see themselves as diaspora from other lands, separated and estranged from each other, they are no more than leftovers of humanity, and to speak of Caribbean culture is a sick joke. Imitate Europeans and we are caricatures of Europeans. However Indian we are, India is what is really authentic. Try as we like to be African, Africa is better.[10]

The Pelau concept is not merely enticingly beautiful in its application, it also signifies the precarious harmony between Caribbean unity and uniformity.

Ever since the defunct and much lamented West Indian Federation in the early sixties, it has been more than evident that the Caribbean has its own individual territorial interest and "nationalistic" awareness which, when multiplied can be considered Caribbean pluralism. Not fully realizing that major power nations never seek relationships with poor countries except for the benefit of the major powers, Jamaica, under its political leader, Sir Alexander Bustamante had declared its alignment with the West and positioned itself to reap the "benefits" of "benign" relationships with North America. A part of that understanding was that if it did not separate itself from the rest of the Caribbean it would not gain its swift upward mobility. It pulled out of the plan and the Federation collapsed. Since the collapse, the struggle to defeat the neo-colonial structure into which the so-called "benign" relationships have slipped, has been waged mostly on the individual front throughout the Caribbean. There is of course the marketing facility known as Caricom, but that too is fraught with difficulties which stem from national awareness and other peculiarities at that level. Caricom does not yet embody the Pelau concept which brings home the realization of strength in the unity of the Caribbean peoples.

From another point of view, the creativity in the argument for the Pelau reality is to be observed carefully, lest Watty be judged as fostering some kind of passive mindlessness within a "pot pourri." Often this is a misconception on the part of the neo-colonial structure. If a metropolitan administration speaks of Edward Seaga of Jamaica as "our man in the Caribbean" it honestly believes that Seaga can single handedly deliver to it the rest of the Caribbean on a silver platter. Notwithstanding the claims to Seaga's role in the invasion of Grenada and also the ousting of Jean Claude Duvalier from Haiti, the United States' evaluation of both the role and its significance for the Caribbean is grossly exaggerated. Obviously there are other leaders who, taking a more progressive stand, would not choose to take sides with the United States on that particular matter. The mere question of sovereignty would be a deterrent. Furthermore, in terms of proximity the military threat that Seaga claimed to have felt in Jamaica from Grenada's socio-political experiment was more contrived than real. Even with the fear of communism the contrivance was simply a lackey role some other Caribbean leaders would never stoop to embrace. Whatever went wrong or right in Grenada, they would feel, ought to have been Grenada's sovereign right to settle. As far as Haiti is concerned, to suggest that it was by Seaga's instrumentality that Jean Claude Duvalier fled Haiti is a diminution of the Haitians' own determination and effort in their struggle for justice. The people have been struggling against tyranny with blood, sweat and tears. Thus the national diversity which exists in the Caribbean is an asset to its dignity and struggle for selfhood.

Beyond the shades of ideological differences, there are also economic peculiarities within the region, even if measured only by degrees. In EPICA's[11] *The Caribbean*, it is interesting to note how the titles of the chapters in the study of each territory in the Caribbean make that clear. The list reads:

> 1. Trinidad: "Capitalism gone Mad." 2. St. Vincent and the Grenadines: Small Island Woes. 3 Barbados: Hard Times on a "Model" Island. 4. The Dominican Republic: Society Without Solutions. 5. Haiti: The Region's Shame. 6. Jamaica: Reaganomics in the Caribbean. 7. Guyana: Pseudo-Socialism and Starvation. 8. Guadeloupe: "You will remain French." 9. The Netherlands Antilles: Reluctant Independence. 10. Puerto Rico: U. S. Colony in the Caribbean.[12]

Each title is indicative of some peculiarity in each country's problem, and indeed each searches for its peculiar solutions. It is all another kind of diversity that is sufficient to warrant speaking of the Caribbean "peoples" instead of the Caribbean "people."

On the other hand diversity should not become a detriment to the unity necessary for shedding the posture of powerlessness because even in the diversity there is a commonality. Jamaica has a bauxite problem and Trinidad has an oil problem but in both cases the denominator is a market problem. If there are shared problems there are shared solutions. Thus the Caribbean, viewed in its togetherness can become a formidable force to deal with. One ingredient that offers prospects for this cementation is shared history. The history of the Caribbean from the mercantilism of colonialism to floundering in the markets of neo-colonialism, delineates its borders and defines its people. By the history of the Caribbean, the Caribbean is the Caribbean.[13]

History as Hope

It is inconceivable that as an election took place in Haiti in 1988, no matter how fraudulent, the people did not hear echoes of 1804 when Haiti stood up to the French army and won. And if hope may be located anywhere in history, Haiti is probably the most suitable to be lifted for its symbols of hope because it is considered the most hopeless of all the Caribbean territories. Hence despite its long history of civil rivalry between Blacks and Mulattos,[14] despite the successive reign of tyrant presidents, despite its poverty ridden state, events suggest that within its own history there are spots of hope created by history itself. The election was by no means the end of Haiti's misery but as an event in its history it stands as a classic demonstration that hope can be snatched out of hopelessness. Even the most powerless can find some source of power. It is therefore crucial that Duvalier's flight from Haiti be recognized as having come about through the instrumentality of Haitians, because here it may be determined that their own liberation praxis is at work.

"History as hope" is born out of the reality that human persons are not passive objects of history. They are also creators of history, and that fact sometimes renders it a redundant exercise to speak about "salvation history." The salvation theory is often latent in the liberation struggle itself. The liberation cry of the poor masses in Haiti, "*Aba la faim! Aba la misere! Aba Duvaye!*" (Down with hunger! Down with misery! Down with Duvalier!)[15] contains the rationale concerning the affirmation of the human self in the *imago dei* and the negation of the oppression and misery as divine disapproval. This is what is meant in the Haitian Bishop's letter of November 1984:

> ...In the name of love which links all the members of the Body of Christ, and in our pastoral responsibility, we have decided to intervene before the responsible authorities to obtain respect for fundamental

rights such as individual freedom, the physical and moral integrity of
every citizen, and the tranquility and peace of the household.[16]

There is no doubt that the church in Haiti was a caring church
all along, but like the missionary church throughout the
Caribbean it had focused its care upon ahistorical factors of
the Christian faith. Theology in history probably meant the
abstract significance of the Christological road from Nicea to
Chalcedon. But in stark contrast to the prior case in the
church's life, when the government official in attendance at
the mass at the Cathedral of Cap Haitien interrupted the
reading of the above mentioned letter and proceeded to criti-
cize the church leaders,[17] the modern church knew what
"situation in life" really means. Furthermore, when in a mass
in the towns of Dessalines and Milot, armed *tontons macoutes*
took up positions on either side of the altar until the benedic-
tion,[18] the church began to understand that it itself had
become an enemy of tyranny and at the same time a symbol of
hope, by its participation in history; and also that the gospel
addresses historical situations for its peace. As the church said
in its letter of appeal to the outside world:

> ...We do not ask for money nor do we demand contributions of food
> and used clothing; that is humiliating. We only demand that which
> money cannot provide: freedom, equality, democracy, justice for
> everyone, work, access to land, and the means with which to cultivate
> the land.[19]

If there is a moral in these deliberations on Haiti, it is that the
common history of the Caribbean creates its own sense of
hope, and that the process of indigenization is the task of
bringing it into full bloom.

History as hope broadens the scope of history to create
frontal and progressive perspectives. The very concept of history as reality is by nature one that looks back. The Hebrews
looked back at their slavery experience in Egypt, the Jews look
back at the Holocaust, and the New World Africans look back
at slavery. Each case comes with its own degree of trauma.
However, there is a sense in which trauma in the history of a
people often becomes the criterion for defining that people.
This is not a discussion of the unwilling guilt of the colonizing

system, which is transposed into further victimization of the victims as if they are responsible for their own enslavement and oppression. This is a discussion of a kind of tunnel vision where the victims themselves see everything through the eyes of the trauma. In which case, for example, when the Jews say "Never again," they must make sure that it does not mean that all Palestinians may be dispossessed to ensure Israel's security.[20] National security should not consist only of ensuring that all future activity be performed for the sake of that security. In other words, if victims of a trauma see themselves as nothing but victims of that trauma and spend their entire energies in retrospection with regards to the trauma, discarding the victim mentality becomes a virtual impossibility.

In the Caribbean the trauma of slavery is not something that will be easily forgotten, or even needs to be. However, when that history provides the rationale for failure it becomes chains instead of guideposts, and liberation for progress becomes a recalcitrant dream. History as hope means shedding the fear created by a slavery psychology, of radicalizing action for change.

Sociology

An appropriate phrase for the Caribbean social reality is "no one is an island," because despite peculiarities, diversity and individual autonomy, no single island or territory does the Caribbean make. It has already been stated that by geography together with history the territories become a unit. It may now be observed that within that reality there is a built-in social responsibility. In consequence of its history the Caribbean territories share a common social identity. Each has been a colonized people. Just as the region's colonial experience is inseparable from its total history, so the Caribbean situation is firmly related to global connections. As European colonies they relate in ways, more than one, to Europe. For example the different shades in complexion of West Indians give a strong evidence of some very intimate relationships between the colonizers and the colonized. That fact, coupled with the fact of the trade in slavery between

Africa and the Caribbean ("Middle Passage"), and also with the arrangement for indentured labor between India and the European plantation owners, has made it possible for very few to deny roots outside of the Caribbean. However, while it cannot be said that the others are of minor importance, in terms of ecological displacement, Africans and Indians are more apt to be caught up in an identity crisis. Since they are in the majority in this respect, it is they who have to face the sociological question, "who are the West Indians or Caribbean people?" Of course, because of the forced participation of the Africans in this Western cultural orientation, there is an intensification of the Caribbean identity situation on their part. They are faced with a further question, "is there a distinct Caribbean culture?" And if there is, what has influenced it? To what extent has it been influenced?

In the final analysis, judged by what is the cultural orientation of the Caribbean, other questions arise and by their very existence demand answers. For example:

1. How is the underdevelopment in the Caribbean to be judged, by conclusions surrounding cultural lag, or conclusions surrounding structural discrimination?

2. In colonialism there are two sides, the dominant and the dominated peoples. The very fact of colonialism suggests that superiority is presupposed on the part of the dominant, just as the dominant presuppose inferiority on the part of the dominated. Is the Caribbean satisfied with the inferiority role or has there been the establishment of a parallel culture even under colonial rule?

3. Since colonizers by the very structure of colonialism separate people from self-actualization and power, is it normal or deviant to colonize?

These are all sociological questions, but while being sociological they raise moral and therefore theological issues. If Caribbean theology means reflection upon the human appropriation of the work of God through Christ as it relates to and deals with the Caribbean context, Caribbean theology must of necessity employ the concreteness of the sociological reality as a tool in the understanding of that context.

The Diaspora Syndrome

Perhaps the only Caribbeans certain of their diaspora status are the Rastafarians who have influenced much of the Caribbean. They began their religious movement in Jamaica in 1930 by endorsing Marcus Garvey's Black consciousness in which Africa was hailed as the mother country for all Negroes. They also support Garvey's doctrine of repatriation for all Negroes living out of the mother country. They called Selasse, then Emperor of Ethiopia, God incarnate and developed a messianism around him and Ethiopia. The movement has now spread throughout the Caribbean to the extent that it may be described as a Caribbean movement as opposed to a Jamaican movement.

At a time when it was fashionable for West Indian Blacks to trace their ancestry to Europe, Rastafarians were not only tracing theirs to Africa but were the leading catalysts for race protest.[21] They adopted some forms of African culture to the extent that their speech included words from an Ethiopian language, and many took no special responsibility for proper syntax in English since it was an imposed language anyway. Up until the early sixties it was not unusual to hear a Rastafarian say:

> Yes when I check it out, I find that my forefather was there and I was taken here as a slave by the Austrians so the captivity of Israel will come again and that means that we have to be repatriated from this land to a next one, to go back to Ethiopia.[22]

However, the intensity of such a statement as made by spokespersons of the movement was beginning to wane as far back as 1963.[23] After the Coral Garden incident in Jamaica where a group of Rastafarians attacked a gas station and a motel, and in which persons, including two police officers, were killed,[24] the police waged an open war on the Rastafarians. As the treatment became more ruthless and arbitrary, with very little objection on the part of the public, the Rasta-

farian spokesperson Sam Brown launched an appeal for justice
on the grounds that they were citizens of Jamaica.[25] This was
a radical change from the citizenship they had heretofore
claimed in Ethiopia. Bongo Dizzy, another of their spokespersons,
later succinctly placed their interest more on the side of
reparation than on repatriation:

> The black man in this country and throughout the West has united
> with the heads of Government in helping to build a better Jamaica, but
> we the black majority who has helped plow the soil, planted the vine-
> yard and gathered the fruits thereof, we are not the benefactors. Those
> who benefit are the protectors. They share the crops, they boss the
> work and own the slaves...the majority of Jamaicans are black—why
> then are not the black supreme here? We want no promises, we want
> fulfillment now. Three hundred years of slavery in the Western
> world—what for? Jamaica's independence means a well without water,
> a treasury without money.[26]

Not only was Bongo Dizzy questioning the race problem in the
country, he was also taking interest in the economic status and
calling for justice in the form of reparation.

Perhaps the Rastafarians had taken a long hard look at the
situation when in 1960 the pioneers who had been sent to
Ethiopia in cooperation with the governments of Jamaica and
Ethiopia, returned and gave their report. The stark reality
was that Ethiopia was just as problematic as the Caribbean. In
any case Ethiopia was not about to take in thousands of for-
eigners even if they were willing to call its emperor God. It
would seem then that Ethiopia was going to be held symbolically as the Messianic Zion while they protested locally for
radical reorganization of structures. After all, this was probably Garvey's own strategy in his "Back to Africa Movement."
Garvey knew very well that not every black person could
physically make it back to Africa. Rastafarians have no particular love for the system that controls Caribbean development or lack of it. They understand the neo-colonial structures and have declared their construction as against divine
intentions for the region. In fact they see the decline of the
economic bases in Britain and North America as fulfillment of
a prophecy of retribution for their sins against the African

peoples.[27] However what seems to have changed, in terms of viewpoint, is the intensity of the "diaspora syndrome" which formerly impeded efforts on their part toward self-development in any serious and systematic way.

If it is this aspect of the diaspora syndrome that William Watty is reacting to when he suggests, in his "Pelau" concept, that if the Caribbean peoples continue to consider themselves as a diaspora they will never experience unity, he deserves to be applauded. However if he means that the Caribbean peoples should disregard all roots beyond the ebb and flow of the Caribbean sea, it needs to be said that such a feat is not possible. Even if it were, the Afro-Caribbean people will place themselves in jeopardy of succumbing to the position that says that the Negro has no past and therefore no culture that is distinctively African. At this point it must be taken into consideration that because all other West Indians have been afforded some dignity and freedom in the retention of some of their culture, the Negro situation comes with more persuasion to have itself dealt with carefully. A prominent portion of the slavery rationale was constructed on the myth that the Negro had no culture. The question, therefore, as to whether the Caribbean situation begins within the Caribbean itself, becomes more acute when it is directed to the Afro-Caribbean. Furthermore, because of what may have been lost in ecological displacement and the psychological domination in slavery, in which only Afro-Caribbeans have been involved, it is important that the response be clear.

The Myth of the Negro Past
Kenneth Stampp, in his book, *The Peculiar Institution*, lists three basic myths on which the system of slavery was excused, and therefore on which it thrived in the New World:

1. God with divine foresight and planning developed the Negro physique for hard labor. Their bodies and strength were simply provided the space and opportunity to perform that which comes naturally.[28]

2. With an extremely low intellectual capacity the Negro was incapable of those cerebral functions necessary for the creation, development, and management of societies, therefore the Negro's natural lot was that of a slave.[29]

3. Furthermore, a certain brutishness and barbarianism innate in the personality of Negroes made it necessary for them to be controlled with the harshness which befitted their nature. For that reason slavery in the New World was good for them because it provided them with the opportunity to see white culture in its purest benevolence.[30]

Needless to say, Stamp takes the opportunity to indicate that these fallacies are based upon a total misapprehension of the Negro's past. The portions of Africa from which most of the slaves came had well-developed cultures. Their economies were based on intricately created agricultural systems and craft production and entailed the principles of demand, production, sale and purchase. They produced meaningful art, colorful and rich folklore, and created complex theological perspectives.[31] Leonard Barrett, himself a West Indian, concurs with Stampp and suggests that if culture means complex organization of knowledge, beliefs, art, law, morals and customs, West Africa, prior to and during the slave trade not only demonstrated the possession of a very high culture, but in its ecological displacement, that culture brought some influence for good to bear upon the Western World. [32]

Of all the distinctiveness of the West African culture which came with the slaves to the New World, Barrett argues that religion has been the most vital institution. He suggests that an understanding of this religious institution gives insight into common systems of beliefs which in turn disclose a common cultural structure.[33] This fact is vital not only to the comprehension of the Euro-American evangelization process in the Caribbean but also to what is basically acceptable to the process of Caribbean indigenization of theology. The importance escalates even further when we hear Barrett saying that:

Religion for Africans was, is and ever shall be the source of life and meaning. It is in religion that they live, move and have their being... the religious world view of the Africans contributed most to their survival in the New World.[34]

What this discussion proves so far is the fact that the Caribbean does not begin with its geographical boundaries. Africa has played a major role in the development of any culture that is indigenous to the Caribbean. So the next important question is how these factors may be used to facilitate the theological process that may be called distinctively Caribbean. Donald M. Chinula suggests that the answer lies in a concept called Pan Africanism.

Pan-Africanism and Caribbean Theology
One of the old sociological principles regarding slavery and colonialism is that dominated people, including slaves, make gradual psychological adjustment to accommodate the burden of domination and servitude. It is a survival mechanism, and when the period of domination is protracted, that accommodation becomes increasingly the absorption of the will of the colonizer.[35] It is not clear how much of this as a factor Donald Chinula is willing to take as inevitable as he judges Jamaica's most serious problem to be an exocentrism which translates into self-hatred on the one hand and love of the masters' goods and lifestyle on the other.[36] However he himself being an African (Tanzanian) suggests that Pan-Africanism is the only road to a theology that will liberate the island from this particular disease. Chinula defines Pan-Africanism as:

...an ideology of black unity and liberation. It asserts that all persons of African ancestry or descent, irrespective of varying shades of color, geographical location or acquired life styles, are an African people who share the following common characteristics: (1) They are black, biologically, symbolically or politically; (2) they have historically been an oppressed humanity, broadly speaking, and largely remain oppressed to this day; (3) their oppressors have been principally Euro-Americans motivated by racial hatred and economic greed; (4) their oppression has left them demoralized, debased, feeble, confused about their true identity and disunited; (5) they are in dire need of redemption under God;

and (6) such redemption must eschatologically look towards the establishment of a united and defensible African nation to guarantee the
regained freedom.[37]

"Africa for Africans" as Pan-Africanism has declared ever
since Marcus Garvey introduced it, is a worthwhile symbolism
for Black people everywhere. Consequently, as far as the idea
is concerned, that sociological categories may be used as a tool
for the development of a theology within the Caribbean for
the Caribbean, that symbolism is indispensable. The concept
of Africa as "motherland" evokes a sense of national pride
which itself fosters a kind of "spiritual" symbiosis between
Afro-Caribbeans and other Africans everywhere. It also helps
to provide the sense of roots and cultural foundations necessary for the overcoming of the colonially contrived "rootless-
ness and culturelessness" of Caribbean beginnings.

On the other hand, despite the fact that Jamaica (for whom
Chinula proposes Pan-Africanism) is ninety-five percent black,
its real problem is rooted in colonialism and neo-colonialism,
the latter working through an institutional classism created by
colonialism. There is still no guarantee that from a practical
standpoint African unity is exemplified in Africa itself where
colonial education has created the same class system in which
the Jamaican "topanarists" are no different from the African
"evolues."[38] In other words the "symbol of blackness" in and of
itself is not enough to counteract the stark economic fallout
from chronic classism.

Secondly, the convenience of ninety-five percent of
Jamaica's population being of African descent should not allow
the temptation to develop a Jamaican theology as separate and
apart from a Caribbean theology, because in the final analysis,
Jamaica's Africanness serves as only one aspect of its Caribbean
distinctiveness. Jamaica is Caribbean and not all Caribbean
peoples are of African descent. A Pan-African perspective
could very well be an imperialist attitude to those of Indian
descent who, for example, would have to subsume their Indian
culture under the dynamics of the African culture.

Finally, from a practical and structural, therefore socio-economic and political standpoint, there is some evidence that

Pan-Africanism is probably no more achievable now than when Marcus Garvey first proposed it in 1917. It is quite true that Africans look back at Garvey's genius with great respect and openly admit the lasting effect of this influence upon their lives, and in some cases, leadership. Yet at its proposal many denied the viability of Pan-Africanism. Theodore G. Vincent writes:

> The work of Garveyites in colonial Africa was hampered not only by government repression but also because the movement did not have wide enough appeal. The Universal Negro Improvement Association was simply too radical for most middle class Africans...professionals, civil servants and tribal chiefs generally avoided a movement which talked loosely of revolution.[39]

Vincent admits that W. E. Dubois's version of Pan-Africanism was more intellectually acceptable to middle class Africans.[40] However it too failed to retain systematic support and as Jeremy Murray-Brown recalls:

> Dubois was an American negro scholar who had first brought the Pan-African idea to the attention of the world by intervening at the Paris Peace Conference which followed the First War and urging the acceptance of the principle of self-determination for all colored people. Further conferences were held in Brussels and London, Paris and Lisbon, but after the fourth, which met in New York in 1927, the movement lapsed due to lack of African support.[41]

Ironically, Murray-Brown goes on to point out that "Africa for Africans" gained a new edge[42] when Kwame Nkrumah and his young supporters, tired of a gradualist approach to African independence, questioned anew the legitimacy of violence. Among the other African greats whose names are now in the indelible ink of history are Jomo Kenyatta and Patrice Lumumba, both of whom were interested in Pan-Africanism and yet were unable to bring it to full flower and permanence in structure. The colonialists have always known just how to exploit the tribalism (political and otherwise) of Africa to ensure disillusionment in Pan-Africanism. In fact when Patrice Lumumba became the bold advocate of "the United States of Africa," it was not the possibility of the dream that enraged his neo-colonial antagonists. It was the audacity of the dreamer.[43]

And yet, this is not to chide Africans for the failures of Pan-Africanism. It is simply to reinforce that the benefits to be gained from Pan-Africanism are not to be sought in its structural perfection but in its philosophy. For in it is a powerful philosophy of spiritual unity. As Lumumba himself used to say:

> ...despite the boundaries that separate us, despite our ethnic differences, we have the same awareness, the same soul plunged day and night in anguish, the same anxious desire to make the African continent a free and happy continent that has rid itself of unrest and of fear and of any sort of colonialist domination.[44]

As far as the Caribbean is concerned, its immediate context will determine what its theological content will be. Its cultural past will only help to shape the context.

The East Indian in Caribbean Culture

The first batch of East Indians landed in the Caribbean in 1838, soon after emancipation. They came to provide indentured labor. Indentured labor is different from slave labor in the sense that the former is contracted and paid for. This fact alone places the East Indians in a different status from that of the Africans at their arrival in the Caribbean. The Africans were captured and traded. The East Indians provided labor in contract between their government and their new employers. It is true that the Indians had their share of cruelty meeted out to them, in that they were whipped and treated to starvation rations,[45] but the fact that the Government of India could intervene so that the contract was suspended for a time acknowledges that their status differed from that of the Africans.

Furthermore, while the Africans were not only uprooted from their culture but were also forcibly cut off from it, the Indians in another status maintained their cultural ties with India. Of course it was at the point where the Indian culture was at its strongest that the church found it necessary to become most active, because by their Moslem and Hindu faiths

they were considered to be heathen.[46]   But this very fact
makes it clear that the Caribbean reality can no more ignore
Africa than it can India.

Philosophy

If history presents the Caribbean indigenization of theology
with a location, and sociology presents it with a description of
that location, it is philosophy that supplies the system by which
the process comes together.   Philosophy helps to determine
the point of departure in the task.   Since this is philosophy in
delineation of a system which implies not only meaning but
also boundaries, it is not so much the history of philosophy in
its broadest function which is important.   The need is to
develop "a philosophy" in terms of a perspective and view
point.   Hence the theological process develops its own philosophy, informed, of course by some philosophical school or
schools of thought, sympathetic to its particular perspective.
Although it is not an easy task it is not impossible for a project
of the nature of Caribbean indigenization to develop a
"philosophy" by which that project is governed.   In any case,
there is the scope of choices for such development because
philosophy has a tendency to defy general applications.   For
example, Paul Tillich, who has successfully used philosophy to
determine some boundaries to his theology, points out that it
is impossible to give a single definition for philosophy that
covers all aspects of its use.[47] He took that view from the fact
that each philosophical perspective takes on the subjectivity of
the philosopher who proposes and constructs it.[48] All of this is
most relevant in the development of theology within a particular context such as the Caribbean and has to be said at the
very outset because the Caribbean perspective has located a
problem with philosophy that needs to be investigated.   This
investigation is indeed the path to the choice of philosophical
perspective.   Burchell Taylor describes the problem as follows:

> Caribbean theology, because of its very nature, will have to make use of
> interpretive tools that we do not usually associate with the theology we
> have been familiar with. The primary and almost exclusive interpretive
> tool used by the traditional, imported (or as some would say imposed)

theology has been philosophy, whether it is philosophical idealism, existentialism, linguistic analysis or the like. The reason for this must in large measure be due to the methodology of such a theology. This theology reflected in ideas and concepts. Such ideas and concepts were not reflected upon in a vacuum, consequently, the finished product would be influenced by the context in which the thinking was done. It must be so influenced. Yet the ideas reflected upon were not necessarily directly related to issues raised by the context. Philosophy then proved to be a useful tool to such a self-consciously detached exercise and abstract reasoning process.[49]

The Marxist Option

It may be acknowledged here that Taylor does not suggest that philosophy must be totally disregarded in the Caribbean theological process. In fact he indicates that Marxist social analysis, which is in itself a philosophy, has been used successfully in some liberation formats. Taylor suggests the mere Marxist title of an analysis should not be enough reason for the Caribbean process to by-pass it. The salient point here is that Marxism becomes a relevant issue for Caribbean theology, not merely because of its concrete socio-economic and political interest, but because any assertiveness in the political arena, even toward non-alignment, on the part of small nations such as those in the Caribbean, is usually judged as Marxist in intent if not in process. Given this reality and the fact that Latin American liberation thought has successfully used the Marxist analysis as a basic interpretive tool, Caribbean theology does itself no harm in at least examining some of its prospects as a philosophic viewpoint.

On the other hand it is fair to say that some Caribbean theologians such as Edmund Davis do not think that it is necessary even to mention the Marxist social theory with respect to the development of Caribbean theology as liberation theology. Davis writes:

Liberation theology cannot be identified with Marxist theory, which regards the economic infrastructure alone as the significant factor responsible for the transformation of society. It cannot be equated with any form of economic determination. On the contrary, it holds that infrastructure and consciousness are mutually interrelated.[50]

Apart from the fact that Max Weber contends that Christianity, particularly Protestantism, believes in economic determinism, some Marxists may think that Davis holds a very limited view of the Marxist social analysis. From a practical point of view, for example, Fidel Castro sees absolutely no reason why Christians and Marxists cannot be "strategic allies."[51] He freely admits to the philosophic differences between Christianity and Marxism, but suggests that there are broad areas of cooperation.[52] When asked whether to be Christian implies the necessity to be Marxist, he responded:

> There is a great coincidence. There are some points that are strictly philosophical which are not a fundamental problem. Marxism seeks an explanation, like all political doctrines, of determined phenomena, of determined laws. We believe that there were great advances. Now, well, one cannot love universally and be antisocialist. One cannot love universally and be anti-communist or anti-Marxist, in its social meaning. It is more. There is no reason for them to present themselves as two antagonistic things and if they converge 90 percent of the time, then let them coincide there and let us work there and let us simply respect those points where convergence does not exist.[53]

Further, Cuban theologian Sergio Arce has posed the idea that the Christian-Marxist reality has moved beyond the mere level of the search for mutual cooperation. For him, the Christian church has lagged behind in its God given duty of providing prophetic witness to the world. Since Marxism has become more adept at providing that witness,[54] it is necessary to see socialism, for example, as one of God's ways of speaking to the church's ineptitude.[55] The church must now, like Jesus, receive the water from the Samaritan woman (the Marxists) and then go on to prophesy as to the meaning of divine grace.[56]

Obviously there are several points of view as to whether Marxism may be used as an interpretive tool for Caribbean theology. However, the arguments gathered into a fragile consensus seem to suggest that if there is no place for Christian-Marxist cooperation, there is at least room for a Christian-Marxist dialogue.

The Abstractness of Philosophy

If it is merely concern for the concreteness of the socio-economic and political perspectives that precipitates Caribbean objection to the use of philosophy in its abstractness, the issue is most relevant. However it has another side, in that there has been an almost natural evolution in philosophical schools of thought, leading from the very abstract to a more concrete structure.

Since Paul Tillich uses philosophy so successfully in his theological scheme, one may take the liberty to not only illustrate Taylor's frustration but also to examine the necessity of philosophy, with one of Tillich's definitions of philosophy. After stating the relationship between theology and philosophy Tillich writes:

> The suggestion made here is to call philosophy that cognitive approach to reality in which reality as such is the object. Reality as such or reality as a whole, is not the whole of reality; it is the structure which makes reality a whole and therefore a potential object of knowledge. Inquiring into the nature of reality as such means inquiring into those structures, categories, and concepts which are presupposed in the cognitive encounter with every realm of reality. From this point of view philosophy is by definition critical. It separates the multifarious materials of experience from these structures which make experience possible. There is no difference in this respect between constructive idealism and empirical realism.[57]

Tillich's statement here may very well provide some kind of spring board into liberation theology, and even into Caribbean theology. Strangely enough the phrase "reality is not the whole of reality," is meant to bridge the gap between the sacred and the secular, revelation and human experience. What it posits is that an object is never merely a "single" entity. An object comes with its own peculiar meaning, that which explains it, its philosophic base, so to speak. Furthermore that meaning, although it transcends the empirical context of the object, has to be interpreted within its context. Therefore as Immanuel Kant would put it, phenomena (the concrete, seeable, touchable) and the noumena (the unseen, spiritual) together make up reality.

For this reason Tillich's theological starting point is differ-ent from Karl Barth's, in the sense that although Barth is not using obvious philosophical language, his theological frame-work is idealism. Idealism begins with the *a priori*, the given idea or revelation. On the contrary, Tillich's view is that the starting point for theology is in the human experience, while recognizing that the human experience, as empirical as it may be, is not complete unto itself. Even in its most concrete sig-nificance it is at least surrounded by its meaning, and meaning leads to transcendence.

This reasoning does two things for liberation theology: (1) It supports the idea that the starting point of theology is the human experience. It is natural for one to know hunger long before one knows that there is a God who cares. Even so, one's knowledge of God has to be in one's "human" experi-ence, nowhere else. (2) It helps to confound the criticism that liberation perspectives are purely materialistic. Yet if some poor hungry person were handed Tillich's statement as a tool for deciphering the meaning of her/his poverty and hunger, such a person could die in the process long before the meaning becomes clear. One may then say that Tillich is not writing for the poor hungry Caribbean person. In that case Burchell Taylor's response would be, "that's the whole point." However, suppose the poor hungry Caribbean person could, by using Tillich's statement, find some kind of meaning for his/her poverty, where would that lead? Would the position be any less abstract?

It may help to note that Burchell Taylor is not alone in raising the argument regarding the insufficiency in abstract philosophy for the concreteness of human existence. Histori-cally speaking two of the persons who have raised the same questions are Soren Kierkegaard and Karl Marx. Soren Kierkegaard, who is sometimes called the father of existential-ism, as far back as the 19th century, wrote:

> ...Western philosophy since the Greeks has been preoccupied with the idea of Essence, the general and universal features of anything, rather than with concrete, individual, human Existence, the former being counted more real (because unchanging) than the latter. Consequently,

Western philosophy has been intellectualistic and rationalistic. It has not only been irrelevant so far as illuminating life is concerned but has actually obscured the truth about human existence. The fundamental categories of classical philosophy (Soul, Virtue, Substance, Accidents, essence, existence) are all impersonal and fail to do justice to the basic character of human life as change, consciousness, process, movement, passion and decision. In short, they fail to indicate the historical nature of human existence.[58]

However, even here the fact that such a critique resembles a statement lifted directly from a liberation text, should not be allowed the position of enticement where existentialism becomes synonymous with liberation theology. For example, Kierkegaard, even in proposing the concreteness of the human situation in which human knowledge is realized, described that knowledge as only a miracle in which in an extraordinary moment of benevolence, divine intervention supplies the genius to make it possible.[59] Furthermore, the human person is as unsure of the knowledge as of its source, even if that person maintains a posture of acceptability only through the felt need for such knowledge and the leap of faith which presumed its possibility.[60] All of which fosters the same subjectivism which privatizes evil while ignoring the systems which create oppressive structures. A position such as Kierkegaard's does identify human sinfulness but it does not make distinctions in which the victims are identified and their redress specified. It does not sum up the certainty with which liberation theology sees God taking sides with the down trodden and hears God speaking out against the political systems that oppress them. Yet the fact that people like Kierkegaard saw the traditional church as remiss in its responsibility to present the true gospel while indulging in relentless defense of its own failure,[61] provides liberation theology with some of the thinking half of its praxis and also some ground rules with which to step forth in its quest to the concreteness of context.

In the case of Karl Marx, he examined Hegel's idealism and found a bankruptcy that was detrimental to historical reality. Hegel had developed philosophical arguments that could have been applied to the understanding of some basic historical categories. Ironically, although he developed these arguments from observations in the socio-economic and political realities of his Prussian context, he would not apply them in such a context. He skillfully devised his arguments through the dialectic method pursuing thesis, then antithesis, finally finding the synthesis for both. This methodology could very well be applied in the industrial development of his situation in the specific context of labor struggles between employer and employee. Of course, simply posing labor as the synthesis between employer and employee could hardly have solved any serious industrial conflict, because at the center of the industrial conflict is the question concerning fair assessments of the value of labor, when that labor is demanded by ruthless profiteering employers from weak and defenseless employees. Nevertheless, given the contextual base, the philosophical theory could have aided contextual releivancy. But when Hegel argued that the thesis-antithesis-synthesis position really belonged to some transcendent nous (mind), and that the theory was to be understood purely in terms of "idea," it became a very abstract, intellectual exercise. Hence, it was at this juncture that Karl Marx took the argument and did what is often referred to as "turning Hegel upon his head."

Marx argued that the conflict between thesis and antithesis is real and alienating, as is observed in the concrete historical world of the employer and the employee. Consequently the synthesis is not some benign understanding of the application of labor. It is a matter of a deadly struggle for real structural liberation, in real history, because power is never donated.

The Possibility of a Philosophy of Liberation
There is the possibility that the Caribbean theologians are wittingly or unwittingly dealing also with a more basic methodological problem than the abstract nature of philosophy. William Watty, addressing the possibility of Caribbean theology as liberation theology, writes:

> Like Black theology, African theology, Asian theology, it represents both an eclipse of Western theology and the liberation theology from the suffocation of Western formulations and methodologies.[62]

Watty says this in full consciousness that formulating new methodology must entail a more serious process than mere "debunking."[63] Thus he asks not pessimistically but in objective contemplation of the task:

> Who are we to formulate a new missiology? Whence this confidence that we are not also children of our time and prisoners of our situation? Whence do we derive this objectivity and detachment which will enable us to succeed where our predecessors have failed?[64]

This problem of course, is by no means uniquely a Caribbean problem but a Third World one. As early as 1965 some Latin American thinkers had been questioning whether it is possible to do philosophy in underdeveloped countries. Enrique Dussel, an Argentine philosopher, theologian and historian, recalls that the questions became progressively insistent to the point where they were asked not merely of Latin American underdevelopment, but of all dominated cultures. He writes:

> A little later the question was put another way: Is it possible to philosophize authentically in a dependent and dominated culture? That is, the facts of underdevelopment and then of dependence and the fact of philosophy appeared to be mutually exclusive or inclusive only with difficulty. These facts reshaped themselves into a problem, into the central problem of philosophy of liberation: Is a Latin American philosophy possible? With time it grew into: Is a Latin American, African, or Asian philosophy of the peripheral world possible? Peruvian Augusto Salazar Bondy...answered courageously: No! No, because a dominated culture is one in which the ideology of the dominator has been adopted by the dominated—by the colonized, Memmi would say.[65]

In other words, it is impossible for colonized people to develop a philosophy, particularly a philosophy of liberation, because they have so internalized the thought process of the colonizer that it is impossible for them to think outside of that thought pattern.

Of course, if this posture ever receives a permanent status, the question as to the possibility of the indigenization of theology in the Caribbean becomes moot. That is to say that without a method that is inclusive of a philosophy, theology that is by nature liberation, new and contextually Caribbean is probably not possible. However, Dussel has not only found others who insist that philosophy in the periphery is possible, he himself concurs:

> It appears possible to philosophize in the periphery—in underdeveloped and dependent nations, in dominated and colonial cultures, in a peripheral social formation only if the discourse of the philosophy of the center is not imitiated, only if another discourse is discovered. To be different, this discourse must have another point of departure, must think other themes, must come to distinctive conclusions by a different method.[66]

This makes a very interesting issue especially when coupled with William Watty's contention raised with traditional theology:

> For all its magnificence and pretense at comprehensiveness and universality, it was essentially constricted, parochial and myopic. It is no accident that no modern Western theologians ever tried to relate their various theologies to what has been and still is the basic reality of the West, namely its dominance over the rest of the world. None of them showed the least interest in the living experience of two-thirds of the human race...None of them wrote a single paragraph on imperialism or colonial exploitation. Call it neglect or oversight, it demands serious theological investigation.[67]

This means that whatever approach is taken in the Caribbean search for a theology that addresses its context, the process must move beyond that which Dussell refers to as the "Center," by which he means Euro-American perspectives. He suggests that if a different philosophical approach is going to be found it must be sought in the tension between the center and the periphery as both stand juxtaposed. In this way there is an engagement which is the very opposite of the investigation that merely treats the situation in its most abstract sense. Furthermore, for Dussel that philosophical option is the recognition that its theme must be the "praxis of liberation."[68] It is the theme that suggests a new point of departure. It begins with politics and makes the order of the option, politics, ethics and philosophy. Politics introduces ethics and ethics introduces philosophy.

It would appear, at least at face value, that this philosophical option would suit the Caribbean approach to theology, in terms of the choice of the facilitating tools, namely history,

sociology and philosophy. One supportive factor is that when
Dussel talks about the scheme in the order of politics, ethics
and philosophy, by politics he means history.

a. History, then for Dussel is the description of facts in the
human condition. In the case of the Caribbean it would mean
the philosophy that governs the dealings of the colonizer
toward the colonized. This means that one must work within
the "periphery" without imitating the "center" and yet begin
with the center.[69] One begins with the center because one
cannot hope to understand the nature of Third World
exploitation without first understanding how the foreign policy of the First World is related to what is considered national
security. As Dussel puts it:

> It is impossible today, for example, to avoid the problem of the imperi-
> alist ideology of national security, which justifies the exercise of world-
> wide geopolitical power.[70]

b. The second step in the option is to treat history to an ethical
consensus, because it is in the ethical construct that the true
meaning of the explanation of facts makes the process real.[71]
The question of ethics is not merely concerned with what the
center has done to the periphery but also what happens when
the Christian perspective within the periphery is confronted
by power that is hostile to its well being.[72] Yet, although the
ethical consensus may be no easy feat, William Watty suggests
elsewhere where it may lie. Despite any critical analytical
method that may be applied to it, the Bible as the ethical word
of God is the most dependable consensus for ethics.[73] Watty
says:

> ...a serious theology of liberation does not stand on a dubious historical
> event, but on the purposes of God as Creator and His purpose for crea-
> tion.[74]

As long as it is understood that the center has used and can
use the Bible to justify its own position, the periphery has the
right to claim that when the Bible speaks in the words of the
"Magnificat" (Luke 1:46-55) it is laying down "peripheral"
ethics.

c. Finally, the ethical construct must be translated into praxis, which is the development of a philosophy of political action designed to cause change.[75]

If this option shows nothing else it shows that the possibility of this scheme for Caribbean indigenous theology would identify Caribbean theology as a theology of liberation.

Notes

1 Cracknell, Basil E., *The West Indians*, Kingston, Jamaica, W.I. Kingston Publishers Limited, 1974, p. 25.

2 Ibid.

3 Ibid. p. 25.

4 Mitchell, David I., "Haiti", ed. David I. Mitchell, *New Mission for a New People*, U.S.A., Friendship Press, 1977, pp. 56.

5 Ibid. pp. 56-57.

6 Neehall, Roy G., "Christian Witness and Mission in Caribbean Development", ed. David I. Mitchell, *With Eyes Wide Open*, Jamaica, W.I. Christian Action for Development in the Caribbean (CADEC), 1973, p. 23, citing William Demas, The Political Economy of the English Speaking Caribbean, Barbados, CADEC.

7 Neehall, Roy G., "Christian Witness and Mission in Caribbean Development", ed. David I. Mitchell, *With Eyes Wide Open*, Jamaica, W.I. Christian Action for Development in the Caribbean (CADEC), 1973, p. 23. Citing William Demas, The Political Economy of the English Speaking Caribbean, Barbados, CADEC.

8 Watty, William, "Struggling to Be," ed David I. Mitchell, *New Mission for a New People*, U.S.A., Friendship Press, 1977, p. 107.

9 Ibid., p. 107.

10 Ibid.

11 EPICA—Ecumenical Program for Interamerican Communication—a non-profit organization with offices in Washington, D.C., is dedicated to the understanding of the socio-economic and political struggles of Latin America and the Caribbean.

12 Sunshine, Catherine A. ed. *The Caribbean: Survival, Struggle and Sovereignty*, Washington, D.C., EPICA, 1983, pp. 133-176.

13 Smith, M.G., *Culture, Race and Class in the Commonwealth Caribbean*, Jamaica W.I., Department of Extra-Mural Studies, University of the West Indies, 1984. p. IX.

14 Mitchell, David I., "Haiti, ed. David I. Mitchell, *New Mission for a New People*, U.S.A. Friendship Press, Inc. 1977. p. 56.

15 Sunshine, Catherine A., *The Caribbean: Survival, Struggle and Sovereignty*, Washington, D.C., EPICA, 1985, p. 150.

16 Ibid. p. 151.

17 Ibid. p.151.

18 Ibid.

19 Ibid. p. 151

20 Buehrig, Edward H., *The United Nations and the Palestinian Refugees*, London, Indiana University Press, 1971, p. 15.

21 Nettleford, Rex M., *Mirror Mirror: Identity, Race and Protest in Jamaica*, Jamaica. W.I., William Collins and Sangster (Jamaica) Ltd., 1970, p. 33.

22 Peenie Wallie, Vol.1, No.1, Jamaica 1973.

23 Nettleford, Rex M., *Mirror Mirror: Identity, Race and Protest in Jamaica*, Jamaica. W.I. William Collins and Sangster (Jamaica) Ltd., 1970, p. 33.

24 Ibid.

25 Ibid. p. 61.

26 Ibid. p. 61.

27 Owens, Joseph, *Dread: The Rastafarians of Jamaica*, Kingston, Jamaica, W.I., Sangster, 1976, p. 77.

28 Stampp, Kenneth M., *The Peculiar Institution*, New York, Random House, 1956, p. 10.

29 Ibid. p. 10.

30 Ibid. p. 10.

31 Ibid. pp. 12-14.

32 Barrett, Leonard E., *Soul-Force: African Heritage in Afro-American Religion*, Garden City, New York, Anchor Press/Doubleday, 1974. p.16

33 Ibid. p. 17.

34 Ibid. p.16.

35 Lee, Alfred McCheng, ed., *Principles of Sociology*, New York, Barnes and Noble, 1969, p. 222.

36 Chinula, Donald M., "Jamaican Exocentrism: Its Implications for a Pan-African Theology of National Redemption," *Caribbean Journal of Religious Studies*, Vol. 6, No. 1, April 1985, p. 46.

37 Ibid. p. 47.

38 Topanarists and evolues are both pseudo-aristocrats.

39 Vincent, Theodora G. *Black Power and the Garvey Movement*, San Francisco, Ramparts Press, 1972, p. 177.

40 Ibid.

41 Murray-Brown, Jeremy, *Kenyatta*, New York, E.P. Dutton & Co., Inc., 1973, p. 253.

42 Ibid. p. 253.

43 Van Lierde, Jean, *Lumumba Speaks: The Speeches and Writings of Patrice Lumumba 1958-1961*, trans. Helen R. Lane, Boston, Toronto, Little Brown and Company, 1972, pp. 60 & 61.

44 Ibid. p. 21.

45 Hamid, Idris, *A History of the Presbyterian Church In Trinidad, 1868-1968*, Trinidad, West Indies, Rahaman Printery, Ltd., Lewis Str., San Fernando, 1980, p. 21.

46 Smith, Ashley, *Real Roots and Potted Plants*, Mandeville, Jamaica, West Indies, Mandeville Publishers, 1984. p. 11

47 Tillich, Paul, *Systematic Theology*, Volume One, Chicago, The University of Chicago Press, 1973, p. 18.

48 Ibid. p. 18.

49 Taylor, Burchell K., "Caribbean Theology," *Caribbean Journal of Religious Studies* Volume III, No.2, September 1980, p. 21.

50 Davis, Edmund, "The Social and Spiritual Implications of a Theology of Liberation," *Caribbean Journal of Religious Studies*, Volume V, No.1, April 1983, p. 49.

51 Arce, Sergio, *The Church and Socialism: Reflections From A Cuban Context*, New York, Circus Publications, 1985,p. 184.

52 Arce, Sergio, *The Church and Socialism: Reflections From A Cuban Context*, New York, Circus Publications, 1985, p. 184.

53 Ibid. p. 184

54 Ibid. p. 46.

55 Ibid. p. 184.

56 Ibid. pp. 50-51.

57 Tillich, Paul, *Systematic Theology*, Volume One, Chicago, The University of Chicago Press, 1973, p. 18.

58 Harvey, Van A., *A Handbook of Theological Terms*, New York, McMillan Publishing Company, Inc. 1978, p. 92.

59 Popkin, Richard H. and Stroll, Avrum, *Philosophy Made Simple*, Garden City, New York, Doubleday and Company, Inc. 1956, pp. 186-189.

60 Ibid.

61 Ibid. pp. 186-189.

62 Watty, William, *From Shore to Shore*, Kingston, Jamaica, Cedar Press, 1981, p. 42.

63 Ibid. p. 44.

64 Ibid. p. 94.

65 Dussel, Enrique, *Philosophy of Liberation*, Trans. Aquilini Martinez and Christine Morkovsky, Maryknoll, New York, Orbis, 1985, p. 172.

66 Ibid. p. 172. f

67 Watty, William, *From Shore to Shore*, Kingston, Jamaica, Cedar Press, 1981, pp. 41-42.

68 Dussel, Enrique, *Philosophy of Liberation*, Trans. Aquilina Martinez and Christine Morkovsky, Maryknoll, New York, Orbis, 1985, p. 172.

69 Ibid. p. 172-173.

70 Ibid. p. 174.

71 Ibid. p. 174

72 Bonino, Jose Miguez, *Toward A Christian Political Ethics*, Philadelphia, Fortress Press, 1983, p. 22.

73 Watty, William, *From Shore to Shore*, Kingston, Jamaica, Cedar Press, 1981, pp. 43-44.

74 Ibid. p. 45.

75 Dussel, Enrique, *Philosophy of Liberation*, Trans. Aquilina Martinez and Christine Morkovsky, Maryknoll, New York, Orbis, 1985, p. 174.

Chapter Four

Sources and Method for Caribbean Theology

Sources

Alfred Reid, reacting to a "right wing" campaign against the pursuit of indigenous theology for the Caribbean, makes the following remark:

> We are being asked to believe that liberation theology is not biblical but springs from some inanimate philosophy alien both to Scripture and to our history.[1]

He then argues that not only is liberation a biblical perspective but also that the history of the Caribbean supplies the source for its own theology.[2] The Caribbean experience provides the source for its theology.

James Cone, the pioneer of Black liberation theology, had already said that sources are the creative components which give character and relevance to a theology.[3] Hence for Cone the components which form the source for Black theology in the United States are:

1. The Black experience which comes in direct reference to the suffering of Blacks.

2. Black history which is relating blacks to their journey from Africa into slavery and beyond.

3. Black culture which is the creative expression of experience and history.

4. Revelation which is the divine hermeneutic that translates history and experience by divine involvement.

5. Scripture which is authentic and authenticating witness to divine revelation.

6. Tradition which is theological reflection upon the history of the Christian church.[4]

Sensitive though not apologetic about placing revelation fourth on his list of sources, after experience, history and culture, Cone moves to explain that sources in Black theology must be taken as a package.[5] Yet the order of the ingredients in the package is of grave importance. As he puts it:

> I do not think that revelation is comprehensible from a black theological perspective without prior understanding of the concrete manifestation of revelation in the black community as seen in the black experience, black history, and black culture.[6]

Thus the Caribbean indigenization process in theology takes its cue from a thoughtful precedence when it points out as sources:

a. Faith in the tension between "Enculturation and "Acculturation," and

b. The relationship of Caribbean experience to the biblical record of divine concern for the powerless.

Faith in Tension Between Enculturation and Acculturation
Enculturation: Enculturation is being used here to represent a kinship to socialization, yet as a principle that moves beyond socialization to inculcate the specificity of a particular culture.

Sociologists admit that culture is not an easy entity to define. The main problem is to make the decision on what to admit or exclude in the definition. Broadly speaking, however, culture is all that is thoughtful and meaningful within human society by which life is organized, to the extent that it promotes togetherness and continuity for generational heritage. Children learn it from their parents and so do not have to start anew with each birth.[7] Even more specifically:

> Culture is the design for living of a group whose members share a given location, feel responsible for one another, and call themselves by the same name. The culture of such a group (or society) consists of (1) solutions to the problems of survival; (2) the ideals and values that shape rules of conduct; and (3) tools and other human made objects (artifacts or material culture).[8]

In view of this definition one must here admit again that the Caribbean is by no means homogenous in its culture. This admission has to do with more than the "phenotypical" differences in physical character of varying races. Quite apart from the multiplicity of the pre-Caribbean heritage in Africa, India, China, etc. there are cultural peculiarities to different territories. For example, what is "ackee" in Western Caribbean is "guineppe" in the Eastern Caribbean and vice versa. "Bullah" is only a small cake in Jamaica but in Barbados it is a vulgar reference to some kind of sexual deviance. However, as long as these differences are viewed in the light of the fact that there are more serious commonalities than differences, James Cone's definition of Black culture becomes a useful analogy for Caribbean theologizing. Cone says:

> Black culture consists of the creative forms of expression as one reflects on the history, endures the pain, and experiences the joy. It is the black community expressing itself in music, poetry, prose and the other art forms.[9]

When this area is taken as an additional aspect to what has already been said by way of defining culture, one develops a healthy respect for commonality. A study of the territorial contributions to a *Carifesta Forum* reveals some of the depth of commonality of expression out of a mutual history and experience among the Caribbean territories. The voice of Nicholas Guillen of Cuba is one that speaks out of historical pain:

> Thus it was that, very shortly after the discovery, Governor Rojas could send a report from Havana to the King to say "The Indians are all gone." How could it be otherwise? The Spanish penetration took place under the sign of cruelty and death. Because of this it has been possi-

ble to say, with terrible irony, that "the cross which the European carried in their conquest could not have been the one on which Christ
died for the redemption of the world, but one of the other two crosses
from Calvary which belonged to the thieves...the place which these
original inhabitants of the island left vacant was occupied by a species of
"surrogate autochton" (Dino Don), the Negro from Africa, more culturally developed than the Caribbean native, though not earmarked for a
less cruel destiny.[10]

But the voice might just as well be that of Jan Carew of
Guyana because the message is the same and its source is the
same kind of experience. The voice of Rene de Pestre of Haiti
is no less aware of the content of history and experience in the
colonial Caribbean. In fact it touches the core of the problem
of homogeneity and poses the answer in the commonality of
historical experience when Rene de Pestre says:

And so, in order to understand the significance and the sociological and
anthropological value of the problem of our identity one must place it
in the history of social relations in our islands. The struggle for this
identity, long before finding expression in our literatures, has had its
place in all stages of the history of our societies. This fight has taken
many different forms in relation to the historical conditions in each
island. The problem of identity is closely linked to a central fact in
Caribbean history—slavery. And what was slavery but anti-identity by
definition?[11]

It is a fact then that whether one is listening to the voice of
Nicolas Guillen from Cuba on the "National Identity and
'Mestizaje'" or Sylvia Winter from Jamaica on "Talk About a
Little Culture," or Aime Cesaire from Martinique on "Discourse on Colonialism" or Edward Kamau Brathwaite from
Barbados on "Caribbean Man in Space and Time," one is
hearing voices which are conscious not only of a Caribbean
historical experience but also of the painful process of
"deidentification" within that experience.

This discourse has declared that enculturation is being used
here to represent a deeper form of socialization. Socialization
is a necessary part of human existence because it would be
impossible for a baby to develop into its human self without
contact and relationships with other human beings. Therefore:

Socialization is the process whereby one learns how to behave in a given society and develops a sense of self.[12]

It is a process of learning which involves a person's eating, drinking, controlling body functions and in fact organizing a behavior system in relation to the demands of society.

The point is, however, that socialization done in a culture different from the one in which a child is born is still socialization. After a few years in the United States some West Indian parents are extremely surprised at how their children not only lose taste for West Indian foods but also how confused they become with the names of those foods. In fact quite often there is almost complete disorientation with regards to lifestyle when young West Indians living abroad return home. It is quite clear that the young can become easily socialized into any culture to which they are constantly exposed. This fact makes it necessary to add a further dimension to socialization that is specifically related to a particular heritage. This dimension shall be identified as enculturation. With such focus enculturation, though related to socialization, is a principle which moves beyond it because enculturation means being steeped in the specifics of a particular culture. For example, the United States business persons who in recent times ventured upon the Japanese stockmarket as a counterattack on what some consider Asian over-involvement in the United States economy, found that it was necessary to know more than the Japanese language to be successful in Japan. They encountered a distinct body language that is uniquely Japanese. It is not superficial communication because since one's psychology is a product of one's culture, that body language would be a part of the Japanese psyche. It put the United States persons at a disadvantage since they could neither understand it nor duplicate it. It is a nuance so subtle and so exclusively Japanese that it is scarcely identifiable by the foreigner.

There are reasons for these nuances and often they are developed out of a survival technique of people whose survival is at constant risk. Since it becomes an innate part of the people it persists even after the risk no longer exists. For example, the indiscriminate use of the word "man" in ordinary West Indian speech would easily be construed in certain United States societies as insensitivity to the problem of the gender gap. Yet if the phenomenon were researched it would more likely reveal that the practice has nothing to do with the male/female dichotomy. It is more likely a constant effort to satisfy a psychological need to affirm "manhood" as opposed to "boyhood." There is no doubt that the colonial custom of addressing grown colonized men as "boys" has something to do with the risk factor that exacerbated this situation of nuances in its own cultural particularity.

It is true that some analysts such as Maslow contend that enculturation as general education toward the conformation to cultural patterns and norms, needs sometimes to be challenged and overridden to release once more the natural naivete that produces progressive innovativeness such as is demonstrated in art.[13] However the results of this innovativeness are usually beneficial to the culture itself and not merely to the individuals who challenge the tradition.[14] Yet enculturation is by no means to be judged as the vehicle that chains a people to meaningless tradition. It is the means by which organization and transition take place within the culture for the stability of that culture. On the other hand, the colonizers, with the tendency to treat as superstition that which they do not understand, and also because they desire to be in control, have played havoc in the lives and culture of the colonized.

Acculturation: Even if acculturation in the Caribbean were limited to slavery in the region, the process would still have been colossal. Sidney Mintz concludes:

> The precise number of enslaved Africans who reached the New World alive will never be known, nor will the numbers who died in slaving wars and in the hideous coffles to the coast, during the Middle Passage, or before being debarked in the Americas. Even if we accept the radically reduced estimates of the number of African slaves who reached this hemisphere, New World slavery may well have been the most massive acculturational event in human history.[15]

Acculturation differs from enculturation in the sense that the former is the imposition of distinctly foreign culture upon another culture.[16] The use of the word "imposition" here does not mean that acculturation is always forced. One must acknowledge that there is such a thing as voluntary acculturation in which a particular culture makes the conscious adjustment to accommodate tenets of another culture. In fact in a broad sense, because of the fact of international communication and trade, most cultures make themselves subject to ranging degrees of change inspired by other cultures. However in the case of slavery there is no question but that "imposition" refers to involuntary acculturation in its strictest sense. Acculturation in the Caribbean is more than the horrors of the "Middle Passage." Beside the particularity of slavery there is the whole idea of cultural assault under the larger umbrella of colonialism and neo-colonialism. E. Adamson Hoebel writes:

> Slave taking from alien peoples is something else again. The forcible removal of individuals from their home societies and their injection into an alien one requires anguishing cultural adjustments on their part. Conquest and political subjugation with or without slavery, has even greater acculturative effects, for the conquered must accommodate to the rule and pressure of the conquerors in their own territory, often with little or no choice.[17]

In the case of the Caribbean the anguish of the peoples has been generated not only by the fact of geographical displacement, but also the forcible sociological and religious adjustments. The Africans were forced into cultural alteration by the chains of slavery while the Indians were duped into bargains which ultimately produced for them a life style that fell well beneath their expectations. For example, the deliberate practice of the British colonialists to limit drastically the number of women among the indentured Indians who migrated to the Caribbean, so altered the lifestyle of the migrants that serious social crises developed among them.[18] Africans had already suffered trauma related to family separation and "stud farm breeding" and a host of other dehumanizing factors. Relative to the anguish of cultural displacement also is the fact of religious berating. Once it is taken seriously that despite what the colonizers believed, the new arrivals were not religionless, it must be realized that with the clash of cultures there was the clash of religions. While it is true that a scholar such as Melville Herskovitz in *The Myth of the Negro Past* has pointed out a certain ease with which syncretism developed in the New World between Christianity and some of the African river religions, because of similarities in the baptism rituals, it is evident that a tension developed in the faith experience between enculturation and acculturation. African religious survivals alone in the Caribbean are a testimony to that fact. Rex Nettleford writes:

> The early efforts to discourage the spread of ancestral African religions led to an active defiance and a startling survival in such expressions as Kumina in Jamaica, Shango in Trinidad, Cumfeh in Guyana and Obeah all over the region.[19]

Caribbean acculturation was an attempt to force people to disregard their own psyche.

Enculturation Versus Acculturation

One of the first theological questions cultural displacement raises is whether God has anything to do with the origin of culture. Paul suggests some words which may address the question: "From one single stock God not only created the whole human race so that they could occupy the entire earth, but God decreed how long each nation should flourish and what the boundaries of its territory should be" (Acts 17:26). Of course this text has been used extensively by some racial separatists and some racial supremacists to justify their positions, but it comes with enough balance to defy glib applications to this end. The fact that it is from "one" stock that God has created the whole human race is suggestive that what Buhlmann calls the "Creation Covenant" has no room for racial and cultural supremacy. As for the boundaries being created by God, it is probably in reference to the fact that indeed God is ultimately responsible for cultures. One is cognizant of H. Richard Niebuhr's attitude to culture in this respect that:

> Culture is the "artificial, secondary environment" which man superimposes on the natural. It comprises language, habit, ideas, beliefs, customs, social organization, inherited artifacts, technical processes and values.[20]

Culture, he goes on to say is "human achievement".[21] However, Charles H. Kraft in full recognition of Niebuhr's emphasis makes the better point that once God is acknowledged as the Creator, the fact that human beings possess the ability to be culture producing entities is congruent with another fact, that God bears some responsibility for the origination of human culture.[22] Of course this argument can be stretched to make God responsible for anything that the human being is capable of. Be that as it may, since within culture lies the value system and therefore the norms by which people live harmoniously, it seems to be an unavoidable human need. Moreover, the idea of culture raises such a question of unique human requirement that culture must be related to whatever divinely inspired moral law or laws such culture may be capable of.[23] This in itself does not subtract importance from Niebuhr's real case which is against cultural impositions, because in that definition he warns that culture cannot be assessed as if religion were not a permanent part of it. Nor can the religious significance be limited to Christianity.[24] So it must be taken into consideration that the African and Asian cultures came into the New World with their own guidelines which included the religious, when Kraft says:

> Furthermore, since culture for some time now has pervasively conditioned all people, we may assume that God created humanity with at least the capacity for culture. Indeed our present evidence leads to the conclusion that there is within humans the necessity for culture. Human beings do not seem to function well in the absence of clearly defined and consistent guidelines for behavior...Much psychological stress and dysfunction is the result of one or another kind of breakdown in such social support systems. Friction between groups is another result of a lack of or inconsistency in behavioral guidelines.[25]

These cultures that knew no separation between the religious life and the secular life came into immediate conflict with European Christianity. Yet if God is responsible for the origin of European culture, God is also responsible for the origin of African and Asian cultures, which raises the second theological question: Is God identified with culture within particular boundaries?

Faith and Divine Cultural Bias

Charles Kraft, who has studied this question at the point of contact between the missionary church and the colonized, suggests that some people, at least by their action, have responded and are responding in the affirmative to that question.[26] In what, borrowing from Niebuhr's format, he labels "God against culture," he shows that the problem has been prominent since the first confrontation of Christianity with Hellenism.   Early New Testament Christianity divided culture into two segments: that which was within the pale by virtue of its acceptance of Christ and that which was without, by virtue of the opposite. The latter was spoken of as the "world" and was considered intrinsically evil.[27] Kraft points out that this attitude has perpetuated itself through the ages and aspects of the church to the modern scene in which:

> In a more particular form such an antagonistic attitude toward culture is manifested by those who oppose politico-economic systems like communism, socialism, or capitalism, or nationalistic or religious movements on the basis of the assumption that God *could not* work within such systems or movements.[28]

In fact the missionary/colonial effort at discouraging the new immigrant's culture in the Caribbean was due to the idea of "God against culture," and the later church support of right wing neo-colonialism has no other root. From the beginning the colonizers took it much for granted that the other cultures involved within the scope of influence were inauthentic by virtue of what they deemed Christlessness. It goes without saying that such attitudes have their consequences. From actual case studies in the work of missionaries, Kraft has discussed the point that evangelization with a strong cultural bias often misses the local concerns. It becomes so "moralistic" from its own bias that it brings the colonized into judgment merely with the foreign culture as yard stick. As a result the colonized acquiesce to a religion without conviction.[29] According to Ashley Smith, this is the reason Christianity in the Caribbean is merely a kind of potted plant. Kraft's argument is that often colonized persons become Christians without repenting of those things which trouble their consciences.[30] The things most on their minds may have to do with communal survival and inter-group relationships. The problem is that in the acts of inauthenticating the local cultures, the missionary church has always made the mistake of transporting and imposing the needs of the metropolitan center, no matter how irrelevant that may be to the dominated cultures.[31] But does the "potted plant" idea mean that there is no legitimate way of considering God within culture and whether there are ideas of the universal significance of morality?

Culture and Divine Immanence

Barbara Ward of "The Economist of London," in her discussion of the connections between rationalism and ideology, once admitted that the unique contribution of Jewry to the world is the idea of a God who is capable of moral indignation on behalf of the weak. She wrote:

> The Jews confront the enormous inequality of human society once it emerges from its tribal simplicity and proclaim God's profound concern for the poor. It is not simply that alms-giving is a duty—other cultures produce such obligations. It is that in some way the miserable and outcast are the Lord's chosen and deserve His special blessing.[32]

The point here is that though not even the missionary church is going to pit God against culture purely for the sake of cultural stratification, there is theological precedence that God takes sides. In fact this is the very crux of the liberationist position that God takes sides with the poor. It is true that Ward may not have been speaking directly in favor of liberation theology, but the inference is inescapable. Indeed her viewpoint is well backed up by Sergio Rostagno who knows both the Bible and liberation theology:

> In the ancient East the socially and economically feeble were considered the people with whom God had a special relationship...The fact that Yahweh places himself on the side of the poor person (Ps.146) also means that he intervenes to raise up the lowly and punish those in high places. This is asserted in strong and manifesto-like terms in 1 Samuel 2:1-10.[33]

Yet even if the late Barbara Ward were addressing the validity of liberation theology for Third World nations, as a non-Third World person she would have been a voice in the wilderness. In the Caribbean situation it is clear that the other half of the reason for the missionary/colonial discouragement of the new immigrant cultures was the theological belief regarding "God in culture." But it had not occurred to the Europeans that the God of the Hebrew Bible could be in the cultures they stratified as being beneath them. There is hardly any doubt then that a popular European belief was that God was in the European cultures authenticating their inception, their proliferation, and every machination in those processes. Hence William Watty is under no illusion about the reasoning behind the "political domination and social fragmentation" of colonialism and neo-colonialism in the Caribbean. He contends that what has not been heretofore explored, is the fact that both have been inspired and bolstered by a theological foundation, as faulty as that theological principle might be:

> From the Conquistadores to the CIA, from the massacre of the Indians to the blasting of the Viet Cong, from Pizzaro to Nixon, from the bulls of Alexander VI and Julius II to the Manifest Destiny of America the theology has been consistent that the European has been given a historic mission to rule and guide the world as it sees fit; and to exterminate the Arawaks and plunder their gold for European coffers, to enslave Africans and accumulate fabulous wealth from the booming sugar industry, to seize the Isthmus of Panama and exercise overlordship over the hemisphere is to do God a service.[34]

If Grenada is a sovereign country with all the rights acquired thereto, what gives the United States the "imperial" right to invade it, bombard it, dismantle its government and set up one with which it is comfortable? It is more than a political conclusion. It is at least a theopolitical one in which United States' right and divine sanction are seen to be intertwined. The conclusion is arrived at with more determined ease because of the United States' claim that Judeo-Christian tradition provides the most significant component of its culture. What Watty means is that the neo-colonialists story of the present is not new, and the only process that can change that trend of theological thought is indigenization.[35] For the Caribbean, indigenization will change a theology that has always been to its detriment, because it is not true that the Euro-American foreign policy has always been God's cultural policy.

On the other hand even indigenous liberation theologians need to heed the warning signals regarding the debilitating dangers of the idea of "God in culture," even on the side of the culturally and economically down trodden, because the risk factor which includes quietism,[36] reductionism and reverse cultural bias, is quite realistic:

1. Quietism, which is more a "consequence of," than an actual wrong, within itself, nevertheless, can become a devastating problem in any struggle as serious as liberation and indigenization. The problem is cited by Sergio Rostagno as a kind of inertia which comes out of a sense of satisfaction, that God is on the side of the weak therefore the weak do not have to do anything about their condition. However, it is also part of a bigger problem that was once a needless concern on the part of the oppressed until the violent confrontation between the Israelis and the Palestinians in Palestine on the occupied West Bank. Even some Jewish people think that the answer to that particular situation is probably that the Israelis, being the most powerful state in the Middle East, need something other than a liberation theology based on their Holocaust experience, to deal with their weaker neighbors. Yet because of the Israeli in the Palestine situation, in which Israel is no longer the oppressed but in the eyes of the Palestinian, the oppressor, the premature question, "What happens when the oppressed cease to be?", (which is usually asked only by the ruling class,) has now become pertinent for others. Furthermore, with regards to the participants in liberation struggles it is possible to have their sense of urgency dampened by preoccupation with that question. The problem with the question is that it contains either implicitly or explicitly another question: "Where does the God in culture go when the particular culture is no longer an oppressed one?"

2. Reductionism in this sense is a specific theological problem in which God becomes so entrapped "in culture" that

divine influence is limited to that of a tribal Deity. When some Caribbean theologians register certain reluctance to subscribe to the particularity of a Caribbean theology, it is probably some of this reductionism that they sense as problematic. Of course "God in culture" is not the only way of acknowledging divine participation in the particularity of human experience, but a God who is limited to that particularity is hardly one who is large enough to liberate to the utmost.

3. The reverse cultural bias ought not to be judged with the same measurements as the recent position on "affirmative action" in the United States where the "right wing" has defined it as "reversed discrimination." It may be said that reversed bias becomes an important issue only because liberation theology lays claim to divine bias. However, that idea must be balanced with another thought, that liberation theology has always said that its position is not merely for the liberation of the oppressed, but also that in that process, whatever is over turned or dismantled, is for the benefit of the wholeness of society. Following on that point it may be noted here that Charles Kraft raises a valid critique when he says that:

> Within Christianity a God-endorsing-my-culture perspective often stems from the God-against-culture position.[37]

Yet liberation theology does not necessarily have to be on the defensive if it is always cognizant of the fact that the process of fighting oppression of the weak is the same one that seeks to stem the tide of the world disaster by nuclear carelessness and the "greenhouse effect" through human greed.

Divine Transcendence of Culture
The conclusion that God is above and beyond culture, untouched and unmoved by it, is at times more enticing than at others. It is most popular when there are more frequent occurrences of those natural disasters which insurance companies call "Acts of God." What raises more questions for the area of theodicy is that these disasters are inclined to take

place in cultures that can least afford another iota of pain. For example there is drought related famine in parts of Africa while there are calamitous floods in other parts. Among the poor of Latin America and Caribbean, earthquakes and hurricanes throw in disarray the gallant efforts at survival. Nature's war seems to be arrayed incessantly against the poor. Indeed, to add insult to injury, in those powerful countries where their destiny is controlled, the politicians who care more about right ideology than the welfare of the weak, continue to win elections and be drafted as the holders and wielders of power; that despite the intercessory prayers of thoughtful and progressive Christians.

However, to argue that God by the fact of divine sovereignty endorses the pain of the weak is to argue into a position of "faulty theodicy."[38] It makes God a racist and a caretaker of the oppressive establishments of the world. Yet, to argue on the other hand that the forces that create havoc for the weak are beyond the capability of God to restrain, is to place severe limits upon the sovereignty of God, to the extent that God is less than God. Therefore, faced with two seemingly exclusive alternatives, some people conclude that God is above and beyond culture. In this sense God cannot be made responsible for human experience especially when it entails suffering, and nature does not appear to be out of divine control. Even with that kind of disclaimer, however, the God above and beyond culture is not without its problems.

If the oppressive situations of the world are judged purely by human standards they are never seen for their true severity and therefore the perceived cure is never sufficiently radical. Secondly, without divine intervention of some kind, in the redress to the powerless, settlement is dependent purely on the good will of the oppressor. And liberation is never a gift from the oppressor. Thirdly, without any hope of divine intervention the powerless become the eternally hopeless. There has to be some way then, in which God can be in culture to aid the powerless and yet not be limited to or by that culture.

Transcendence and Divine Intervention in Culture
If it is true that God is the creator of the human impetus toward culture, God cannot then be against culture for its own sake. If it is true that God is not against culture for its own sake but is on the side of the powerless, and since powerlessness can be a cultural problem, is there a possibility that God can operate within culture to redress imbalance without total containment by culture itself? There is indeed a position that God is above culture but does operate in and through it.

When the Antilles Pastoral Institute, in a Roman Catholic viewpoint, made an assessment of the need for an indigenous theology in the Caribbean, it made some striking admissions. Ronald Graham, commenting on *A.P.I.'s* '71 consultation writes:

> While they acknowledge that many foreign ministers who have worked in the Caribbean conducted a generous and pastoral function, members of the A.P.I. 1971 were aware that failure frequently followed when foreign priests lack a certain psychic and sensitive maturity.

> Where the foreign priest was unable to adapt and integrate within the West Indian environment, where he lacked the humility to make his own contribution without negating or destroying what is different, there has been waste, frustration and bitterness.[39]

To rectify this situation it was proposed that "the Institute" should assist in collating and disseminating knowledge of Caribbean life, sponsor cultural programs, collaborate with existing cultural centers to incorporate regional art and learning in liturgy and worship.

This is highly appreciative of the fact that such adjustment is hardly enough to create indigenous theology but as a part of Roman tradition the authority for such a stand had to be sought. The authority here found was the Decree on the Missions from the Documents of Vatican II.:

> 1. That they may be able to give this witness to Christ fruitfully, let them be joined to those men by esteem and love, and acknowledge themselves to be members of the group of men among whom they live. Let them share in culture and social life by the various exchanges and enterprises of human living. Let them be familiar with their national and religious traditions, gladly and reverently laying bare the seeds of the Word which lie in them.

2. The manner in which the evangelization of these peoples is to proceed is incarnational —"the same way that Christ is bound Himself by the social and cultural conditions of the persons with whom He conversed." Due to the past progress of the missions in setting up the Church virtually everywhere in the globe, the focus of missionary activity in our era is less on geographical expansion and more on making the church a living and active presence within and native to the various cultures of non-Christian peoples. Dialogue and cultural adaptation are given more than usual emphasis in what follows.

3. Christ himself searched the hearts of men, and led them to divine light through truly human conversation. So also His disciples, profoundly penetrated by the Spirit of Christ, should know the people among whom they live, and should establish contact with them. Thus they themselves can learn by sincere and patient dialogue what treasures a bountiful God had distributed among the nations of the Earth. But at the same time, let them try to illumine these treasures with the light of the gospel, to set them free, and to bring them under the dominion of God their Saviour.[40]

Here again it is almost unnecessary to point out that some of the language used in this passage does not quite escape the old style that is associated with Christian imperialism and paternalism, but in terms of its authorizing function, it is clear on some positives. One positive is the recognition of the authenticity of culture itself by its divine endorsement, regardless of the location of that culture. That is indeed a tremendous evolutionary step from what Herve Carrier recalls from the Vatican archives:

In his evangelical Inscrutabili (1878) Leo XIII came close to what we would today call the problem of culture. Against the revolutionaries of 1870, he sought to illustrate how the church by spreading the light of the Gospel, has dedicated itself to the advancement of humankind, by its fight against barbarism, superstition, backwardness and moral degradation as well as by promoting education, moral progress and intellectual refinement.[41]

The journey itself has been fostered by the admission that all culture is "under the dominion of God" (transcendence) and by the same token "Christ is bound Himself by the social and cultural conditions of the persons with whom He converses" (immanence).

In the idea of God being above culture, yet acting in and through it, there are answers to at least two questions which may be asked of the host culture in the process of indigenization. The questions have to do with (1) whether equality among cultures is acknowledged to exist; and (2) whether God takes sides in the struggle for that acknowledgement.

1. Richard Niebuhr makes the point that when culture is defined to exclude the significance of the organization of "civilization," the definition is too narrow.[42] Of course "civilization" is a technical usage here to "designate the more advanced, perhaps more urban, technical and even senescent forms of social life."[43] Yet the colonial and imperial political agenda seems to ignore the other half of Niebuhr's warning, which is that limiting culture to "civilization" thus designated is also far too narrow a view.[44] At face value it does not seem to be such a revolutionary statement by Niebuhr, of course, but when placed alongside major power activity on the world scene, it demands an audience. It is not a wasted statement, when human worth is being measured strictly by Western civilization. Cultural and national respect is dependent upon economic strength and nuclear capability. Moreover, what multiplies the problem is that the church does not really make much effort to separate its beliefs from that of the business community. Indeed the situation has forced Niebuhr to take to task someone as important to the theological enterprise as Ernest Troeltsch; for Troeltsch had suggested that Christianity is so "inextricably intertwined" with Western culture that one in it could not present Christ apart from it, and one without it could not receive Christ without becoming a part of it.[45] The equality of cultures expressed in the God above culture and yet operating in and through it, is not reached through matching economies and military strengths, because like Cuba the rest of the Caribbean needs to seek out alternatives to the systems that are promoted by selfishness and greed and which in turn promote more selfishness and greed. Otherwise the subsequent step from "transferring power" will not be "transforming power." In any case the equality comes through a certain reciprocity of cultures made possible by the fact of divine sovereignty over all cultures:

You have put on the new self, which is being renewed in knowledge in the image of its Creator. Hence there is no Greek or Jew, circumcised or uncircumcised, barbarian, Scythian, slave or free, but Christ is over all, and is in all. (Colossians 3:10-11)

This reciprocity is expressed in the annals of the World Council of Churches among the reports on significant studies and statements made over the years in the name of the Church. And J. Van der Bent reaps the following from the 1983 Vancouver Assembly of the World Council of Churches.:

It was re-affirmed that cultures express the plural wonder of God's creation, that each culture has life affirming and life denying aspects, and that Christ judges and transcends all cultural settings. It was recommended that a search for a theological understanding of culture should be initiated, and that the role which secular and religious ideologies play in the formation of culture should be reassessed. The last sentence of the report reads: "We need to look again at the whole matter of witnessing to the Gospel across cultural boundaries, realizing that listening to and learning from the receptor culture is an essential part of the proclamation of the Christian message.[46]

2. Perhaps among the most serious objections shared by those theologians who are unwilling or reluctant to endorse the specificity of a Caribbean theology is the fear that a theology called Caribbean cannot be also Christian. That objection on their part, however, cannot be considered apart from a possible schizophrenic tension between the affirmation of an equality among cultures on the one hand and a notion of the superiority of Euro-American culture on the other. As for the schizophrenia, there is more than a strong signal to label it "unfounded." On the basis of culture no European culture has the right of superiority. The German claim to cultural superiority was the same situation that deteriorated into Nazism. On the other hand the reluctance as a consequence of the question concerning the particularity of Caribbean theology in juxtaposition to the generality of Christian theology may serve to bring a warning to the developers of Caribbean indigenous theology. The warning is that Caribbean theology has to be carefully shaped in order not to alienate its own context. Yet if Caribbean theology must be Christian theology, it still has the responsibility to be indigenous, since indigenous

theology may not be developed outside of the experience of the people, and since the most denigrating assaults in that experience have been cultural ones; Christ must perform his most effective liberative work within the culture of the people. Hence something basic to the new Caribbean perspective is the question in the face of colonial authenticity, how does God propose restitution?

Methodology for Caribbean Theology

William Watty, in a discussion of the question and topic "What is Caribbean theology?" finds it unnecessary to lay down a proposed method of doing Caribbean theology, because of the abstractness that proposed methodology is noted for.[47]   He suggests that Caribbean theology should be "stories" or "testimonies" of lived experiences.[48] Although this must have been judged by his audience as evasive tactics, his point is vintage understanding of the liberation position on the subject of methodology. It is akin to what Gutierrez calls the "second act."[49] Gutierrez calls theology from the liberation point of view, the "second act" because it is "reflection" (testimony if you will) on what has already been taking place. Yet even the testimony must be presented with a structure, and that for important reasons of communication.

Even if Caribbean theology is liberation theology, it cannot escape the questions concerning method. It is within its right to make its own quota of criticism of traditional theology in this respect, because within the idea of methodology itself is the question regarding the abstractness of philosophical programming. Transported through its abstract methodological principles traditional theology has always been academic in structure. Ultimately, however, it has to face the issue on its own grounds where, on the other hand, liberation theology has always claimed a more concrete stance with a special kinship to theodicy. It springs from the grass roots praxis relative to suffering experience in the interpretations ordinary folk give to the divine concern over their plight. What happens in the Basic Christian Communities in Latin America, where the study of "the word" is done primarily through lay leadership, is a prime example. The "word" is the authenticating factor regarding the praxis in which they are engaged. Yet that theology must be communicated with the understanding that liberation has the task not only to "transfer power but also to transform power";[50] in which case Caribbean theology as liberation theology warrants a methodological structure.

The fact that the tools of history, sociology and philosophy, along with the sources which include experience have had their systematic effect upon the task of indigenization of theology in the Caribbean, is enough to suggest a method. Though by no means unique, original or even exhaustive, those same factors endorse a structure that suggests three distinct areas of development.

1. In the first place it makes an assessment of the historical position of its people in the particularity of their experience. In the case of the Caribbean where the colonial socio-economic situation has not kept pace with missiological religiosity, the analytical process focuses upon the socio-economic and political situations which place the Caribbean in conflict with the metropolitan centers with colonial and neo-colonial power and control.

Even at this early stage of the methodological process, praxis is occurring. Not only is there categorization of the position, in the sense that there is an awareness of the sociological reality of being bracketed among the poor and powerless of the earth, but as a powerless people they are developing a critical understanding of their particular situation. It is reflection upon their experience, which is not merely to admit to powerlessness but to be spurred toward an ideological question as to why this powerlessness should not exist.

2. The second stage is the broadening of the contextual question where the Caribbean context is submitted to worldview. It has already been alluded to in prior discussions that some of the objectors to a Caribbean theology are afraid of the isolationism in the particularity of the Caribbean context. It is in this second stage that the real attempt at allaying that fear is made. The attempt is made where the broader context is brought into focus at the point where the "center" is con-

fronted by the marginally positioned, Third World versus First World, Caribbean versus Euro-American categories.

It is here that the idea of liberation doing the double task of "transferring and transforming power" makes sense. Specific cases of specific people, within specific contexts, with specific hopes and aspirations are all particularized, but the aim of liberation theology is to transform all of society. Hence an understanding of the broadened context in which the particular experience appears will allow for the wider horizons of desired change. For example, to establish an interest in the "Black Experience" is quite legitimate in its particularity. However, the "Black Experience" is a part of the human experience, so when the interest in the Black experience is corrective in nature, it is a universal corrective. Black liberation is ultimately the transformation of the human situation.

3. The third stage is the strict theological stage. Liberation theology in general brings to the Caribbean indigenization process some of its stigma. Its elaborate employment of the tools of the social sciences has allowed, though not condoned, an identification of the product with the tools.

Admittedly the first two stages of this method are more ideological than theological, if ideology is interpreted in the popular sense. In this sense ideology means a slanted view of reality to create a distortion which supports a particular political bias.[51] Conversely considered in its less popularized significance, ideology is a point of view, and a point of view is common to all.[52] However, it is when that point of view is carried into the split between rich and poor, powerful and powerless, and forced to take sides that ideology stands on the threshold of theology.[53] For to speak about a God that takes sides is to admit that theology comes with its own ideology. Yet James Cone is right, liberation theology that is not Christ centered is not Christian theology.[54] And Cone also points out that the process of liberation is expressed when it is said that Christ has liberated the powerless to fight for their own freedom.[55] Hence the final stage of the method has to do with the human appropriation of what God in Christ has done for them.

Caribbean Experience and Biblical, Social Concerns

Kortright Davis, who has given tremendous leadership to the Caribbean Conference of Churches and therefore to the indigenous quest, writes:

> The Bible provides the main source for our identification of a method of theological interpretation in the Caribbean – the search for a theology which arises out of the living experiences of the people of the region as they respond to realities as they perceive them.[56]

It is very interesting that Davis should consider that along with the particularity of the experience of the people, Scripture as a source prescribes the methodology of their theology. For by method, it may be supposed that Davis means the "categorizing" of this theology. It is understood that Caribbean theology is indigenous theology made so by its contextual roots. However, it must further be determined whether, when expressed, it is the Caribbean way of looking at the traditional perspectives, or part and parcel of the perspective of the "underside," thus falling into the category of liberation. Even so, the liberation perspective may not be treated as some annexation, secondary to "important" theological thought.

Juan Luis Segundo, after stating his disgust with the habit of those "circles" of European theology which consider liberation theology to be a single "burst of enthusiasm" or "a passing fad," went on to attempt a correction of the misconception:

> What is designated as "liberation theology" does not purport to be merely one sector of theology, like "theology of work" or the "theology of death." Liberation is meant to designate and cover theology as a whole. What is more, it does not purport to view theology from one of many possible standpoints. Instead it claims to view theology from the standpoint which the Christian fonts point up as the only authentic and privileged standpoint for arriving at a full and complete understanding of God's revelation in Jesus Christ.[57]

For a number of reasons it would now seem necessary to use Segundo's statement as a reinforcement of the authenticity of liberation theology. One reason is that at the point at which the Biblical record is submitted as a source for the indigenization process, it must be recognized that this source is a universal one. It is common to all theological perspectives, especially the Euro-American tradition, and Caribbean theology must declare itself regarding its emphasis in that use. On the other hand this is not to say that liberation theology needs to indulge in biblicism by picking out a couple of texts such as 1 Samuel 2 and Luke 4 to bear the brunt of the Biblical authority for its slant. Indeed if Segundo is right what is necessary is not a few passages to bear out a liberation viewpoint, but the rubric which reveals that the Bible is really a liberation story. Alfred Reid, Suffragan Bishop of Montego Bay, has already suggested that the liberation theme runs through the Bible from start to finish as "a golden thread."[58] In fact he thinks that if the liberation portions of the Bible were "excised" there would not be much of a Bible left.[59] Of course it is one thing to lay claim to a place in the general liberation theme as that relates to Scripture, but it is quite another to claim a contextual peculiarity and give it specific Scriptural authenticity.

If this should become a real question for Caribbean theologians, perhaps it can be answered in part by two Caribbean contributions. The first one is from Kortright Davis who proposes that in terms of choosing the Bible as a source for doing Caribbean theology, that process has a task:

> To understand Scripture itself and to translate it into appropriate terms in the Caribbean culture, as well as to understand that culture and translate it back into categories which can be compared with Scripture.[60]

Here, in the interaction between contextual experience and Scripture there develops a kind of reciprocity that makes it possible for divine judgment and vindication to be applicable in both at the same time. When God judged Pharoah, God judged the slave masters of the Caribbean peoples. When God said "No" to Israel's slavery, God says "No" to Caribbean slavery, colonialism and neo-colonialism. The second contribution is from Sehon Goodridge, principal of Codrington College, who suggests that:

> Perhaps the greatest task in rediscovering the importance of the Scriptures is one of communication and transculturation, i.e., looking for "cultural equivalents."[61]

Surely, "cultural equivalents" must be more intricate than mere textual references. Cultural equivalents should have something to do with some exegetical rigor that brings cultural repression into confrontation with Biblical ethics. For Goodridge cultural equivalents are more than mere academic record, they are to be internalized by the people, making Biblical ethics a relevant part of their cultural experience.[62]

Notes

1 Reid, Alfred, "Truth and Liberation", *Caribbean Journal of Religious Studies*, Vol.V. No.1, April 1983, p. 40.

2 Ibid. p. 41.

3 Cone, James H., *Liberation: A Black Theology of Liberation*, Philadelphia, J.B.Lippincott Co., 1970, pp. 50-51.

4 Ibid. pp. 54-70.

5 Ibid. p. 63.

6 Ibid. p. 63f.

7 Lowry, Ritchie P. and Rankin Robert P., *Sociology: The Science of Society*, New York, Charles Scribner's Sons, 1969, p. 98.

8 Hess, Beth B., Markson, Elizabeth W., and Stein, Peter J., *Sociology*, Second Edition, New York, Macmillan Publishing Company, 1985, p. 56.

9 Cone, James H., *Liberation: A Black Theology of Liberation*, Philadelphia, J.B. Lippincott Co, 1970, p.60.

10 Guillen, Nicholas, "National Identity and Mestizaje" ed. John Hearne, *Carifesta Forum: An Anthology of Twenty Caribbean Voices*, Jamaica W.I., Institute of Jamaica and Jamaica Journal, 1976, p. 35.

11 de Pestre, Rene, "Problems of Identity for the Black Man in the Caribbean", ed. John Hearne, *Carifesta Forum: An Anthology of Twenty Caribbean Voices*, Jamaica W.I., Institute of Jamaica and Jamaica Journal, 1976, p. 61.

12 Hess, Beth B., Markson, Elizabeth W., Stein, Peter J., *Sociology*, Second Edition, New York, Macmillan Publishing Company, 1985, p. 109.

13 Maslow, Abraham H., *Motivation and Personality*, Second Edition, New York, Harper and Row Publishers, 1970, pp. 171-172.

14 Ibid.

15 Mintz, Sidney W., *Caribbean Transformations*, Baltimore, The Johns Hopkins University Press, 1974, p. 9.

16 Hoebel, E. Adamson, *Anthropology: The Study of Man*, New York, McGraw-Hill Book Company, 1972, p. 663.

17 Ibid. p. 663f.

18 Hamid, Idris, *A History of the Presbyterian Church in Trinidad 1868-1968*, Trinidad, W.I., 1980, pp. 32-34.

19 Nettleford, Rex M., *Caribbean Cultural Identity: The Case of Jamaica*, Kingston, Jamaica, Institute of Jamaica, 1978, p. 18.

20 Niebuhr, H. Richard, *Christ and Culture*, New York, Harper and Row Publishers, 1951, p. 32.

21 Ibid. p. 33.

22 Kraft, Charles H., *Christianity in Culture*, Maryknoll, New York, Orbis, 1979, p. 103.

23 Ibid. p. 104.

24 Niebuhr, H. Richard, *Christ and Culture*, New York, Harper and Row Publishers, 1951, p. 32.

25 Kraft, Charles H. *Christianity in Culture*, Maryknoll, New York, Orbis, 1979, p. 104.

26 Ibid. p. 104.

27 Ibid. p. 105

28 Ibid. p. 105.

29 Ibid. p. 247

30 Ibid. p. 247.

31 Augustus, Earl; Julien, Terry and Graham, Roland, eds. *Issues in Caribbean Theology*, Port of Spain, Trinidad, Antilles Pastoral Institute, 1974, p. 44.

32 Ward, Barbara, *Nationalism and Ideology*, New York, W.W. Norton and Company Inc., 1966, p. 42.

33 Rostagno, Sergio, "The Bible: Is an Interclass Reading Legitimate?" ed. Norman K. Gottwald, *The Bible and Liberation* (Revised Edition of A Radical Reader) Maryknoll, New York, Orbis, 1983, p. 64.

34 Watty, William, *From Shore to Shore*, Kingston, Jamaica, Cedar Press, 1981, p. 17.

35 Watty, William, *From Shore to Shore*, Kingston, Jamaica, Cedar Press, 1981, p. 18.

36 Rostagno, Sergio, "The Bible: Is an Interclass Reading Legitimate?" ed. Norman K. Gottwald, *The Bible and Liberation* (Revised Edition of a Radical Religion Reader) Maryknoll, New York, Orbis, 1983, p. 64.

37 Kraft, Charles H., *Christianity in Culture*, Maryknoll, New York, Orbis, 1979, p. 107.

38 Jones, William R. *Is God A White Racist?* Garden City, New York, Anchor Press/Doubleday, 1973, p. 105.

39 Augustus, Earl; Julien, Terry and Graham, Roland, eds. *Issues in Caribbean Theology*, Port of Spain, Trinidad, Antilles Pastoral Institute, 1974, p. 38.

40 Ibid. p. 39f.

41 Ibid. p. 17.

42 Niebuhr, H. Richard, *Christ and Culture*, New York, Harper and Row, 1951, p. 32.

43 Ibid. p. 32.

44 Ibid. p. 32.

45 Ibid. p. 30.

46 Van Der Bent, Aus J., *Vital Ecumenical Concerns*, Geneva, World Council of Churches, 1986, p. 8.

47 Watty, William, *From Shore to Shore*, Kingston, Jamaica, Cedar Press, 1981, p. 10.

48 Ibid.

49 Brown, Robert McAfee, *Gustavo Gutierrez: Makers of Contemporary Theology*, Atlanta, John Knox, 1980, p. 43.

50 Rostagno, Sergio, "The Bible: Is an Interclass Reading Legitimate?" ed. Norman K. Gottwald, *The Bible and Liberation*, Maryknoll, New York, Orbis, 1983, p. 69.

51 Hardegree, Joseph L., Jr. "Bible Study for Marxist Christians: The Book of Hosea," ed. Norman K. Gottwald, *The Bible and Liberation*, (Revised Edition of Radical Religion Reader) Maryknoll, New York, Orbis, 1983, p. 99.

52 Ibid.

53 Ibid. p. 99.

54 Cone, James H., *Liberation: A Black Theology of Liberation*, Philadelphia, J.P. Lippincott Company, 1970, p. 197.

55 Ibid p. 202f.

56 Davis, Kortright, *Mission for Caribbean Change: Caribbean Development as Theological Enterprise*, Frankfurt and Main Berlin, Verlag Lang GMBH, 1982, p. 127.

57 Segundo, Juan Luis, "Capitalism Versus Socialism: Crux Theological," ed. Rosnio Gibellini, *Frontiers of Theology in Latin America*, Maryknoll, New York, Orbis 1979, p. 241.

58 Reid, Alfred C. "Truth and Liberation," *Caribbean Journal of Religious Studies*, Vol. 5, No. 1, April 1983, p. 40.

59 Ibid.

60 Davis, Kortright, *Mission for Caribbean Change: Caribbean Development as Theological Enterprise*, Frankfurt and Main, Berlin, Verlag Lang GMBH, 1982, p. 127.

61 Goodridge, Sehon, "The Domestication of Theology", *Caribbean Journal of Religious Studies*, Vol. 1 No.2, July 1976, p. 38.

62 Ibid. p. 38.

Chapter Five

Issues in Caribbean Theology

Basic to the Caribbean theological enterprise are some specific issues which seek their own clarification within the process itself. These will not appear in the same sequence as in the contents of most traditional theological treatments. In fact the topics are not the same since they come out of the sense of reality made pertinent by the questions being asked within and about the process of indigenization which is itself a localized process. There are eight such issues to be highlighted in this chapter, although they by no means exhaust the list of questions raised in the process. They are: the problem of contextualization, demythologizing missionary Christianity, neopietism and recolonization, remythologizing local traditions, human beings versus systems, humanity and transcendence the Caribbean Christ, and poverty and eschatology.

The Problem of Contextualization

In reference to its function in theological education, Edmund Davis defines the process of contextualization by saying:

> Contextualization expresses succinctly what we mean by the capacity to respond to the context. As dynamic process of theological education it challenges us to relate theological reflection to the life-situation and the life-experiences of a particular people within a particular community.[1]

This definition is relevant not only in the purely academic reference of an indigenous theology but in the application of this particular kind of reflection in community life. Yet even among some of those who support the larger principle of indigenization there are some nagging doubts which engender vacillation between the extremities of the "universal" and the "particular."   Between those points a number of sub-issues arise, namely (a) whether contextualization is not compartmentalization. (b) If it is, how does it relate to the other compartments which are different liberation perspectives?   (c) How do all these perspectives relate to Christian theology as a universal perspective?   When these sub-issues face the Caribbean situation squarely the main question which emerges is: If indigenous theology is compartmentalized theology, is it possible that Caribbean theology has imposed serious limitations upon itself to the extent that the perspective is totally isolated at the very point of its inception.

Horace Russell's point on the subject referred to earlier gains extra significance at this juncture. His argument is that although theology almost by nature must have a tri-focus in its point of departure, namely (a) God, (b) Humanity and (c) cosmos, the area of cosmos has been neglected.[2] It has already been noted that that argument can be used to bolster Burchell Taylor's highlighting of the necessity of the concrete in the theological perspectives of the Caribbean. However, when Russell's emphasis is coupled with his question it may be seen that some of his emphasis on cosmos is not merely in reference to "world" as concrete space, but to "universal" as opposed to "localized" thought. He asks:

> Might there also be the suggestion that this mixture of peoples, characteristic of the region is not an accident of history but an integral part of God's design for the world?[3]

Which point then underscores his concern with isolationism. The very fact that Caribbean theology would isolate its own context as the basis of its subject matter, could also mean isolating its perspectives from the general perspectives of Christian theology and therefore impede its own validity.

Compartmentalization and Relativity

This particular concern in not new, at least not to liberation thought. It relates to the wider problem of relativity in which questions concerning the limitlessness of the number of liberation perspectives may arise in different contexts and in their relationship to one another. How Latin American liberation theology relates to Black liberation theology is a question which may be multiplied numerous times if one takes into consideration the variety of liberation perspectives. For example, there are even curious differences in position between Black liberation theology and womanist theology and theology through the eyes of the feminist majority is different from womanist theology which is theology through the eyes of the female minority. Of course, since each position argues out of its own unique experience it becomes necessary for each to speak for itself. However, that is not the end of the problem because as each position addresses its situation there are those who believe that it must be careful not to lose its universal liberation concern.

Donald M. Chinula, commenting on the problem, says the following about African and Caribbean theology:

> Their desire to jettison Euro-American theology and supplant it with indigenous theology is as much a desire for liberation as is Black American preoccupation with dismantling the oppressive structures of this society, or the black South African cry to overthrow the alien theology of apartheid. But should African and Caribbean flirtation with liberation be so narrowly circumscribed? Do they not need a theology which explains, in Jesus' name the oppressive institutions of sexism, classism and tyrannical or corrupt regimes? Do God's people not need salvation from these evils? It is obvious that they do.[4]

Ignoring in Chinula's statement the unfortunate choice of words such as "preoccupation" and "flirtation" and also ignoring the narrow definition he obviously gives to colonialism and neo-colonialism so as to allow it to exclude racism and classism, it is possible to take up with him the broader question of universality. For example, the question of sexism is a pertinent one for the Caribbean, and Chinula's reference to it here is reminiscent of Jacquelyn Grant's addressing it from the perspective of a Black female theologian and pointing out some long time ago that the situation is paradoxical. She said then:

> In examining Black theology it is necessary to make one of two assumptions: (1) either Black women have no place in the enterprise, or (2) Black men are capable of speaking for us. Both of these assumptions are false and need to be discarded.[5]

On the other hand she had already admitted that:

> ...there is a certain validity to the argument that any one analysis—race, class or sex—is not sufficiently universal to embrace the needs of all oppressed peoples.[6]

It is inevitable that Caribbean theology within its process of disengagement from the colonial and neo-colonial traditional perspectives of dominance, deals with the questions of racism and classism and therefore relates to all perspectives which deal with these issues. If those are universal considerations, they have not escaped the general analysis. Sexism, of course, is another whole issue which has yet to be considered in any significant way. Yet one important point that has to be made is that as long as experience plays a major role in the development of liberation perspectives, the uniqueness and validity of each experience has to be the point of caution between the poles of the universal and the particular. Even so, there is a sense in which it is the liberation need that creates the relativity among all liberation perspectives. Whether the need has to do with sexism, racism, classism or some other perspective, the need to be liberated from the condition finds its counterpart in any other of the needs.

Isolationism and Reductionism

In the process of establishing the fact that history and sociology must of necessity be among the tools for doing Caribbean theology, Russell makes a curious statement:

> Sociology and the Natural Sciences can be called negative and it is undeniable that "truth" of a sort has emerged from these studies. Whether the truth which emerges from these studies can be called theological truth is another issue.[7]

The statement is curious in that it seems to underscore the obvious that the social sciences are not in themselves bearers of theological truths. Their truths may come with theological significance only so far as they share the same ideological reference with theology. Therefore if Russell is not stating the obvious, he is probably raising in a subtle way, criticism with which liberation theology has been bombarded over the years, that liberation theology in its use of the social sciences to illustrate categories of human experience and worth has forfeited the right to be identified as Christian theology. For one reason or another liberation themes have been drawn under a cloud of suspicion by some with regards to their Christian content. Leonardo and Clodovis Boff cite some of the innuendo:

> It is likewise bruited about that the theology of liberation is an entirely "secularized" theology—that it reduces faith to a strictly earthly ideology, hope to purely temporal eschatology and love to nothing but a political practice.[8]

When it comes to the question concerning contextualization, Donald Chinula is right in indicating that Caribbean theology shares the space in which that criticism is leveled. He recalls that one as important to the indigenous enterprise as John Mbiti registers open reservations with regards to the validity of at least Black liberation theology in this respect.[9]

Yet Mbiti taken seriously forces a non-Christian definition upon the total Protestant faith which by virtue of its Reformation roots, by his definition, would be invalid. Mbiti, in addressing a liberation perspective says:

> One would hope that theology arises out of spontaneous joy in being a Christian, responding to life and ideas as one redeemed. Black theology, however, is full of sorrow, bitterness, anger and hatred.[10]

For here Mbiti's problem with the perspective is not simply with its language, but also how closely it identifies with its particular context. In his critique, therefore, he chooses either to ignore the reality of the struggles within Christian history, or he is advocating that there should be a permanent separation between theology and historical contextual experience. There is little evidence in the history of the Christian church to support a theological movement emerging from some passive and tranquil joy.

It is probably not possible to charge the Caribbean's Horace Russell with Mbiti's position, or any other position, for that matter, since Russell's style through the medium of this particular paper is to raise issues without taking sides. Yet the questions raised are usually indicative of emphases in areas of concern. So in the discussion concerning the emergence of the New Caribbean person in her or his own right, Russell says:

> ...it might be conceivable that the future lies in a particularizing of history. Thus a possible Caribbean concept of man could be that of man localized, and bereft of a divine reference.[11]

Does he mean that the lapse in divine reference in regard to this human person is an inevitable result of being subjected to localization and particularization? If so Russell's conclusion could very well be that the possibility exists that particularization in contextualization is indeed reductionistic. If so would he go as far as to allude therefore that Caribbean liberation theology within itself could not be Christian theology?

On the other hand the charge of reductionism earns its permissibility only if contextualization becomes culpable not only in terms of complete inversions between the spiritual and the political, but also in substituting the one for the other. The point is that it is hardly possible for Caribbean theology or any other liberation perspective to fall into that trap. Indeed the charges and fears when examined seem rather unfounded because not only do the liberation perspectives usually emphasize a holistic interest covering the spiritual as well as political, but also as Leonardo and Clodovis Boff see it, often:

> Here we are dealing with precipitant, simplistic and terrified interpretation. Surely no interpretative code but an ignorant, ill-willed, or terror stricken one could read "political too" as "political only," "earth too" as "earth only" or "also, and especially the poor" as "only the poor."[12]

In any case, the picture is warped in the portrayal of the Caribbean Church engaging in politics while identifying it as theology. A truer portrait is one of the church in its spirituality finding it impossible to escape the socio-political realities of its world, for at least two reasons:

a. The line between the sacred and the secular is not as theoretically distinct as it was once perceived to be. Technological advancement has been so pervasive in society that it is fraught with all kinds of social and moral significance worthy of theological interpretations. Furthermore human existence is so politicized that the church which does not prepare itself to understand the significance of the relationships between these realities and the spiritual reality is a church that is not relevant to modern society.[13]

b. If there is such a thing as Caribbean theology, it was born out of a reaction to the European religiosity which can hardly be divorced from the politics of colonialism, expansionism and imperialism. Caribbean theology like other liberation perspectives, however, because of its contextual interests is less disposed to disguise its ideological and political concerns. This fact can hardly be said of the traditional Western perspective which wraps its political bias[14] in spiritual garb and pretends to be apolitical. The former is more honest.

Demythologizing Missionary Christianity

In the non-technical use of the word "mythology" (muthologia) it simply means the telling of stories. Furthermore, telling stories is a perfectly legitimate part of theologizing. On the other hand, demythology would suggest a rearrangement of that story telling to effect some form of change.

Ever since the concept of "demythologizing" was popularized by Rudolf Bultmann, people have seized license to use it in different areas of theological thought. This case is no exception. It is being used here to describe a process Caribbean thinkers employ to "deactivate," so to speak, the missionary theological expositions that are antithetical to indigenous efforts at self-actualization. With the effects of colonial evangelization in mind, this is indeed a legitimate if not a noble duty. It is at least psychologically necessary. Albert C. Outler says:

> The Christian view of the human, needs to appropriate the psychotherapeutic ideal of psychological autonomy, that is, one's self-direc-

tion undistorted by superego tyrannies and the arbitrary interventions of other persons.[15]

Terry Julien, Director of Catechetics in Trinidad, in setting the stage for the discussion on the part "tradition" plays in missionary Christianity and how it is used in the Caribbean as an impediment to the process of indigenization, made the following insightful comment:

> It seemed to me that the discussion up to a point assumed that missiology today simply meant adapting the traditional methods of evangelization to the mentality and needs of the present day Caribbean peoples. To me it seemed that the missiology envisaged justified itself by maintaining its continuity with the traditional missiology reaching back through Europe to the original preaching in Palestine.[16]

With the kind of reverence the evangelized people have for the church's Palestinian roots, any claim within this context to an unbroken link to the "Early Church" is designed to intimidate the   process of indigenization.   It is estimated that the enthusiasm to clash with those who walked with Jesus, and the descendants of a tradition inherited in its "ancestral purity," would be very difficult to muster. The cultural excess baggage that has been accumulated by the church over the centuries is often canonized under the umbrella of "Apostolic Succession." Therefore Julien would exhort the indigenous process not to be intimidated, but to be bold enough to perform its own demythologization of that excess baggage in tradition.[17]   At the very beginning there must be a decision as to whether defense of the tradition is defense of Jesus or of Christendom. Defense of the latter is usually bound up with cultural stratification.[18]

If the tradition were examined purely from the stand point of "a journey" from Palestine, it would show its own ambiguities at its very root where kerygma and myth came to play upon questions concerning the very underpinnings of the faith. Julien points out that the basic question was whether Jesus meant only to reform Judaism (as the Judaizers claimed), or if the movement was a break from the cultural roots of Judaism (as the Hellenists claimed).[19]   The answer to these questions, of course, lies in the determination of what was in the mind of Jesus. It is not a new theological problem, except for the precedence it sets for the Caribbean context, and in this case the Hellenists were forced to begin the cutting of the umbilical cord which tied the "New Way" to Judaism, to avoid further cultural impositions upon it.[20] It goes without saying that Julien perceives an apt parallel to this in the Caribbean situation:

> I felt that our model should be based on the answer to the question whether the history of God's salvation in the Caribbean began with the entrance of European Christians into Caribbean history. All the conquered peoples of the European Empire have had to face the kind of claim made by a British historian of Africa, that "the history of Africa is really the history of Europe in Africa." So too, in the effort to develop a Caribbean missiology, we must face the widespread view that salvation history in the Caribbean began with the arrival of the Europeans and their Christian religion. In these countries at the moment a pervasive movement of de-colonization is taking place which refuses European Christianity as the Gentiles before them refused Judaic Christianity. The primary danger before us is not so much dissolving Jesus into a "Christ myth" but frustrating the desire of Jesus to become more incarnate in Caribbean peoples and Caribbean culture.[21]

Nor does the necessity to demythologize for the sake of indigenization lie merely in the area of cultural impositions where the religion of the colonizer becomes a source of legitimacy for the process of colonization. There is ample evidence of this need in the doctrinal and organizational areas of the traditional legacy to the Caribbean church from missionary benefactors. And last but by no means least of the myths to be shattered is the Euro-American self-appointed guardianship of global morality. Of course even in these areas it will not be easy to separate these problems from culture.

Doctrinal Myth
In many cases doctrines are developed out of specific cultural needs with religious perspectives. But that which is easily applicable to a certain situation is often antithetical to another, because there are so many distinct needs and basic differences in different cultures. Yet basic to the task of colonial evange-

lization, has been the imposition of doctrines shaped in and for a culture far different from the colonizer's. In the case of the Caribbean, perhaps most detrimental to certain developments within the region are the doctrines concerning sin and secularization.

a. *Sin in Cultural Reference*: Robert J. Schreiter, a member of the "Metropolitan Center," in an examination of the ways in which theological indigenization takes place underscores the importance of tradition in religion. Yet for him the cultural chauvinism that usually accompanies colonial missiology lurks in religious tradition in its reference to doctrine. He expresses it thus:

> The experience of the cultural rootedness of theology rebounds again on a local community when it engages the church tradition, entering into that dialogue to test, affirm, and challenge its own understanding of the gospel. We now know that what had often been called the Christianization of a people was in fact their Westernization, depriving them of their own past. When encounter reminds these churches of their enmeshments with that colonial past, the situation becomes even more difficult. Instead of being nourishing, the encounter becomes alienating, and tradition is held at arm's length. What often results is that the tradition comes to be understood positivistically (a surface reading of its culture texts, based on assumption from the culture of the reader) or if it is read selectively (only those texts form the tradition that affirm the identity of the local church), or it is not read at all.[22]

In citing this statement, one does not intend to suggest that Schreiter proves the necessity to discard tradition in the life of the church. It is meant, however, to highlight ways in which some components of tradition are so irrelevant to the indigenization process that the need to demythologize tradition becomes of paramount importance. It bears elucidation here, however, that demythologizing means more than the translation of traditional themes into the terminology of the local context.[23] The process has to do with what concerns cultural roots and foreign doctrine.[24] If the themes are not symbolic of anything in the indigenous culture, and yet are forced to fit in by a mere language transfer, the process belies any meaningful reciprocity between tradition and indigenization.

One example of this has been the attempt to develop an African theology of Original sin in sub-Saharan regions. When there is no myth of the Fall in in local culture, it becomes hard to build a local correlate of an ancient doctrine.[25]

The point here is that the indigenous culture may accept imposed inappropriate myth for years through the very tradition that is basic to the faith. But because the doctrine has no counterpart in the indigenous culture the acceptance is succumbing to paternalism, and paternalism fosters the spirit of accommodation,[26] which in itself is a barrier to conscientious response, not only to problems of justice but of sin and salvation. Which fact suggests that, not only does indigenization have to examine the concept of sin in terms of how its missionary interpretation has impacted the Caribbean cultural context, but also the long list of other doctrinal components of tradition to correct any immobilizing effect of the myth surrounding them. So Alfred Reid, in redefining sin, rightly disagrees with the notion that the term should refer merely to personal and privatized failure:

> Sin is also one and indivisible. Sin is not only what is done in the bedroom but also what is done in the boardroom and in the banking institutions, and we cannot credibly claim to be saved and sanctified when we have, in fact, been seduced to become the bedfellows of injustice. The basic sin is idolatry. That old-fashioned word, 'idolatry' is a fairly good description of what millions of people do when they cover up and bow down before those who have set themselves up as the demi-gods of the modern world.[27]

b. *Secularization of the Gospel*: T.O. Beidelman in his research on colonial evangelism in parts of Africa found that although the indigenous people had a cultural conception of religion encompassing all aspects of everyday life, the consensus of the Christian Missionary Service was to observe and teach the very opposite. To supply one of many proofs to the effect, Beidelman quotes R. Cush, one of the important theorists of the Church Missionary Service as saying in an 1898 missive:

> I am entirely in favour of the Lay Evangelists, the female Evangelist, the Medical Evangelist, whenever Gospel-Preaching is the substantial work; but when it is proposed to have a pious Industrial Superintendent, or an Evangelical tile-manufacturer, or a low church breeder of cattle or raiser of turnips, I draw my line.[28]

It is hardly necessary to point out that the colonially evangelized persons could scarcely expect this missionary enterprise to address in any significant way the injustices of the colonial system. This attitude affected not only the missionary concept of sin as a private issue but of salvation which could never be of any systemic value to the local community. In any case, since the missionary church itself operated as an instrument of social control it was not likely that it would have been willing to change the colonial system as a whole. In fact, according to Beidelman's findings, the colonial political powers were often more willing than the missionary church to release some areas of control to the indigenous people. As the missionary church wielded its power over the life of the local community it became more marginalized, even as it became apparent to the church that marginalization could keep the local people docile, and thus prevent them from realizing their dynamic and creative potential. The church also learnt that one of the most effective means of marginalizing the people was not only by emphasizing the sacred-secular split, but by placing some very important developmental requirements on the secular side of the split. Education was one such item to be placed on the secular list, because the missionaries realized that the lack of it on the part of those they sought to control could be a very successful tool for social control. So Beidelman points out that although the application of mere common sense would suggest that educating the Africans would prove more beneficial to both the missionary church and the colonial government, there was extreme reluctance on the part of the church to take the Africans beyond signing their names and reading the Bible. The particular fear was that the educated African would automatically become a malcontent.

Geoffrey Williams of the Guyana Institute of Religious and Social Studies, drawing upon some of the relevant research in the area, heard similar sentiments which he relates to the Caribbean situation. He refers to a specific case regarding the evangelization of Sukumaland (Tanzania) where the missionaries had convinced their converts that "to be a good Christian, it is necessary to be a bad Sukuma."[29] The reference does much to verify that in many cases the missionary church was more interested in the people's docility than in their self-actualization. When it comes down to the Caribbean situation, the process of education, based on the same principles which prevailed in Africa, forced upon the people a chronic case of classism,[30] and demythologization will have wrought a miracle if it rids the territory of the effects of that classism. The colonial education process, which in fact owes most of its ingenious application to the church, did not fail to pass on the rank consciousness of Europe. As a result, higher education, pursued as a ladder to the social pinnacle and a source of empowerment, became inverted from the dangerous medium of secularization for the masses to the prize of the privileged intellectual elite.[31] Perhaps where education in the Caribbean has been most detrimental is at the point in the inversion where it is given without reference to the indigenous situation.[32] It did not matter that the education offered was hardly related to the indigenous culture as long as it groomed the indigenous people in the ways of the "master," and therefore to be psychologically dependent. As Geoffrey Williams describes it in Guyana:

> The curriculum of the denominational schools were as to be expected, modeled on the British public school system and hence did not cater either for an education geared to local needs, or situations. It has been noted that secondary education in Guyana aims at producing an educated elite whose ambitions are oriented anyway from the home situation usually to those countries whose models of culture they have self-appropriated, instead of catering for the needs of a majority of the population.[33]

Indeed, Guyana owes the serious shortage of teaching specialists in the country to this very fact.

Guardianship of Morality

On the questions of culture and communication, it has already been indicated that communication even to the point of voluntary acculturation has been inevitable for the Caribbean region. It can even be acceptable. However, when colonizers disregard principles of reciprocity in communication by forcing their ways upon others, it becomes a serious imposition.

Even if the value system they push is good for people other than themselves, the fact of its imposition makes it unwholesome. Yet the truth is that the Euro-American value system is not always good and right. As William Watty takes pains to show, evidence of the fallacy of moral adjudicator is to be found in abundance in the ashes of the "World Wars":

> ...the question was bound to arise out of the debris of the world wars, for in those catastrophies, the triumphalism of Western Christendom and the moral superiority of Western Civilization collapsed...The perpetrators of the barbarity were not "heathen lands afar" but Christian nations of the West. Adolf Hitler rose to monstrous power and supervised the genocide of the people in the heartland of the Protestant Reformation, and Mussolini fulminated his fascism and raped Abyssinia in the shadow of the Vatican. The first atom bombs were dropped by a nation on whose coins are engraved "In God We Trust."[34]

In fact the evidence in the debris of the world wars is merely an extension of the commitment to the kind of expansionism in which the end justified the means. Needless to say, the means includes genocide and the like. Furthermore it is one thing to defend any atrocity on the grounds that people are always children of their time; it is quite another thing to justify for all time the morality under whose rubric the atrocities have been done.

Neo-Pietism and Re-colonization

Recolonization Threat

The idea that re-colonization could take place in a real literal sense within the Caribbean, is now not as juvenile as it could have once sounded. Since the invasion of Grenada and Panama by the United States in recent times, and of the Dominican Republic formerly, the proof of the willingness of a major power to use military force to destroy and replace unpopular political structures is quite open and apparent. Of course even after mention of those events, one has not begun to touch all those delicate questions concerning the possibility and probability of covert activity through "intelligence" organizations to ensure favorable political structures wherever necessary. Yet when Caribbean theologians speak of a re-colonization threat, they are not warning against pending overt military overpowering of the whole Caribbean region. They are however thinking of ways in which the power of thought can hold so much psychological sway over people that it immobilizes their efforts to self-actualization.

A diligent interpreter of this threat of re-colonization is William Watty. He perceives it as a condition which runs the gamut from the imposition of foreign theological concepts, through internally generated ideas of an exilic existence to the intensification of the socio-political structures of neo-colonialism.[35] Basically the importance of Watty's interpretation at this juncture is the assurance it creates that the threat exists. The question of "neo-pietism" being a part of that threat is raised by persons such as Ashley Smith and Sehon Goodridge.

Pentecostalism: It is necessary here to establish why it is important to identify the case as one with neo-pietists and not merely Pentecostals. The main reason is that not all Pentecostals are neo-pietists in the sense in which "neo-pietist" is being used. That is not to say that there is no problem between the indigenous process and the Pentecostals who may not be considered to be neo-pietistic.

Kortright Davis, pointing out the doctrinal differences between the traditional churches and the Pentecostals, shows that one of the main reasons the Pentecostals refuse to take up membership in the Caribbean Conference of Churches is their fear that that association with the "established churches" will confuse the "conversion experience" that took them away from those churches in the first place.[36] It is rather ironic that when the Pentecostals broke from the established churches it was partially in renunciation of the same tradition that the established churches, in search of indigenization, also seek to break with. Yet the most distinguishable difference between the established churches and the Pentecostals is the self-same tradition. As Davis puts it:

> The historic churches have traditionally emphasized that which is given and unalterable in the Christian tradition, while the newer churches have tended to emphasize that which is known and recognized in the present experience.[37]

Davis goes on to muse that indigenization must of necessity
bring the two emphases together for the kind of creativity its
success demands.[38]   Theology also has its own strange
"bedfellows"; but Davis is right.

Actually, the Pentecostal renunciation of the tradition selects
from the tradition portions of its theology which support the
body-soul dualism in the human person, then separates the
soul for emphasis, and becomes concerned only with its salvation. As a result it postpones the rectification of the ills and
injustices of the present world for some future redress in the
next world:

> Better days are coming by and by, When we reach the city in the sky.
> My troubles will be over — And heavenly joys flow over — Better days are
> coming by and by.

Their brand of "existentialism," which does not go beyond
concern for salvation of the soul, does not help the plight of
the suffering of the poor and the marginalization of the fran-
chiseless. It is succinctly put by Sehon Goodridge who says:

> The Christian gospel demands that those who know God and respond
> to him as disclosed in the life, death and resurrection of Jesus Christ
> should share their experience with others. There is all the difference
> in the world between sharing our Christian faith and manipulating
> people by a kind of theological stance based on rewards and
> punishments, the threats of hell and the assurances of heaven which we
> hear so glibly emitted in some of our religious broadcasting. This kind
> of theological propaganda, despite communicating a wrong image of
> God, does promote a kind religiosity which might be intended to salve
> the conscience, but does great violence to the human personality. So
> what should be "good news" is very often "bad news."[39]

Another part of the problem with Pentecostalism is the area
of a certain kind of "providencialism." Providencialism is the
kind of theological perspective which encourages people "to
leave it all in the hand of God." The attitude does well for
personal faith claims but it so minimizes the importance of the
human effort in the struggle, that the fight for liberation is
always somebody else's fight. So while this kind of Pentecostalism is worthy of much praise for its strength of faith, it
must also be admitted that its "otherworldly" positions amount

to an apolitical stance. An apolitical stance does not generate the praxis destined to cause social change. Yet if that is all that Pentecostals did, or did not do for the process of indigenization which seeks social change, it would not mean much more than what the aviation people would term being a "drag." It is merely more dead weight to be carried. However, it is one thing to be a drag, it is quite another to be in active opposition.

Neo-Pietism

When Ashley Smith looks at the subject it begins to be apparent that there is quite another dimension to the Pentecostal situation. Strategically placed in the following necessarily long quotation from Ashley Smith's book, *Real Roots and Potted Plants* are a number of nuances which more than suggest that when he talks about the evangelists to whom he had made prior reference as "neo-pietists," he is not talking about a few misguided regionals who are willing to postpone their own social adjustments till they get to heaven. He is talking about powerful doctrinaires who are really using their apolitical stance as political activism. Smith writes:

> The Jew in the Roman colonies was a non-citizen and could only see the fulfillment of the promise of the gospel in another age; the slave and indentured labourer and subsequently the dispossessed and disinherited in the Caribbean region have seen personhood, freedom, and genuine fellowship (even with the bearers of the Good News) as that which could be possible only in an age to come, or perhaps in another country. For very few Afro and Indo-Caribbean Christians, has life in the Christ accommodated the affirmation of either their own humanity, the land of their birth, their ethnic forefathers, the elders and heroes of their island or sub-continental home. Every act of worship, every ecclesiastical event, is for the typical Caribbean Christian, a reminder that this world (the Caribbean homeland and its affairs) is not the home of those who have responded in the affirmative to the claims of the gospel as presented by missionary and evangelist. Illustrative of the excessive "other-placeness" of the Caribbean Christian world view is the notion held by many Christians, especially the evangelical wing of the Church, that one of the evidences of authenticity of one's conversion is one's ability to speak, especially a prayer or verbal testimony with a non-Caribbean accent, more often than not, an "American" accent.[40]

Here Smith has covered the idea of "other worldliness" in the history of colonial evangelism in the Caribbean up to where in the neo-colonial period the principle has become a political instrument of sabotage. And there is no mistake as to where its point of origin is.

The reason for the designation neo-pietist then is clear, for while these people pretend to save the Caribbean from "materialism" they simply delay their enlightenment toward the processes of real liberation. Pointing the Caribbean people steadfastly to heaven, neo-pietists deliberately tranquilize their consciousness for their earthly exploitation. Furthermore when it is realized that even the local neo-pietist groups are backed by foreign organizations far more wealthy than the "established churches" could ever hope to be, the threat to re-colonization becomes increasingly more real. And the task of indigenization becomes a greater one.

Remythologizing Local Traditions

Perhaps a safe way to tackle the question of remythologization is by looking at the idea of myth itself as it enters into the area of mythology. In addition since remythologizing here is an off-shoot from Rudolf Bultmann's principle of demythologization, it may be wise to look at myth from his basic understanding of it. In any case since myth is understood and addressed in a multitude of ways, choosing Bultmann's meaning eliminates the need for endless definitions of mythology.

Bultmann has defined mythology as:

> ...the mode of representation in which the unworldly, the divine, appears as worldly, human, and the other-worldly as this-worldly.[41]

By this definition Bultmann means that myth is important by the nature of its purpose, which is to express divine realities in human terms. Which fact makes mythology more than story telling. It is the description in story of human understanding of human existence, past, present and future and what lies beyond that existence to sustain and motivate it. It is the human way of expressing what appears to be divine mystery. Tied up in that definition of mythology then, are the exigencies of human understanding of life, participation (human and divine), and destiny. It is important to point out that Bultmann does not propose mythology as some objective scientific function, because Bultmann understands the subjectivity involved in the human agency. Where there is only subjectivity there can be unreality. In fact, it is for just this reason that de-mythologization becomes a necessary function. As demythologization is borrowed in the Caribbean situation it has become necessary to apply it to the missio-colonial structures to see what myths have helped, through the deficiencies of their particular human agencies, to hinder self-development among the colonized. The question for the moment is, why is it necessary to do re-mythology in the process of indigenization?

The question concerning whether re-mythology in the Caribbean sense is necessary is answered when a certain response is given to the general question: Is myth necessary? That answer has already been broached by Bultmann's definition of mythology. Yet even if Bultmann's definition were considered to have some special Christian bias, scholars other than Christian have found that human beings of whatever age and clime have this "endearing insistence on carrying quasi-mythical modes of thought, expression, and communication into a supposedly scientific age."[42] As a result of this seemingly necessary function of myth, after the process of demythologizing of the missio-colonial structures there needs to be new myth taking the place of the dwarfing myth. In any, case taking William Watty seriously on the question of "debunking," demythologizing the Euro-American tradition can very well be judged as debunking. Therefore it is the development of that which is new that makes the progressive difference. That is the difficult part of the Caribbean situation because mythology has to walk the narrow road between memory of roots and colonial acculturation. No wonder Watty warns that (1) Any wholesale transportation to the Caribbean situation of foreign theologies such as Black liberation, Latin American liberation theology is re-colonization of the

Caribbean.[43]   (2) If even the great respect for the Afro-or
Indo-roots should cause the Caribbean people to feel a sense
of impermanence on the Caribbean scene, it is to succumb to
re-colonization.[44] (3) To imitate the structures one criticizes is
to surrender the search for freedom and self-development.[45]

So then, what are the unimposed traditions of the
Caribbean? With that question it suddenly becomes obvious
that with all the exceptions to Caribbean re-mythologizing, the
options for the seed-bed for myth are very few indeed. Yet
Watty suggests that it is in those narrow confines of the young
Caribbean culture[46] that this new mythology must take place
and where the new theology must be done because the new
theology must be of a distinct character. Part of the process of
re-mythology of course authenticates the new culture. Therefore Watty says:

> What we require is a lot more stories, more real-life situations, more
> testimonies (and I mean real testimonies) more biographies and more
> autobiographies (and I mean real autobiographies). And then, even
> then, we might only be able like Moses with his face hidden in the cleft
> of the rock, to glimpse the backside of God as His glory passes by
> (Ex.33:17-22), and exclaim with Job out of the mystery of his affliction
> "Lo, these are but the outskirts of His ways, and how small a whisper do
> we hear of Him! But the thunder of His power who can under-
> stand?(Job 26:14)[47]

The implication for mythology in this premise is parabolic
in the sense that stories are myth. They are not myth in the
sense of being useless fable, but in the sense that a parable is a
way of expressing a central truth. This time it is the story of
the Caribbean understanding of its experience with the rest of
the world and with God. The process involves examining
experience in the light of Scripture. Jose Comblin, in another
setting with similar conditions once said:

> ...there comes a point when we must make explicit our experience of
> the Gospel mission, when we must examine it critically and synthesize it
> in carefully worked out concepts. This obligation is not properly that
> of the missionaries, but of the church itself. The church must interpret
> what exactly is going on in the mission experience, appraising the
> input and scope of its novel features. It must try to comprehend the
> signs of the times offered by that experience. To do that, the church

must go back to its sources, reread its texts, and critically re-examine its past traditions that may have been unwittingly canonized.[48]

As it has been noted, while it is true that the European Christian experience had to be transported to some degree through the European cultural experience, the process of evangelization does not have to give licence for claiming the "home" experience as the only authentic experience, thus rendering the host experience not only inferior but inauthentic. Therefore as the process of indigenization sheds this baggage of imposed inferiority it affirms its own worth. By virtue of the Caribbean context, the perspectives that emerge are "Caribbean." The "new" here is the operative term because such perspectives arise out of a new perception of God's dealing with the Caribbean situation. New perceptions arise out of a new self-awareness.

Human Beings Versus Systems

Facing the Christian as a topical engagement, the choice between persons and systems is not difficult. Christians are supposed to choose persons as more important than systems. But the engagement is not as simple as it presents itself at face value, as any area of liberation theology well knows. There are intricacies involving provision such as the query as to what one intends to do with the persons or with systems. Basically, the precarious journey is between the scientific analysis that creates reductions which amount to meaningless components, and the political (often conservative) analysis that creates compartmentalized groups with stereotypical labels. In the one case the human being is reduced to a mere specimen for analysis. In the other, one gets thrown into a group to become a non-person, in any case. Hence the Caribbean theological issue concerning human personhood in the world of systems has developed. Nor can the theological process remove itself from the responsibility of its own caution. Even as it does not allow other processes to reduce the human being below the boundaries of human dignity and the human spirits, so

Caribbean theology recognizes its solidarity to be with persons. The work of liberation must take place among the people.

The question of "Humanity in the Divine Image" has come into the Caribbean discussion through the Antilles Pastoral Institute in their attempt to wrestle with some of the issues in Caribbean theology. It is interesting that as they prepare to introduce the issue they utilize the Biblical text, Acts 10:28:

> But God has been showing me that we ought not to speak of any (human being) as profane or unclean.

What makes the choice of the text interesting is that when in the context of the discussion there is the inclusion of the words, "What God has *cleansed*," the emphasis being on "cleansed," the transposition from "diet" to "people" becomes a little troublesome. In other words the application implies the possibility of the "non-personhood" of a people until some kind of acceptable change is made. Therefore, the Institute has to make the clear distinction between what the people of the Caribbean have always been, on the one hand, and what for some time they had been perceived to be, on the other. In this case, the missionary church must make the adjustment in perception about the people, their culture, and their humanity.

But the Caribbean discussion on humanity has progressed beyond the point at which decisions are made as to whether to include the Calypso or Reggae into liturgical experiences as a mark of accommodation to the local culture. Though that is itself an important issue, a more important one in terms of human value is the area of the discussion concerning a certain "spirituality" in the Caribbean person. Sergio Arce-Martinez of Cuba says:

> I believe in the human being as a spirit, who is a created conscience and therefore I believe in his/her responsible freedom. I believe in the human person who is not the mere result of the forces of the environment and of heredity, but who is free to obey God, and to be responsible before God and before others, human brothers and sisters. I believe the human person chooses whom to serve, God or mammon. I believe the human person can say to God, "I love you!" or can say to God, I abhor you!"[49]

Arce said this after arguing passionately against the reduction of the human being to Andrew's "mountain of atoms" or Pascal's "cane that thinks."

In our modern world there is a certain empiricism which demands that everything must be broken down to its observable constituent parts. Thus even the analysis of situations creates such compartmentalization that adds to the already overemphasized individualism of most of our Western economic and social realities. It aggravates the tendency to the selfishness and greed that motivate much of the so-called "free enterprise system." On the other hand, as a result of all the efforts at counteracting the problem of rugged individualism the basic human worth tends to get lost in the shuffle of the system. As that situation impacts upon the Caribbean it forces considerations that affect the very core of the Caribbean existence. The process of indigenization must seek with great passion to avoid the "lumpen" syndrome which Edmund Davis will not allow the Marxists to forget.

The name "Caribbean" is worthy of its unifying image and influence. It brings a group of people from a relatively wide area of concentration and presents them as a unit of concerns, varied, perhaps, more in degrees. Yet what the theological process must guard against in this designation, is the tendency to treat *en masse* the region's case to the extent that the Caribbean peoples become reduced to some faceless structure with a tag that says, "Caribbean." Dr. Dale Bisnauth, commenting on the task of the theological enterprise in the pluralism that exists in the Caribbean, posed the following remarks:

> Our contribution both to the search for directions for development and to the process itself must be the insistence that development must have a human face, whatever the value of the economic-cum-political ideological and programmatic approaches to the enterprise. Our clear, unambiguous declaration must be that development is about people. To put it another way: it is the good of people that justifies the means of development at every stage. And this primacy is not about "man" or "mankind" in the abstract, but of human persons in their concrete relatedness to one another in particular contexts of geography and other environmental realities.[50]

Bisnauth's comment is from the "prolegomenon" to his treatment of Caribbean pluralism, but are most cogent to the area of the discussion where the human being is judged against the system. The statement is highly reminiscent of a pronouncement of Jesus: "The Sabbath was made for the human being, not the human being for the Sabbath" (Mark 2:27), because in so saying Jesus has sanctioned forever the human person above the system.

Neo-colonialism does not always present itself as a personal enemy. It is an elaborate system couched in the political halls of the metropolitan centers such as London, New York and Washington, Paris, West Berlin and Bonn. Once in a while it is possible to refer to some head of state as anti-Third World, but in the majority of other times the neo-colonial enemy is not personally available for confrontation. It therefore has to be judged by the liberation process as the system that it is. This is why it is so important to liberation theology that neither the concept of sin nor the concept of salvation be privatized. Producing a procedure to remedy a privatized situation when the problem is systemic, leaves the situation out of sync with its cure. But as Bisnauth points out, even as liberation theology is busy organizing its assault upon the systemic evil, it runs the risk of limiting its concern to the remedy of systems, forgetting its primary function of liberating persons.

It is true that the systems affect people to make them poor and powerless, but it is for that same reason that dismantling the systems really means dismantling the power they hold over the people. Anyone who has worked with any kind of liberation process knows only too well that some of the gaps between theory and praxis must be filled by the willingness of the people to overcome. That willingness is created in psychological and spiritual liberation, both of which are not system reality but people reality. The affirmation of the human being over systems is only a part of the theological affirmation for the Caribbean. There has to be a reason for this affirmation. If the reason encompasses all of humanity, it becomes the equalizing factor for all of humanity, negating every rationale for domination whether of colonial or neo-colonial significance. Caribbean theology therefore owes it to its context to examine whether that equity in human dignity is not affirmed in the concept of the *imago dei*.

Psychological Difference

When Abraham Maslow studied the making of the human personality, he discovered some very important factors relative to the concept of need. Consequently he could divide needs into categories of "lower needs" and "higher needs." Lower needs are among those that are basic to survival. Higher needs are more evolutionary in the human developmental system. One such higher need is the need for self-actualization.[51] What is very interesting and most relevant to the present discussion is the fact that Maslow says that while human beings share some needs with other living creatures(need for food with all living things; need for love with the apes) self-actualization is the only need unique to the human being.[52] Furthermore the need for self-actualization is a universal need among human beings. It is obvious then that deliberate processes of underdevelopment violate basic law governing the expatiation of the human condition. If self-actualization may be listed in psychology as one of the realities basic not only to the uniqueness of the human being but also the universality of humanity, to prevent self-actualization in anyone or any group of human beings is to be in serious violation of a human principle.

Economic and Social Gaps

Higher needs of the human self notwithstanding, the lower needs are never meant to be treated as if they bear no importance to human development, or even its survival. In fact, because of the nature of some of these lower needs one recognizes the importance and the detriment in not having them met long before sensing that some higher needs exist. There is the necessity to eat long before the desire for self-actualization. Hence it may be interjected that eating should not have to include the appetite for the prime meat whose production deprives the poor of large quantities of protein (soybean) in order to induce the right tenderness. Even so if Marx is taken seriously on this score, "use value" is defined directly in terms of "need".[53] Hence prime meat is valuable only because people think they "need" it. But as Michael Manley makes the consequential point:

> ...there is ...what is sometimes described as the appetite for conspicuous consumption. This attitude includes the assumption that there is a right of access to consumer goods regardless of productive contribution. It expresses itself in an unthinking appetite for and production with consumer goods, but a disinterest in productive responsibility.[54]

Which point raises the inevitable question about labor: For there are those who, while satisfying their most exquisite cravings, conspire to devalue the means and people by whom that satisfaction is provided. As Horace Russell observes it on the Caribbean scene:

> It would seem that the Caribbean man has been conceived of in terms of a 'producer.' The emphasis upon man as producer and production as the *summum bonum* would seem to minimize the rather less pronounced, but equally important element in Caribbean selfhood.[55]

There are people who chop sugar cane from before dawn to after dusk six days a week without earning enough to supply their own basic needs. One should not be "sentenced" to malnutrition because one is only a cane cutter or a grass cutter, at least not while others live at relative ease off the fruits of that same labor. When this happens, some basic principle governing equity in the value of human beings is being violated.

History and Self-Actualization

There is a movement of time and the occurrence of events within which the human being is not simply a spectator. This sequence is the creation of history, and the human being is part of it. That is to say that the human person is an agent of history, to the extent that history itself is partially a human creation. In addition to the fact that history is partially created by the human person, the participation in historical events is often planned. When that planning directs or alters a particular course of history it presents the human person as being in charge of some awesome responsibility; responsibility that in a sense sets her/him apart from the other animals and nature. A dog may run across the street and cause an accident in which someone with some great gift for which the world is waiting is put out of commission. Some kind of change that would have been wrought through that gift is then cancelled and an historical event or events are turned aside. Yet the dog has no ability to sit and plan to cause or avoid an accident. It is only the human being who can say, "I have arranged it so that I will have a surplus coming to me next year, therefore I will demolish my granaries and build bigger ones." It is this reflective ability and the ability to plan, that makes the reality of future relevant, and eschatology promising and compensatory.

Humanity and Transcendence

Future, eschatology, and self-actualization on the agenda of the human person easily earn for him/her the designation *homo viator*.[56] He/she moves within history in search of fulfillment even more than an end. Even so there are events of history over which human control is either quite limited or nonexistent. In Armenia the people can construct safer houses, in the Caribbean they may concentrate on hurricane resistant roofs, but both the earthquake and hurricane, so far, are beyond human control. Apart from the inability to be in total control, there is the problem of the pros and cons of individual choice. One person's sense of realized eschatology is expansionism in all its ruthless acquisitiveness, while that of another person's is greater justice to a greater number of people. Operating within the same scope of history, not only will both sides create some kind of jostling milieu but there will also develop eventually a sense of futility. It is the human futility that makes this situation more problematic than otherwise. It requires therefore, another position; one which transcends the futility of history.

The futility in history as encountered in the Caribbean situation is mostly due to domination. Those who study the condition conclude that domination, being as sublimal as it is overtly physical, demands counteracting efforts of enormous proportions. In this Caribbean reality the necessity to break through the barriers of human futility is as real as it is anywhere else, and its indigenizing process has its work cut out and stockpiled. Dr. Luis Rivera of Puerto Rico has no illusions about it:

> Liberation theology should also have this witnessing character testifying to the tenacity of the human spirit, resisting the fatalistic acceptance of the apparent hegemony of the structures of oppression upon the historical potentialities of our collective existence. It has to witness to the capacity of mankind to cultivate our ability to develop new visions of reality and to fight for their historical realization despite the many defeats and many causes of disillusionment.[57]

When the Caribbean theologians introduce the subject of "The Caribbean Person," they demonstrate that they have come to grips with this issue. It extends itself beyond the socio-economic and political aspects of liberation theology. It advocates a dimension called "The New Caribbean Person" who through psycho-theological principles must live the new prospectives, so that Caribbean self-actualization may occur. This new Caribbean person is in full recognition that the point of transcendence of the futility of the human condition is God in Christ. This is the Gospel message. Jan Lochman, perhaps unwittingly, supports the Caribbean position by saying:

> The gospel treats the world in utter seriousness. At the center of the gospel stands the proclamation of the incarnation of God. But exactly and specifically, it is the incarnation of God. If God is ideologically denied, man is threatened to become dissolved in his history, his society, and his future, and he becomes imprisoned in his immanence and his worldly projects. The penultimate becomes the ultimate for him. His total destiny then depends on his accomplishments. He lives with the possibilities of happiness and euphoria as they emerge in the moments of his success. But he also lives in frustration and despair as they are given in the situation of defeat and guilt.[58]

Perhaps this is why some Marxist projects meet with failure because they are not allowed to transcend their own history. On the other hand, it is here that the locus of power lies for the Caribbean colonial and neo-colonial redress, because it is the transcendence procured through "newness of being,"[59] created in the reality of the incarnation of God in history. It creates the impetus for the right to regional independence and also to participation in global perspectives.

The Caribbean Christ

It is not the most investigated in the indigenization process, but Christology in the Caribbean context is the most crucial area in the Caribbean perspective. It is crucial for at least three reasons (1) Christian theology is centered in its Christology. Once Caribbean theology has identified itself as Christian theology it is concerned that it expresses the Christ reality within the Caribbean context. (2) It further decides how it expresses the Christ reality within the Caribbean context. That means that it decides what the Caribbean Christ looks like, and how the locus of liberating power, through the transcendence made available by the Incarnation, is transferred to the Caribbean context. In doing so, it gives consideration to what some may describe as the possible enslavement of Christ to a single context. This has to be avoided. (3) When the context, indeed even the ideological point of view, is representative of religious and non-religious pluralism what does Christ do? In other words, in the pluralism of the Caribbean, Caribbean theology must aptly describe what is soteriology.

A pertinent and particular point in the Christ debate in the Caribbean is whether the necessity for a Caribbean Christ has truly arisen. Clifford Payne of Trinidad, who has given some systematic body to this discussion, suggests quite clearly that there is hardly a doubt that the necessity exists.[60] No other than a Caribbean Christ can address "the deepest needs of the Caribbean people." And having satisfied the debate that the Caribbean context is sufficiently a particularized one, Payne moves on to answer the questions pertaining to the universality of the Christ who must at the same time remain Christian.

Payne's way of affirming the universality of Christ is made apparent in his statement:

> ...we must not complain that the Europeans "Europeanized" Christ. Christ had to become a European in order to deliver Europeans from evil. This helps to understand why, when the Europeans shared Christ with us, it was a Europeanized Christ that they shared.[61]

Alfred Reid of Jamaica seems to confirm Payne's point of view when he says:

> What we have to understand is that liberty is one and indivisible. Inner spiritual freedom in the context of objective oppression is a noble thing but it is incomplete, and it is inadequate as a manifestation of the complete and final victory of Christ over all forms of evil.[62]

Here the acknowledgement of the universality of Christ does more than admit that Caribbean theology is Christian theology. It is arguing also that even if contextualization to some extent runs the risk of the "cultural captivity" of Christ, Caribbean theology is willing to admit that in Christology the universal as well as the contextual significance exists. The reason for the Caribbean acceptance of the universality of Christ is that evil has its own universal significance. If one believes that the work of Christ has to do with the cure of evil, and if one is unwilling to accept some notion that evil has no meaning except as violation of something within the personal self, one can hardly not accept the comparable conclusion that the efficacy of the work of Christ is not privatized. Of course, privatization of Christology from a personal perspective is one thing, contextualization from a particular ideological standpoint is another.

One of the main problems with the universalization of Christology is the danger of repeating only Christological abstractions which do not represent anyone. This is more significant when the position is taken that indeed God is not neutral in the arena of hurt and powerlessness for some. In a Caribbean world where the dominated community cries out for redemption, Christ the liberator can hardly look like the colonizer, for in that case where domination is rampant it is the Christ of the dominant who will be forced to deal with the case of the dominated. In which case, the dominated are put at a disadvantage. Clifford Payne, describing the arrogance of that fallacy, goes on to say:

> ... we must admit that they (the Europeans) did not exert themselves over what might be the likely consequences of the "natives" experiencing Christ as a foreigner, since for them the natives were children living in the darkness and in need of both the love of Christ and the civilizing influence of Christian peoples; that is to say in need of becoming little Europeans.[63]

So even though Payne envisions that the process takes time, the Caribbean Christ must be Afro-and Indo-Caribbean; which means that the Caribbean Christ identifies with the people among whom the marginalized may be found and whose sense of culture is an instrument in their liberating process. It goes without saying that some disagree.

Richard J. Neuhaus, taking Gustavo Gutierrez and the particularistic categories of liberation theology to task, once said:

> It makes all the difference in the world...whether an image places Jesus with the poor or with the rich, with the oppressed or with the oppressor. The problem, of course, is that terms such as oppressed and oppressor and notions about what might be done to change their relationships are uninteresting abstractions until related to concrete and usually conflictual movements, struggles and political parties. Jesus, knowing the temptations we would face, cautioned his disciples against saying "Lo here! or Lo there!" as though we could with absolute certainty identify the presence of the Kingdom in history.[64]

Furthermore, according to Neuhaus, it is quite a futile endeavor to get the gospel message to come in solidarity with any side:

> Serious Christians have been forced again and again, often reluctantly, to respect the gospel's stubborn resistance to being used; it remains unenlistable and unrecruitable.[65]

These statements have done their own work in creating the suspicion that Richard Neuhaus will not be convinced of a divine bias even with Luke 4:18-19 as evoked by Caribbean's H. Clifton Niles, who himself is convinced that:

> ...the only valid option for the church is the example of the Lord. Jesus made the lot of the poor, despised and oppressed of the earth his own as is evident from his incarnation, ministry and death. He identified with them in their poverty and in their hope and perceived his own mission as the means of their hope being realized.[66]

Nevertheless, while the oppressed, of all people, may not be able to point into the present in total recognition of "the will of God being done on earth as perfectly as it is done in heaven", they are perfectly aware of what oppression is. Subsequently, if they take the historical Jesus seriously as portrayed in the gospel they usually know whose side Christ is on anyway, because the historical Jesus informs the church of what Jon Sobrino calls "the intention"[67] of the timeless Christ. In the end then the oppressed know how they will be unshackled and by whom.

Finally Caribbean theology must decide how soteriology becomes effective within the Caribbean heterogeneity. Dr. Dale Bisnauth of Guyana, in his article "Religious Pluralism and Development in the Caribbean"[68] has been very thorough in his description of the vast number of religious roots and currents existing in the Caribbean. When the political views and non-religious perspectives are added to the religious diversity, it is not difficult to understand Bisnauth's contention that most conclusions about Caribbean homogeneity are gross exaggerations. Furthermore the situation raises questions relative to the efficacy of the meaning and work of the Caribbean Christ in the midst of that kind of diversity.

With regard to heterogeneity however, it is never as frightening as it is made out to be, when it is analyzed from the perspective of unity versus uniformity, a point that has been examined elsewhere in this discourse. It may do well to say here, however, that even Bisnauth admits that diversity sometimes plays a positive role in the process of development.[69] If this were not true St. Paul would have wasted a good portion of his time composing 1 Cor. 12. In fact if one takes the elements of language, race, economics, social categories and religion, operative within Bisnauth's analysis of Caribbean diversity, one finds that (a) they exist to one degree or another in any given one of the territories, and (b) they are a part of the same system that necessitates a liberation strategy for the region. Therefore diversity among the people may not be judged in its minutest detail. It should be judged within the broader application of the definitions of national communities which entail relationships cemented by history and geography, shared world view, and some kind of developmental dream.[70]

In the final analysis, the liberation that the Caribbean seeks is the right to build its community and develop its dream. If this is the main perspective shared within the pluralism of the Caribbean, the Caribbean Christ is already at work within that same pluralism. Michael McCormack is thoroughly convinced that soteriology is possible within the diversity of Caribbean pluralism. Because of its interest in the development of the human society, he calls the whole process "the new humanism" and exhorts the church to see to its success:

> In the movement towards a more human society the churches must show solidarity with the new humanism and with the forces for change in the region. This means refraining from denigrating criticism of the non-Christian forces for change and from concentrating on the negative aspects of society. Solidarity means working with such forces and stressing the values in their work, which are beneficial.[71]

Ashley Smith is even more explicit in his argument when he says:

> Any Christian who takes the incarnation seriously is fully aware not only of God's affirmation of the world but also God's involvement in the process of bringing the world to perfection through the continuing work of Christ. Of course, no one with a developed understanding of God's activity in the world is so naive as to assume that God works only through Christians or those Christians who are ordained to special responsibilities with the body of Christ.[72]

Poverty and Eschatology

Even before the United States invasion of Grenada there were people who sized up the fears, the miscalculations, the desire to dominate, and the enormity of metropolitan politics and power, by more than what they call "vibrations." They understood all the dynamics at work in the Caribbean, and under their power, understood the reason for hopelessness. One such person is Dr. Reinhild Traitler whose poetry put in uncanny sarcastic but prophetic words, events yet to come:

Again
the buccaneers are roaming the waters
Birds of prey
circle the skies

The cries of the boy next door
shot in the head by police
pierce the night
Nobody knows the offence

Maybe he was a thief
Him, he had no money
no work
Him lazy
dreaming of the revolution

The faint fragrance
of easy life fills the air
The smell of perfume and sun lotion
or burnt skin
White flesh on white beaches
An abyss
of steel bands
black slaves
The sweat of the cane fields
Bitter taste of freedom
rum and coke

At night
sometimes
the incantation of the past
the slow movements
of your body
as you walk
tell the story of a struggle
and the story of a victory
calypso pride
We haven't sold our souls yet

But the saviours are coming
The guardians of the free world are coming
With transnational corporations under their
wings
Hell's angels
the drug pushers are coming
the little mafias in the service of the big
bosses
The missionaries and their radio stations are
coming
Salvation in the sweet by and by
The Caribbean Basin Initiative is coming
our deliverance from
Che Guevara and Fidel Castro and
those little Maurice Bishops
with their fancy utopias

The marines are coming
the death squads are coming
Security is coming at last

law and order
The silence of the churchyard

Oh those hopes of our early years
I feel your heart
trembling with pain
as the shadows grow

But the anger
but the anger
but the anger
of the drum
Man
is maybe dead
is maybe dead
is maybe still alive.[73]

There are two dimensions in the function of eschatology. The concept becomes important for liberation when the liberation perspective stands in the tension created by the paradox of hopelessness on the one hand and divine promise on the other. This is the first dimension. The second dimension is the position of hope. This position is not some passive inaction but a positive spiritual introduction to the future, enabling the future to reach back for elevating intercourse with the hopelessness of the present.

Eschatology and Caribbean Social Analysis

The eschatological need in the Caribbean develops itself despite liberation pronouncements, hence William Watty's innovative address: "Liberation — Popular as Calypso and Rum Punch, But Caribbean People Now Less Free."[74] Despite liberation, the areas in which freedom has not been realized have been left virtually unchanged since the earliest years. The labels on the systems may have changed but the domination and marginalization are intact. In fact the systems of exploitation, if anything, are larger and far more intensified than in the past. Despite the title he gives to his analysis, Watty does not blame the condition of the unfree upon liberation itself. Indeed he suggests that liberation is not a new concept within the region. It had been known to the original citizens who resisted the Spanish conquest, and to the Africans who escaped and fought for freedom. In which case liberation has functioned at least as the "first movement." However, liberation, though popular in present day awareness has been accepted with many misconceptions because the principles of the bondage are accepted with some misconceptions. So Watty indicates that liberation carries the symbol of hope, yet a hope that is often delayed, and to understand the lack of freedom despite the presence of the liberation concept, the nature of the bondage must be properly understood:

> Certainly we are none of us free as our forebearers hoped we would be by now. In order, therefore, to understand the meaning of Caribbean liberation, we ought to identify more precisely the nature of bondage by which we are still shackled.[75]

Watty then goes on to analyze the situation:

1. Very present on the Caribbean scene is neo-colonialism as expressed through imperialistic political confinement which has little or no regard for territorial sovereignty. As Watty sees it:

> After all these years we are still not free to live our own lives, to take our own decision and choose our own friends without foreign interference and harsh reprisals. After all these years we are still a besieged and subjugated people in the Caribbean.[76]

Watty's comments are not merely philosophical reflections. They are based on historical reality as described in the neo-colonial patterns of domination. It is not difficult to make the assumption that he is thinking about the United States objection to Grenada's revolution and Jamaica's experiment with democratic socialism. He probably remembers United States marines in the Dominican Republic and the situation that obtains there even now. Moreover his contention is that although the United States is very much free to do what it pleases, these territories which are supposedly politically independent dare not do anything against the will of the United States. They are virtual slaves in their independence and national sovereignty.

2. Secondly, the neo-colonial control of the marketplace and therefore the economies of the territories, makes it impos-

sible for the Caribbean people to rise above indebtedness and therefore subservience. So Watty says:

> We find ourselves enslaved to metropolitan countries and transnational corporations whose only aim is profit, and which leave us, after all these years, an exploited and plundered people.[77]

Caribbean production is totally dependent upon implements produced in the industrialized countries. While the price of these implements keeps escalating the price of the goods they help to produce keeps falling. The multinationals demand of the Third World situations, enough exemptions and low wage control to ensure astronomical profits. Besides, they manipulate cultures to cause cultural shifts that result in the creation of new appetites, and that for the goods they produce. The Caribbean territories, as most Third World countries, overspend just to produce but never earn enough to service debts and improve living standards. As they are forced to devalue currency to meet loan standards, the debts multiply in value by the decreased value of currency. With no hope of recovery and self-development they are forced to assume more and more the position of the beggar.

3. Resultant upon this state of "underdevelopment" is the fact that more people become marginalized:

> The worst forms of poverty are still rampant. There are still too many of our people rotting in festering slums without the basic minimum of the amenities necessary for decent civilized living. There is a steady rise in unemployment and under-employment which leaves too many of our brothers and sisters under a cloud of hopelessness and demoralization and degradation and frustration.[78]

4. There is a lack of unified effort among the Caribbean peoples, partly because they have been deliberately polarized. Hence there is a severely restricting lack of trust. The result of all this is that:

> There is less freedom of movement in the Caribbean today, less possibility of internal migration, less chance of persons who wish to start life anew and rebuild their future in another territory than at any time since emancipation.[79]

5. Perhaps the greatest obstacle to liberation is the Caribbean affirmation of its condition of domination and powerlessness. This affirmation of domination is not only by suffering people who have become too tired and whipped to resist, but also by those who have become compromised clients of systems of selfishness and greed. As Watty puts it:

> After this long experience of domination we have become conditioned to accept it as a way of life. We have become culturally imitative. We have become a mimic society. We have learned at length to ape well the standards and values of our oppressors...Our thinking has become clogged up with false ideas of what liberation is all about and even those of us who happen to enjoy a measure of liberation from the more obvious forms of oppression such as unemployment, disease, bad housing and poverty fall all the more easily as victims to false values and individualism and selfishness and emptiness of consumer society which make us a hinderance to the real task of liberation and the creation of healthy and stable communities in the Caribbean.[80]

There are at least three reasons for enumerating here, almost anew, the ills caused by neo-colonialism:

1. There are some who believe that neo-colonialism is merely a concept that has no real significance outside the boundaries of the overactive, liberal and very misguided cranium. They conclude that failure to succeed on the part of the poor Third World countries is due to their own lack of initiative, innovativeness and ingenuity. That condition in turn is due to a basic lack of education. For example, Carl Gerstacker, who served as the chairperson of the Dow Chemical Company (1960-1976), takes the position that the United States, far from being guilty of exploiting the Third World, has spent billions of dollars being their benevolent benefactor. The only mistake that the United States has made in this area, cannot and should not be judged from a moral perspective. Moral judgments are unfair and unnecessary when the mistake is simply overestimating the ability of the beneficiaries of United States generosity. The United States thought these poor countries knew "how to fish" therefore it "gave them a fish." Relative to the Chinese proverb "Give a fish, you feed for a day; Teach how to fish, you have fed for life," Gerstacker is convinced that the United States' only mistake is not to have

perceived Third World ignorance with regards to their own process and avenues of development.

Moreover, Gerstacker suggests that even the "simple" mistake of overestimating Third World capability is now being rectified not so much by the government but by the transnational corporations. These multinational bodies, he suggests, are bringing wealth to the people who have never dreamed of it before, and the corporations ought not to be criticized therefore.[81] But when Gerstacker spells out the concern of the multinational corporations only part of it resembles any of the Third World contention as identified by William Watty. Gerstacker says:

> You may object and say that we all have motives of altruism and charity. Indeed we do, or should have, such motives, but they usually come to us after we have taken care of our own self-interest, our own needs, our own family. How many people do you know who would do extra work for the sole purpose of paying extra taxes?

> The salient fact about transnational companies is that they are not pretending to do their work to spread joy in the world or because they want to maintain international peace or because they are inspired by some other lofty motive. No, the fact is these firms are inspired by their own self-interest. But, as I have said, it's self-interest that has brought human kind up out of the ooze.[82]

It is the last sentence in the statement with which most Caribbean religious thinkers need to disagree. Selfishness has not brought the Caribbean out of the ooze. In fact the Caribbean is by no means out of the ooze, but there are no illusions about the self-interest which motivates these corporations operating within its bounds.

2. The necessity of an eschatology comes at the point where liberation praxis is assessed for not only its success but also its viability. The situation, having been evaluated under the sway of unchallenged missionary power and know-how of the past, must at this point be reexamined under the light of the influence of the process of indigenization and liberation. How does the liberation quest stand up to the test of relevancy, bearing in mind the charges of indigenization regarding the unrelatedness of missionary Christianity to the reality of existing situations? That is an important new question.

The phrase "liberation-popular as Calypso and Rum Punch..." is catchy, but the Caribbean liberation themes are by no means frivolous. Caribbean theology has looked at the old way, the missionary way of defining sin and salvation in their most privatized significance, and it has reconstructed those definitions. It has redefined sin to include a systemic responsibility, and salvation to include rescue from those forces that leave persons hungry and immobilized in desire for self-actualization. The Caribbean liberation process has examined the missionary church's view of the Kingdom and has reinterpreted it through Scripture to mean much more than pie in the sky by and by. Now it has come to mean the reign of God in "justice, peace, harmony, and love for each other." Yet, "Caribbean people are now less free!"

3. Finally, redescribing the problem at this point shows the enormity of the problem that the Third World faces, the categories of despair and hope, hence the need for a viable eschatology in the Caribbean perspective.

As far back as 1974, Richard J. Barnet and Ronald E. Muller did a study on the power multinational corporations wield over global economy and their influence over the political systems of the world. They pointed out then that when the annual sales of these corporations were compared with the gross national product of some countries it was discovered that:

> General Motors is bigger than Switzerland, Pakistan and South Africa; that Royal Dutch Shell is bigger than Iran, Venezuela and Turkey; and that Good Year Tire is bigger than Saudi Arabia. The average growth rate of the most successful global corporations is two to three times that of most advanced industrial countries including the United States.[83]

Barnet and Muller are quite conscious of the fact that the size of these corporations is only a fraction of their omnipotence. What is even more awesome about them is the fact that in the development of business and in their "self-interest" they have and wield:

> ...the power to transform the world political economy and in so doing transform the historic role of the nation-state ...In the process of developing a new world, the managers of firms like GM, IBM, Pepsico, GE,

Pfizer, Shell, Volkswagen, Exxon, and a few hundred others are making daily business decisions which have more impact than those of most sovereign governments on where people live; what work, if any, they will do; what they will eat, drink, and wear; what sorts of knowledge, schools and universities will emerge; and what kind of society their children will inherit.[84]

In spite of Karl Gerstacker's protestations regarding the integrity of these corporations, in terms of their intentions to take poor nations "out of the ooze," it is clear that these companies, operating purely on the profit motive, find it more lucrative to do business away from their home bases. So Barnet and Muller hear Karl Gerstacker stating the true case:

I have long dreamed of buying an island owned by no nation and of establishing the world headquarters of the Dow Company on truly neutral ground of such an island, beholden to no nation or society.[85]

For the idea is to be controlled by none while they control all, including their home base country, especially if they need political pressure to be launched against some uncorporative government. They exploit every situation for profit. Moreover, whatever they do in Third World countries, American based multinational corporations on occasions have had their overseas investment account for as much as seventy two percent of their total profits.[86] That kind of profit should not seem unusual if in the Third World they never find the Third World worker worthy of his/her hire. For example, at the same time a company was paying laborers in the United States two dollars and twenty three cents an hour to help manufacture semiconductors it was paying Jamaicans in Jamaica thirty cents an hour to do the same work.[87] While paying two dollars and forty nine cents an hour in the United States to make clothing the same company in Trinidad paid forty cents an hour for the same work.[88]

Eschatology and Caribbean Hope
Frank Cameron's contribution to the Caribbean Conference of Churches' effort at producing new music for indigenous worship in the Caribbean bears some suggestions of an indigenous view of eschatology:

Give me dear Lord, thy grace to see
Each day as it should really be
Encumbered not by yesterday,
Let me live fully all the way.

Unwisely, if my eyes be cast
Too much upon the distant past,
I will not see the task at hand,
Nor use the time at my command.

Today let me no sadness wear
But see tomorrow without fear,
For if I dread the unforeseen
How can I ever on thee lean?

Here are definite strivings to break with the past, and given some political events in Caribbean history, those strivings are well understood. However under the suggestion that even in the area of eschatology there is a gap between the Caribbean reality and the Euro-American emphasis, it is interesting to note that the difference may lie in what is understood by the past. Perhaps it should be noted that this and other "Euro-American" references warrant some qualifying because the scope of that tradition is so wide that it should not be understood as the confirmation of a theological monolith. Of course to pretend that a disclaimer of one sentence can deal with the issue is to belittle the seriousness of the problem, its history, growth and progress in understanding.[89] It is sheer convenience that the title "Euro-American" is used to identify a fraction of such complexity. On that very score, it is interesting to note how Karl Gerstacker, in his anxiety to vindicate multinational corporations, views the Third World's past as it relates to the missionary church. At this point one could almost mistake Gerstacker, the chief North American multinational corporation advocate, for William Watty or Ashley Smith, Caribbean liberation advocates, when Gerstacker says:

> It is true that the basic objective of the church was to spread the good news of the gospel, and it is true that hundreds of millions of people were converted to Christianity. But there is little evidence that this effort greatly improves the lot or solves the problems of the poor, the underdeveloped, the uneducated, the starving. Indeed, some of the world's least Christianized nations, such as Japan, are more prosperous

than the most thoroughly Christianized nations such as Brazil or Latin America generally. Individual missionaries such as those in Hawaii, or missionary nations such as Spain and Portugal, seemed to prosper as they brought Christianity to others—but the less fortunate remained less fortunate. What went wrong? Clearly the church failed to teach those in the back of the bus how to fish, and in fact from our history books we know that the poor were often cruelly exploited by agents of the church in the name of Christ.[90]

The point is that even here the meaning of the past cannot be taken at face value even as expressed from a North American perspective. Yet since it is futile to take all the Euro-American theological expressions relative to this question, each in its individual emphasis, it may be more profitable to evaluate one expression in terms of how it may or may not suit the Caribbean situation. The choice is Jurgen Moltmann's under-standing of the idea of hope. First it may be said that the choice is not arbitrary since Moltmann is one of the pioneers in attempts at bridging the gap between witness and eschatol-ogy by way of an understanding of hope from the Third World perspective.

Yet Moltmann speaks of hope as *"ta eschata hos ta prota"* — "the end is like the beginning,"[91] because he is concerned that the eschatological promise of the transformation of the present can be meaningful only if it is based upon the past.[92] By past, of course, Moltmann means events in time which have been verified by history and human experience. Beyond that there is the possibility of entering into some utopic expectation which exists nowhere except in myth. So although sin is "paradise lost" and salvation is "paradise regained,"[93] paradise is something that belongs to human memory because of human experience. And what may be hoped for in the future owes its appeal and selection to that which already is known as good, because of the past. Therefore all the great movements through history, which have operated on an understanding of an eschatological dimension in the need for change have come with the prefix "re." They have been Renaissance, Reforma-tion, Revival, Renewal, Restoration and even Revolution.[94] "Re" which is looking back at what existed prior to its distor-tions, becomes the barometer for the eschatological promise.

As a result, tradition is very important to hope.   Moltmann says:

> Confronted by hope's possible disappointment, one readily clings to the traditional, to the tried and tested knowledge of old. For whatever has been handed down from antiquity to the present has preserved itself in the past, and whatever has preserved itself must also have verified itself. Where else might one find the criterion for the good in the abundance of new possibilities for the future?[95]

Most Caribbean theologians are agreed that when the immediate Caribbean past is examined the Caribbean Christian experience is a prominent part of the Caribbean experience. However, evangelization and colonization with slavery and indentured labor are all bound up together in its history and therefore form part of that Christian experience. The union was there at the beginning and has continued to exploit the region even in its eschatology. So what does the Caribbean Christian view in retrospect in cogency with her/his eschatological expectations?   What, in the past, given that experience, is "paradise lost?" For even if one assumes ownership of the tradition by which the Europeans brought evangelization, in that same tradition are couched the calculations for colonization and enslavement. As Moltmann himself points out, the movement from the "Old World" to the "New World" was to colonize it so to find freedom.[96] Yet even as Moltmann deals with this "freedom" in time for the colonizers' fulfilling their eschatology, it must be noted the subject fails to note that the same movement made some other people "unfree."

The conclusion here then, is that if nowhere else, in the area of eschatology in Caribbean theology there has to be special reasoning to the idea of hope. This is not to say that Caribbean people have no sense of hope. More than anything else they are aware of hope as is promised in 2 Corinthians 4:7-10.

> But we have this treasure in earthen vessels, to show that the transcendent power belongs to God and not to us. So we are afflicted in every way but not crushed; perplexed but not driven to despair; persecuted, but not forsaken; struck down, but not destroyed; always carrying in the body the death of Jesus, so that the life of Jesus may also be manifested in our bodies.

But the idea of future in relation to the value system of the past will have to be adjusted according to the Caribbean context created by its history. What the Caribbean people remember is how they have been treated. In which case therefore, hope is measured by the denial of rights suffered in the Caribbean. Hope for them is in the ability and will to struggle, and eschatology realized is in the struggle itself toward the dismantling of the structures of oppression to the reality of shared participation in a world God has created for all.

> For in this fight
> we are right
> the earth
> was made for all. [97]

Notes

1 Davis, Edmund, "Contextualization as a Dynamic Process of Theological Education," *Caribbean Journal of Religious Studies*, Vol. 2 No.2. September 1979, p. 30.

2 Russell, Horace, "The Challenge of Theological Reflection in the Caribbean Today," ed. Idris Hamid, *Troubling of the Waters*, Trinidad W.I., Rahaman Printery Limited, 1973, p. 26.

3 Ibid. p. 26.

4 Chinula, Donald M. "Jamaican Exocentrism: Its Implication: Its Implications for a Pan-African Theology of National Redemption," *Caribbean Journal of Religious Studies*, Vol. 6 No. 1, April 1985, p. 52.

5 Grant, Jacquelyn, "Black Theology and the Black Woman," eds. Gayraud S. Wilmore and James H. Cone, *Black Theology: A Documentary History*, 1966-1979, Maryknoll, New York, Orbis, 1979, p. 420.

6 Ibid. p. 418.

7 Russell, Horace, "The Challenge of Theological Reflection in the Caribbean Today," ed. Idris Hamid, *Troubling of the Waters*, Trinidad, W.I. Rahaman Printery Limited, 1973, p. 26.

8 Boff, Leonardo and Boff, Clodovis. *Liberation Theology: From Confrontation to Dialogue*, Cambridge, Harper and Row, 1986 p. 20.

9 Chinula, Donald M., "Jamaican Exocentrism: Its Implications for a Pan-African Theology of National Redemption," *Caribbean Journal of Religious Studies*, Vol. 6, No. 1, April 1985, p. 48.

10 Mbiti, John, "An African Views American Black Theology," eds. Gayraud S. Wilmore and James H. Cone, *Black Theology: A Documentary History*, 1966-1979, Maryknoll, New York, Orbis, 1979. p. 478.

11 Russell, Horace, "The Challenge of Theological Reflection in the Caribbean Today," ed. Idris Hamid, *Troubling of the Waters*, Trinidad W.I., Rahaman Printery Limited, 1973, p. 29.

12 Boff, Leonardo and Boff, Clodovis, *Liberation Theology: From Confrontation to Dialogue*, Cambridge, Harper and Row, 1986, p. 21.

13 Smith, Ashley, "The Christian Minister as a Political Activist," *Caribbean Journal of Religious Studies*, Vol. 2. No. 1 April 1979. p. 26.

14 Collins, Sheila D., "Feminist Theology at the Crossroads," *Christianity and Crisis*, Vol. 41, No. 20, December 14, 1981, p. 343.

15 Outler, Albert C., *Psychotherapy and the Christian Message*, New York, Harper and Row, 1954, p.95.

16 Julien Terry, "Christian Mission, Cultural Tradition and Environment," ed.Idris Hamid, *Out of the Depths*, Trinidad, West Indies, St. Andrews Theological College, 1977, p.9.

17 Ibid. p. 9.

18 Ibid. p. 10.

19 Ibid. p. 11.

20 Ibid. p. 12.

21 Ibid. p. 10.

22 Schreiter, Robert J., *Constructing Local Theologies*, Maryknoll, New York, Orbis, 1985, p. 75f.

23 Ibid. p. 76.

24 Ibid. p. 77.

25 Ibid. p. 77.

26 Smith, Ashley, *Real Roots and Potted Plants*, Mandeville, Jamaica, West Indies, Mandeville Publishers, 1984, p. 86.

27 Reid, Alfred, "Truth and Liberation," *Caribbean Journal of Religious Studies*, Vol. V, No. 1, April 1983, p. 41f.

28 Beidelman, T.O. *Colonial Evangelism: A Socio-Historical Study of an East African Mission at the Grassroots*, Bloomington, Indiana Univeristy Press, 1982, p. 119.

29 Williams, Geoffrey, "Classicism and the Caribbean Church," ed. Idris Hamid, *Out of the Depths*, Trinidad, West Indies, St. Andrews Theological College, 1977, p. 73.

30 Ibid. p. 68-70.

31 Ibid. p. 73.

32 Hawkins, Irene, "Education and its Imbalances," ed. David I. Mitchell, *New Mission for a New People*: Voices From the Caribbean, United States of America, Friendship Press, Inc., 1977, p. 102.

33 Williams, Geoffrey, "Classicism and the Caribbean Church," ed. Idris Hamid, *Out of the Depths*, Trinidad, West Indies, St. Andrews Theological College, 1977, p. 70.

34 Watty, William, *From Shore to Shore: Soundings in Caribbean Theology*, Kingston, Jamaica, W.I., Cedar Press, 1981, p. 52.

35 Watty, William, *From Shore to Shore: Soundings in Caribbean Theology*, Kingston, Jamaica, W.I. Cedar Press, 1981, p. 23f.

36 Davis, Kortright, *Mission For Caribbean Change: Caribbean Development as Theological Enterprise*, Frankfurt, Main, Berlin; Verlag Lang GMBH 1982, p. 189.

37 Ibid. p. 190.

38 Ibid. p. 189.

39 Goodridge, Sehon, "The Domestication of Theology," *Caribbean Journal of Religious Studies*, Vol. 1. No. 2, July 1976, p. 39.

40 Smith, Ashley, *Real Roots and Potted Plants*, Mandeville, Jamaica, W. I., Mandeville Publishers, 1984, p. 11f.

41 Bartsch, Hans Werner, ed. *Kerygma and Myth: A Theological Debate*, New York, Harper and Row Publishers, 1961, p. 47.

42 Kirk, G.S., *Myth: Its Meaning and Functions In Ancient and Other Cultures*, Berkeley, Cambridge University Press/University of California Press, 1973, p. 2.

43 Watty, William, *From Shore to Shore*, Kingston, Jamaica, W.I., Cedar Press, 1981, p. 24.

44 Ibid. p. 23.

45 Ibid. p. 19.

46 Ibid. p. 65.

47 Ibid. p. 65.

48 Comblin, Jose, *The Meaning of Mission*, Maryknoll, New York, Orbis, 1977, p. 3.

49 Arce-Martinez, Sergio, "What is Man," *Caribbean Pulpit*, Kingston, Jamaica, W.I.,Cedar Press, 1983, p. 10.

50 Bisnauth, Dale A., "Religious Pluralism and Development in the Caribbean: Questions," *Caribbean Journal of Religious Studies*, Vol. 4. No. 2. September 1982. p. 17.

51 Maslow, Abraham, H., *Motivation and Personality*, New York, Harper and Row Publishers, 1970. p. 98.

52 Ibid. p. 98.

53 Heller, Agnes, *The Theory of Need in Marx*, London, Allison and Busby, 1978. p. 23.

54 Manley, Michael, *The Politics of Change: A Jamaican Testament*, London, Andre Deutsch Ltd., 1974, p. 64.

55 Russell, Horace, "The Challenge of Theological Reflection In the Caribbean Today," ed. Idris Hamid, *Troubling of the Waters*, Trinidad, West Indies, Rahaman Printery Ltd., 1973., p. 29.

56 Lockman, Jan Milic, "Christian-Marxist Dialogue" ed. Alistair Kee, *A Reader in Political Theology*, Philadelphia, Westminster Press, 1974, p. 5.

57 Rivera, Luis N. "The Mission of the Church and the Development of a Caribbean Theology of Liberation, ed. Idris Hamid, *Out of the Depths*, Trinidad, West Indies, St. Andrews College, 1977, p. 251.

58 Lochman, Jan Milic, "Christian-Marxist Dialogue" ed. Alistair Kee, *A Reader in Political Theology*, Philadelphia, Westminster Press, 1974, p. 7.

59 Tillich, Paul, *Systematic Theology* Volume One, Chicago, University of Chicago Press, 1973, p. 49.

60 Payne, Clifford F., "What Will A Caribbean Christ Look Like?: A Preface to Caribbean Christology," ed. Idris Hamid, *Out of the Depths*, Trinidad, West Indies, St. Andrews Theological College, 1977, p. 1.

61 Ibid. p. 1.

62 Reid, Alfred C., "Truth and Liberation," *Caribbean Journal of Religious Studies*, Vol. 5, No. 1., April 1983, p. 41.

63 Payne, Clifford F., "What Will a Caribbean Christ Look Like? A Preface to Caribbean Christology," Ed. Idris Hamid, *Out of the Depths*, Trinidad, W.I., St. Andrew's Theological College, 1977, p. 1.

64 Neuhaus, Richard J. "Liberation Theology and the Captivities of Jesus," ed. Gerald H. Anderson and Thomas F. Stranskey, C.S.P. *Mission Trends No.3 Third World Theologies*, New York, Paulist Press/Wm. B. Erdmans Publishing Co., 1976, p. 45.

65 Ibid. p. 45.

66   Niles, H. Clifton, "The Functions of the Ministry," *Caribbean Journal of Religious Studies*, Vol. 4, No. 2. September 1982, p. 24.

67   Sobrino, Jon S. J., *Christology at the Crossroads*, Maryknoll, New York, Orbis, 1978, p. 35.

68   Bisnauth, Dale A., "Religious Pluralism and Development in the Caribbean: Questions," *Caribbean Journal of Religious Studies*, Vol. 4, No. 2. September 1982, pp. 17-33.

69   Ibid. p. 21.

70   Ward, Barbara, *Nationalism and Ideology*, New York, W.W. Norton and Company, 1966, p. 17.

71   McCormack, Michael, *Liberation or Development*, Barbados W.I., CADEC (Christian Action for Development in the Caribbean) 1971, p. 18.

72   Smith, Ashley, "The Christian Minister as a Political Activist," *Caribbean Journal of Religious Studies*, Vol. 2, No. 1, April 1979, p. 30.

73   *Caribbean Contact*, Vol. 12. No. 1. Jan/Feb. 1984.

74   Ibid.

75   Watty, William, "Liberation — Popular as Calypso and Rum Punch, But Caribbean People Now Less Free," *Caribbean Contact*, Vol. 12, No. 1, Jan/Feb. 1984.

76   Ibid.

77   Ibid.

78   Ibid.

79   Ibid.

80   Ibid.

81   Gerstacker, Carl Allan, "The Third World and You: The Role of Transnational Corporations in Reducing Poverty," *Church and Society — The Church and Transnational Corporations*, (A Report of the 195th General Assembly of the Presbyterian Church (U.S.A.)) March/April 1984, p. 125f.

82   Ibid. p. 127.

83   Barnet, Richard J. and Muller, Ronald E., *Global Reach: The Power of the Multinational Corporations*, New York, Simon and Schuster, 1974, p. 15.

84   Ibid. p. 15.

85 Ibid. p. 16.

86 Ibid. p. 17.

87 Ibid. p. 127.

88 Ibid. p. 127.

89 It becomes necessary to point out one's awareness of the existence of a more radical development to theology on the Euro-American scene, for example European political theology. However it is just as important to note that even this approach is in the minority and is not enough to make the distinction between traditional and liberation theological positions necessary.

90 Gerstacker, Carl Allan, "The Third World and You: The Role of Transnational Corporations in Reducing Poverty," *Church and Society. The Church and Transnational Corporations*, March/April 1984, p. 126.

91 Moltmann, Jurgen, "Religion, Revolution and the Future," ed. Walter H. Capps, *The Future of Hope*, Philadelphia, Fortress Press, 1971, p. 106.

92 Ibid. p.104.

93 Ibid. p. 104f.

94 Ibid. p. 107.

PART THREE

A CRITICAL EVALUATION

In summary, Caribbean theology has set for itself a specific task and a special way of performing that task. The task of Caribbean theology is to make itself relevant to its context so that where missionary theology has failed, it may succeed in being truly representative of the people. As Caribbean theology performs this task it must take some points under advisement:

1. It must be ready to provide a critical edge even as it assesses the failure in missionary theology.

2. It must be contextual, which means that it begins with the human experience, within a particular context.

3. It must be ideological, which means that it develops a viewpoint by which it measures goodness or the lack of it, as it seeks rectification for the oppressed people it seeks to represent.

4. Its ideological position must itself be in part a biblical paradigm.

There comes a time, therefore, when Caribbean theology must be assessed for its success or failure. That is to say, it has to be assessed as to whether the new voices in their theological praxis can make a difference.

Chapter Six

The Theological Consensus

Some people have argued that theology is in "disarray" because there are so many theological perspectives today. Lonnie D. Kliever, in his book *The Shattered Spectrum*, has shared the opinion that if there is a disarray it did not begin with the more contemporary trends of thought, it began with the Neo-orthodox school which has encouraged within itself the diverse perspectives of people like Barth and Tillich and Bultmann etc. Since Neo-orthodoxy, no one has been able to divide theology into two neat little packages, conservative and liberal. So just as there is no monolith of thought and positions in Euro-American traditional theology, one can hardly be claimed for the Caribbean. It has been said that once Karl Barth, in reference to the popularity and yet diversity in the so called "Barthian School" said, "Thank God, I don't belong to it." The point is that even in one school of thought there may develop several different emphases. So in the liberation aspect of Caribbean thinking and in its process of indigenization there are sufficiently differing views to merit a secondary categorization among the spokespersons and their points of view. Yet even with differing views some kind of consensus may be reached to warrant the title of "a theology," and also may be reached through an examination covering the area from the theologians to their constituency. With this in mind, our next task is to determine who are the theologians of the Caribbean. Who does Caribbean theology?

It has been established that the task of initiating an indigenous process for a theology in the Caribbean has been assumed by the Caribbean Conference of Churches. Under the leadership of the late Dr. Idris Hamid, the Caribbean Conference of Churches began to influence the movement which has persisted to its present stage, even beyond the actual membership of the Council. A reminder that the membership of the Caribbean Conference of Churches comprises a variety of denominational interests should suggest a diversity of emphasis. Yet the parallelism that exists among the emphases is remarkable. Unaware of the *curriculum vitae* of these theologians, one could never tell their church affiliation by their theological emphasis, excepting the few cases where thorough knowledge of Vatican issues betray the Roman Catholic contributor. Yet there are differences which though individual, are more identifiable with ideology or worldview than with denominations. In fact these differences carry enough significance for categorization, that for sheer convenience may be labeled "Left", "Right" and "Center."

The Left

The position of the Left is obviously the most radical of the three. It is not necessarily Marxist though in its worldview it deplores the capitalist principles which motivate selfishness and greed. Yet it should be examined from three perspectives, namely, capitalist, Marxist and separatist, because these are the main emphases in the position.

Capitalist Principle

Whether one can support that stance and not be Marxist is probably a debatable question for the Rightist and Center positions. However, there is something to be said for an argument against selfishness and greed, whether one is Marxist or not. If only Marxists tackle that position then Peter in his handling of the Ananias and Sapphira case in Acts was Marxist long before Marx.

"Anti" selfishness and greed should be more a Christian position than it is Marxist. In any case the anti-capitalist debate raises more questions than those relating directly to selfishness and greed. There is the question of labor. It had been suggested that capitalism by its very nature is alienating because by its design for profiteering there is a built-in tendency to exploit labor.[1] This problem is much more than academic, when Caribbean history comes into focus. Even after slavery, and subsequently with the advent of trade unions, the alienation between management and laborer has been strong enough to force riots and political shifts. Furthermore, as Horace Russell hints at in the Caribbean case for labor and Arts:

> Work to be real must be given a monetary value and so the Arts in contrast are thought to be valueless.[2]

The salience of that position is that pressured by the "more production in less time" philosophy, labor becomes selfishly valuable in the production line and leaves the laborer with no time to celebrate "human energy" in art which is worthy of sharing.[3]

The weight of the concern of the Left about capitalism is to be pitted against its consequences. Since it leaves some people in comparative poverty it makes it harder for them to maintain their faith in Christ. As Ashley Smith says:

> ...those who are chronically poor live in a social environment that makes them incapable of exercising faith. Living in the culture of poverty people have a sense of dependence, powerlessness and helplessness. They become victims instead of agents, fatalistic instead of trusting.[4]

It is alienation described in other terms.

Marxist Principle

If the reference to Marxism is merely that some Latin American theologians have used the Marxist social analysis to exemplify and promote the egalitarianism liberation struggles seek, that reference does not necessarily warrant a Marxist identity for its promoter.[5] Again if the reference simply indicates that Marxist social analysis is itself a philosophy by which liberation theologies are supplied with another kind of philosophical tool, suitable to the concreteness in human experience they seek to emphasize, the supplier of the reference may not necessarily be deemed Marxist. However, there is a greater weight of evidence concerning Marxist

confirmation when the reference is in defense of models of
socialist economy and is supported by theses such as:

> There is no incongruity between Christianity and socialism in that
> socialism offers more hope than capitalism of being more fulfilled and
> therefore more evangelical. That is more like Jesus Christ, who came
> to liberate people from slavery and exploitation.[6]

The Marxist confirmation faces its share of objections and
those who utilize the Marxist analysis are often judged with
prejudicial analysis. They are usually charged with more than
they are guilty of because the selectivity in their use of Marx is
seldom taken into consideration. Of course the Roman
Catholic theologians have a more classic worry since the Vatican has decreed a virtual impossibility in attempting to purify
Marxism for Christian use, notwithstanding the fact that the
theologians who borrow from Marx are usually interested in
only the social analysis. But the exponents fight back. Some
even relate the unqualified attacks upon them as a modern
version of Gnosticism, in that the attacks see intrinsic evil in
the materialist approach.[7] Ultimately they turn to the Scripture citing Acts 4:32,35 and showing that New Testament
Christians were Marxist before Marx ever was.

Given the chronic classism that is rampant in the Caribbean
and the gap between the rich and the poor, the Marxist social
analysis is an extremely handy tool for not only assessing the
problem but for posing a remedy, if it is agreed that it is the
dismantling of the oppressive structures that will bring equality to the region. In any case since neo-colonialism of this
capitalistic and imperialistic nature keeps up its pressure on
the area, some governments, searching for progressive alternatives, keep turning again and again to the Marxist corrective.
At such times, the church, whether it is agreeable or not, is
forced to debate the question, its *pros* and *cons*.

Separatist Principle

This idea of separation is not advocacy for some kind of clos-
eted version of theology. It is a radical approach to theological formulation, which is supported by those who believe
that Caribbean theology cannot be neutral. It is especially

true for those who live in or near volatile conditions such as existed in Grenada. Dr. Leslie Lett's assessment is:

> In Europe and North America theologians could discuss the "death of God" while "theologizingly" sipping tea in a library; in the Third World God is affirmed and it is the theologian who faces death.[8]

In which case even to be neutral in theology is to take sides, the wrong side, because theology represents either "domination" or "liberation" in the Caribbean. One who does not come out on the side of liberation is inadvertently on the side of domination.

If one, therefore, is on the side of liberation one's primary task is that of being confrontational to the Euro-American categories, in a constant process of rejection of ideas and even language patterns. If it were possible to abandon European languages all together, it would be the ideal situation. The basis of this part of Leftist radicalism is that the Euro-American theological perspectives are so intrinsically part of the colonial and neo-colonial structures that theology cannot be separated from politics. The position does not share Derek Walcott's enthusiasm for the "Noble Savage's" triumphant mastery of the "master's" language, because Caliban's ability to speak like the master does not mean that Caliban is as free and equal as the master. The theological scheme for this part of the Left is by no means revisionist in its reformation process. It has to be new, different and indigenous.

The Right

On the other end of the pendulum swing are those who may be numbered among the Right. By virtue of numbers it is probably not necessary to subcategorize into "far Right" even as it is impractical for the Left. Suffice it to say that the Right has a tendency to demonstrate a sense of satisfaction with the status quo in tact. They betray their position with an untimely over-compensation on the side of the spiritual; untimely in the sense that it is usually at the time when others are attempting to bring into focus the neglect of the socio-economic and political concerns within the human condition. For example,

in his sermon one Caribbean person analyses the reasons for
charges that CADEC, the service arm of the Caribbean Conference of Churches, is a communist organization:

> ...I think it is because of an undue emphasis resulting in an unfortunate
> imbalance. You see precisely because the emphasis of CADEC seems to
> be solely on the economic aspect of development, to the disregard and
> neglect of the spiritual, people have begun to wonder whether CADEC
> is endeavouring to upset the present economic order and to change the
> present system. Is CADEC indeed an agent for the spread of commu-
> nism in the Caribbean?[9]

For those supporting this position, even if they are conscious
of some little areas of concern beyond the spiritual needs of
the church, a problem which cannot be cured by aid, they are
more willing to see *no* change than *radical* change. Radical
change of any kind, for them, always carries the communist
potential. Marxism for the Right comes without the possibili-
ties of being divided into areas and the extraction of useful
parts. Marxism for them is Godless communism and communism is people in chains in filthy prison camps in the *Gulag
Archipelago*.

So this kind of theologian claims the task of calling people
back to an understanding of the mission of the church; that
mission is usually defined as the conviction of sin in the private consciousness of individuals and the pronouncement of
available grace for such a condition. It smacks of spiritualizing
the gospel beyond commensurate concern for its social value.
But they contend that:

> ...it is only since Christians have largely ceased to think of the other
> world that they have become so ineffective in this.[10]

Center

Those who stand in the center position do not always lend
themselves to easy assessment, because although they are
never totally Right nor Left they are sometimes given to mood
swings. This means that depending on the situation at hand it
is possible for them to support one side or another. They are
usually moderates and therefore are not usually supportive of
radical and sudden discontinuity. As a result they usually

appear as gradualists and revisionists. There is no intention to convey some disparaging definition of the moderate attitude, for example to suggest that it represents some vacillating chameleon. To the contrary, it is the need to be objective that motivates placing of one foot in either camp for the sake of attempting balance. Gradualism and revisionism are deliberate efforts against radicalism.

Gradualism
Gradualism means that the moderate is always conscious of the rigors of the past but is also conscious of a journey which has offered some upward mobility. To them, the failure of the Euro-American tradition is not enough reason to break away from it. There are ways of working to bring success out of failure. The moderate is therefore quite justified in saying in one breath:

> However, the force of tradition has played an important role in creating many of the existing problems. The Jamaica Church began as a projection of the Church in England. Its primary purpose was to cater to the spiritual welfare of the English settlers. Consequently, metropolitan interests, decisions, and culture were paramount in the colonial church. These factors hindered the process of decolonization in theological education at the local level. The concepts and practices which were adapted and transmitted in Jamaica failed to create a New Man and a New Society, liberated from metropolitan intellectual, psychological, social, political, and economic pressures and influences. This failure handicapped the development of any sense of a Jamaican identity with a new consciousness, new attitudes, and new values. Instead, through the Anglican Church in Jamaica it produced a society which was uncreative and lacking in self-confidence.[11]

And also saying in almost the same breath :

> The emphasis in this book on need for the development of native ministry does not mean that theological education in Jamaica should have developed in isolation from external intellectual, psychological and cultural influences. In order to preserve the universal nature of the Church it is desirable that expatriates should be trained locally, as well as that Jamaicans should be exposed to theological studies in highly developed countries whereby priests from overseas are encouraged to work in Jamaica on a short term basis, while Jamaicans serve on the same terms abroad. The argument in favour of a "Jamacanized" ministry is really a challenge to the Anglican Church to liberate its people from the social and psychological scars of the past and create in them a

new consciousness and self-confidence by discarding the trappings of colonialism and facing the challenges of freedom. It is a call for relevance. And indigenous ministry would mean isolation; it would mean a richer and more creative interaction with highly advanced countries.[12]

Revisionism

Revisionism is related to some extent to gradualism. This is to say that it is quite natural for the gradualist in philosophy to be a revisionist in practice. It does not mean that only gradualists ever set themselves the task of revising the tradition for relevance and new contextual meaning. Yet the gradualist is usually aware of the possibility of theological isolation and therefore chooses to move with caution from the safety of the troublesome old to the unfledged and precarious new. The process comes with its own private source of pressure from the old for the moderate:

> The result of this subtle pressure is that theologians in the Caribbean labour under the burden of having to prove themselves and vindicate the Caribbean before a critical European audience, one that is largely without understanding of the region. It has become a matter of honour to enunciate a theology which demonstrates the value of the Caribbean heritage and at the same time possesses the sophistication of the European theological tradition.[13]

Needless to say the new because of its newness is quite tenuous:

> "Caribbean theology" is an emotive phrase and because of this it is easy to forget that significant questions hover over its use... the phrase "Caribbean theology", because of its connotations, must be used cautiously. Used in its popular sense it may unduly limit the theological enterprise.[14]

In this assessment of the different voices in the theological process, the developmental factor must be taken into consideration. Sheer growth in one's thinking on a particular situation creates change in positions. In the same way one talks about the Early Barth or the Young Luther one must allow for position shifts in these categories. Furthermore, apart from the consciousness of overlapping among the categories given the context of the utterances, "Caribbean theology" is itself a concept in progress.

Who Validates Caribbean Theology?

It is obvious that the quest for an indigenous theology in the Caribbean has met with some serious obstacles, at least objections, from the foreign based missionary church. Many of the local theologians have registered their protest against these objections, saying such objections should not exist or should not be taken seriously. As previously noted, when Edmund Davis talks about Caribbean theology being prepared under the critical scrutiny of the European theological eye, he should be taken seriously in that respect as well as in others. For example:

1. If Caribbean theology sets itself up as a critical entity, it must be prepared to be criticized. Precisely because of the kind of criticism Caribbean theology brings to the Euro-American perspectives, it ought to at least presume the right of some Euro-American traditionalists to confirm or reject the criticism. Noel Erskine does well to remind the Caribbean community that it is to Jurgen Moltmann's credit that he not only took the time to visit within the Americas to seek to understand the issues raised from the "underside" but also to pioneer a deeper understanding of them among his European colleagues, by the adjustments in his own theology.[15] Yet it has been a significant journey for Moltmann himself, at the beginning of which his vehement attack on Latin American theology was due to the very fact that Latin American theologians had been critical of his tradition. It may serve some small but good purpose to remind the Caribbean community that a part of Moltmann's counter-criticism was that the indigenous process had failed because it had made critique of the European tradition its primary emphasis, and when it dealt with real indigenous issues it used Marx indiscriminately to ratify its claims. After all, Marx himself belonged to Europe.[16]

2. Locally, in the sense that Caribbean theology is reflection on a Caribbean understanding of what God is doing in the region, it owes its legitimacy to its constituency. By "local constituency" is meant four basic institutions which either initiate or appropriate the theology. They are (a) the Caribbean Con-

ference of Churches, (b) *U.T.C.W.I.* (c) the denominational structures to which the theologians relate, and (d) even a more immediately localized area, for example, the congregations.

(a) To the extent that the *Caribbean Conference of Churches* has been the vanguard for the organized effort toward an indigenous theology, the theology, in a broad sense, meets with the general criterion posed at the outset by the Caribbean Conference of Churches. As the relevant committees allotted assignments for papers and lectures, they chose the topics pertinent to the project in mind. As these papers and lectures covered a wide area of interests from history, to education, to culture, to literature, to the value systems and the church, they met with the approved agenda of the Caribbean Conference of Churches. The Caribbean Conference of Churches became a validating agent for the perspectives posed. When the challenge went beyond the scope of the Caribbean Conference of Churches's initiation, the motivating influence still remained the essence of the project. However, in that subsequent works came not as a result of being assigned by the Caribbean Conference of Churches, it had no responsibility to their ratification. (b) *The United Theological College of the West Indies* having been stimulated into the pursuit of this indigenous objective deals with the subject academically in contemporary courses. It also, through the forum of *Caribbean Journal of Religious Studies*, encourages a lively debate on both the subject matter and process of indigenization. It is true that they invite spontaneous contributions to this publication, but they also make requests for special analyses. Because of the latter fact and also because they make the decisions on what is printed, it is true to say that this institution has become an agency of validation of the Caribbean initiative.

(c) The *denominational unity* carries some importance because most of the people who assume responsibility for producing contributions, whether voluntarily or by assignment, belong to one denomination or another. Since denominations have special emphases it is safe to assume that denominational interests in some way influence the way individuals approach their tasks. For example, some denominations are more closely connected to the European church than others, and with some the connection is more "spiritual" than physical. This is not to say that the European church is allowed to dictate liberation policy. However, often the closer the connection the more paternalized the local situation, therefore the more reactionary the liberation rhetoric. One must hasten to say however that if there are denominational rules of acceptability, as far as the indigenous theology is concerned, they must be soft rules. Any number of denominations show the aptitude for drastic differences in position among members even of the same denomination. For example there cannot be a sharper difference between two individual's ideological commitment as is shown in the contributions of Edmund Davis and Ernle Gordon, both of whom belong to the Anglican communion.

(d) A more *immediate constituency* places even greater caution upon the theologian. For a theology to be truly indigenous it must have meaning for the people it represents. There is a set of people who, under the direct service of the theologian, whether that theologian is a seminary professor or the pastor of a congregation, form the immediate constituency. Particularly in the case of the pastor these people have more validating power than most others have.

Edmund Davis points out from his experience that in certain areas of the church:

> The term [Caribbean Theology]is viewed with suspicion because the interest in African religious traditions associated with it calls up in the minds of many a return to primitivism. Anglicans of the first and second generation are conservative in matters of faith and morals. For those raised in the closed predicament, theology—most of all "Caribbean theology"—is not only "foreign," but impious.[17]

Here is the crux of the matter that a constituency made up of such persons as are described by Davis would certainly not be disposed to a ratification of the indigenous thrust that looked to its African roots for cultural endorsement. Subsequently, the person who serves this constituency will be severely influenced in his/her theological presentation. In the final analysis therefore, such validations as are sought are truly the prerogative of the needy to give. Perhaps only those who need an indigenous theology of liberation will accept one.

Unanimity in Perspectives

With the possibility that within the Caribbean perspective there are sub-divisions such as Left, Right, and Center, it is hardly necessary to say that uniformity is not a likely accomplishment in Caribbean theology. The question is whether uniformity is necessary for this kind of enterprise. For there is often a certain kind of dynamism in diversity, where the very fact of differing opinions encourages and sharpens debate. Furthermore, seemingly totally opposed positions can come under creative tension even if the only agreement is to disagree.

Uniformity and Diversity

There are areas where diversity is necessarily only partial emphasis, thus creating room for uniformity in other parts. For example, when the process analyzes the historical fact of something as blatant as slavery, no matter who deals with that fact it must be admitted as a fact. The same is true of colonialism as an event of Caribbean history. No one denies that it took place. It is only when it comes to the interpretation of the consequences of both slavery and colonialism that the diversity is strictly installed. Hence there are those who are convinced that those events are a unique atrocity, creating physical and psychological scars of indelible and inconceivable proportions. Others treat it with philosophic casualness, comforted in the conclusion that some of the greatest peoples of the world have been enslaved or colonized at one point or another in history. Still others take the point of view that despite the pitilessness of slavery and the arbitrariness of colonialism, the industrialization which followed upon their heels and the education to deal with it are more than sufficient balance for the atrocities. The consequence of any of these positions is quite evident in the proposals for liberation or indigenization.

Unity in Diversity

At face value the concept of unity in diversity always appears "mythological," especially when within the process there are views diametrically opposed to each other. For example as it has been noted, one Caribbean spokesperson's criticism of the Christian Action for Development in the Caribbean (CADEC), as being associated with Marxism is that it pursues economic development to the total exclusion of concerns for the things of the spirit. This view of course has been identified as Rightist and conservative. When the Left position analyzes the same organization, it is amazing how striking is the contrast in viewpoint:

> CADEC, the development arm of the Caribbean Conference of Churches has received financial contributions from agencies in Western Europe. The Third World has been raided by foreign "Aid" and so CADEC lost credibility because it appeared to be merely serving the interests of transnational corporations...My second criticism is that I was never too sure if CADEC understood the dangers of "developmentalism", which would counteract structural transformation.[18]

Yet when these different viewpoints are looked at carefully it may be observed that unity in diversity may not be a mere myth. Both criticisms of the Caribbean Conference of Churches's CADEC demonstrate that there is room for adjustment beyond the exclusivity of their own positions. Moreover, they are in agreement on the point that the Caribbean Conference of Churches and its service arm have room for understanding and growth. Whatever else is true of the quest for an indigenous theology it cannot stand frozen in time but must, as it struggles against what it deems the enemy, struggle also to overcome its contra-distinctions, for its own growth and power.

Notes

1 Cunnigham, Adrian, et al, *The "Slant" Manifesto — Catholics and the Left*, Springfield, Illinois, Templegate Publishers, 1966, p. 17.

2 Russell, Horace, "The Challenge of Theological Reflection in the Caribbean Today," ed. Idris Hamid, *Troubling of the Waters*, Trinidad, W.I. Rahaman Printery, 1973, p. 29f

3 Cunnigham, Adrian, et al, *The "Slant" Manifesto — Catholics and the Left*, Springfield, Illinois, Templegate Publishers, 1966, p. 19.

4 Smith, Ashley, *Real Roots and Potted Plants*, Mandeville, Jamaica, W.I., Mandeville Publishers, 1984, p. 73.

5 Taylor, Burchell K. "Caribbean Theology, *"Caribbean Journal of Religious Studies*, Vol.3, No.2, September 1980, p. 13.

6 Gordon, Ernle P. "Evangelization and Politics: A British Caribbean Perspective," eds. Arce, Sergio and Marichal, Oden, *Evangelization and Politics*, New York, Circus Inc, 1982, p.102, Citing the report on a 1970 Chilean Bishops Conference.

7 Ibid. p. 102.

8 Lett, Leslie, "Third World Theology: Its Origin and Development," *Caribbean Contact*, Vol 12, No. 1. Jan/Feb 1984.

9 Didier, Atherton, "What is the Mission of the Church?" eds. C.H.L. Gayle and W.W. Watty, *The Caribbean Pulpit*, Kingston, Jamaica, W.I., Cedar Press, 1983, p. 29.

10 Ibid. p. 30.

11 Davis, Edmund, *Roots and Blossoms*, Barbados, W.I., Cedar Press, 1977, p. 111.

12 Ibid. p. 111.

13 Ibid. p. 115.

14 Ibid. p. 115.

15 Erskine, Noel Leo, *Decolonizing Theology: A Caribbean Perspective*, Maryknoll, New York, Orbis, 1981, p. 64.

16 Moltmann, Jurgen, "An Open Letter to Jose Miguez Bonino," eds. Gerald H. Anderson and Thomas F. Stransky, C.S.P., *Mission Trends No. 4. Liberation Theologies*, New York, Paulist Press, 1979, pp. 61-62.

17 Davis, Edmund, *Roots and Blossoms*, Barbados, W.I., Cedar Press, 1977, p. 114.

18 Gordon, Ernle P., "Evangelization and Politics: A British Caribbean Perspective," eds. Sergio, Arce, Oden, Marichal. *Evangelization and Politics*, New York, Circus Inc, 1982, p. 105.

Chapter Seven

The Validity of Indigenization

Truly assessed, the theological constituency in the Caribbean is varied. The variety is an inevitable consequence of the colonialism which by its very nature creates classist structures. Indigenous theology makes no secret of speaking on behalf of those who have suffered most by the alienation that is directed at their social class. Yet, as an agent of re-evangelization, indigenous theology must not only speak on behalf of, but address an audience. Furthermore, if it is to influence change, its audience must include the powerful and the powerless. It is therefore not too early to attempt an assessment of whether Caribbean indigenization is at least poised for contextual influencing.

Possibility of Contextualization
When it comes to contextualization in the Caribbean perspective the stigma of provincialism and reductionism, once and for all, ought to be discarded. If in a very broad sense of the term, contextualization means relating the Gospel message to the particularity of situation, contextualization is by no means unique to the Third World. One could never listen to Karl Barth in certain instances and attribute contextualization exclusively to Third World theology. For example in his criticism of the contradiction between German idealism and the condition of the State, Barth does not even sound like Barth:

> Religious righteousness! There seem to be surer means of rescuing us from the alarm cry of conscience than religion and Christianity...There comes over us a wonderful sense of safety and security from the unrighteousness whose might we everywhere feel. It is a wonderful illusion, if we can comfort ourselves with it, that in our Europe—in the midst of capitalism, prostitution, the housing problem, alcoholism, tax evasion,

and militarism—the Church's preaching, the Church's morality, and the "religious life" go their uninterrupted way. And we are Christians! Our nation is a Christian nation! A wonderful illusion, but an illusion, a self-deception!...When we let conscience speak to the end, it tells us not only that there is something else, a righteousness above unrighteousness, but also—and more important—that this something else for which we long and which we need is God.[1]

Nor should Barth's outburst be allowed to force a retreat from the Caribbean charge of Euro-American theological neglect of the particularity of the social condition in certain areas of human experience. For one thing Barth's social reference above is more the exception than the rule for traditional theology. For another, given the leadership in the role of theological education in the Caribbean in the past, the missionary systematic theology professor would be far more interested in examining the Caribbean student on "the Doctrines of the Word of God," in Barth's Church Dogmatics than in Barth's social analysis of Germany. For yet another thing, Sheila Collins is right when she suggests that liberation theology from whatever perspective:

...is far more honest than the dominant Western theology that masks its political bias, and it is therefore less likely to be used as a tool of any group that wants to maintain itself in power over others.[2]

The point, however, is that no matter how camouflaged the interest in abstract terminology, a theology is influenced by its context.

Contextualization and Indigenization

It would seem that Caribbean theology has come upon a cultural barrier which in turn has created a psychological complex as it deals with contextualizing in its more specialized sense. Yet, since there are two components closely related in the issue, one has to be separated from the other in order to highlight the complex.

The first component has to do with the definitions, whether there is a difference between "contextualization" and "indigenization" and therefore, whether, in the final analysis, there is a choice to be made between them. Dr. Shoki Coe of

Taiwan, as director of the World Council of Churches Theological Education Fund, had occasion to look at both words and form an opinion. His opinion is that although the word indigenization means reinterpreting the Gospel which is then expressed "afresh in the new cultural soil," it is oriented to the past. Contextualization attempts to convey the roots significance of indigenization while leaving an opening for change in the future.[3] The problem here is that the definitions are clear in reference to Asian, African and such contexts, in the sense that Christianity visited them within stable uninterrupted cultures. But in the case of the Caribbean, the Gospel meets cultural transplantations to be further complicated by colonial acculturation.

The second component of the issue, then, is not so much whether indigenization and contextualization are significantly different as it is that after cultural transplantation and centuries of acculturation there is a serious question as to the nature of this soil in which indigenization must take place. The problem leads William Watty to say, perhaps with some cultural embarrassment:

> In another place I have raised what I consider to be objections to the very concept of indigenization as applied to religions, and this has probably arisen out of the particular situation of which I am part in which indigenization cannot, in its strict sense, be applied. It seems to me basic to the understanding of religion in Afro-America to realize that nothing indigenous survives, but everything that we can identify as religious represents an importation and transplantation from another part of the world.[4]

If contextualization encompasses all of the meaning of indigenization as far as the gospel being expressed afresh in new soil is concerned, and indigenization is here considered an impossibility, Caribbean theology is caught in an inevitable deadlock. The deadlock itself is due to psychological complex over cultural awareness. Yet indigenization entails de-colonization and Caribbean theology proposes to do that quite well. However, in the process it has developed the "fear" that anything it brings from the pre-Caribbean experience will rob the Caribbean of its "Caribbeanness," that it is in fact a contradiction to renounce European cultural impositions yet keep what is remembered of Africa or India or anywhere else, and call it Caribbean. Since there are very few of the original Caribbean people left, to identify a truly indigenous culture, Caribbean theology has to move to break the deadlock, if it must become completely viable as an indigenizing and contextualizing agent. One may suggest three ways in which that may be done.

1. It may redefine the process of indigenization and contextualization to suit the uniqueness of the Caribbean situation. It has identified the major contextual problem to be missio-colonial misevangelization whose consequence is lack of theological rationale and motivation for self-determination. Part of the vehicle of missio-colonial misevangelization is cultural displacement. The remedy, therefore, is re-evangelization which must entail some cultural "replacement." But since culture would not have stood still, even if it had not encountered displacement in colonialism, the differences between the Caribbean cultural memory and the pre-Caribbean cultural roots are a part of the natural movement of culture and therefore an important part of the open-endedness of contextualization. Indigenization then is possible, if indigenization is re-evangelization. The other point is that indigenization brings into focus not only the Caribbean context as it stands, but as it is to be shaped; in which sense there is a clearer vision of Caribbean culture as it exists, and also Caribbean culture in the making.

2. Caribbean theology has to take seriously the differences between acculturation and enculturation, the foreign imposition of the former and the voluntary acceptance of the latter. When culture is imposed it has to be done through the preconception of superiority of the imposer, for which reason there is every justification for the Caribbean reaction to missio-colonial evangelization. On the other hand, very few cultures can claim not to have been affected by some other culture. For example, the Western world, though reluctant to admit it, has absorbed tremendous influences from its slave culture also. However, when the choice is voluntary the adaptation is of a different nature. Thus the United States can lay claim to an "American culture" despite the convergence of

many cultures into the formation of the United States, and it can do so with constant reference to the "Old Country" whichever that may be. So that which is not imposed upon a people from some self-aggrandized superior position does not necessarily work against the authentication of such a people's cultural value. On the contrary it may work to enhance it.

3. Caribbean theology needs to overcome the stigma of what in the pre-Caribbean portion of the people's memory it often refers to as "primitivism." Because these "leftovers" from the pre-Caribbean experience are an authentic part of the Caribbean culture, they are an important component of the movement now identified as "contextualization." Noel Erskine is right in warning that theology falls quite short of taking the totality of religious experience seriously when it ignores them.[5] Caribbean theology of course has made some effort to study some of these "leftovers" but mostly from "an above" socio-religious research position. There has been little effort to recognize in them suitable value systems for the process of indigenization. Incorporating these values into the theological process means that Caribbean theology is free to exhort its constituency into seeking its identity in its past as well as in its future.

Context and Economic Heterogeneity
Within the context of Caribbean theology there is a potential audience of a variety of groups. These groups are partly a consequence of colonial stratification and partly a consequence of levels of awareness in the survival milieu.

1. There are groups of Caribbean people who have managed to benefit from colonialism and neo-colonialism. By the definition of neo-colonialism which is favored in this project the structure is a foreign imposition upon the economic, political and therefore the social life of the Caribbean. However, in many ways neo-colonialism is virtually inoperable unless it finds some internal agency as its medium. It is the people who serve in the creation of this internal agency who stand to benefit from the structure. They further complicate the situation by being the resisters of change in that they support usually the missionary church in all its "pomp and cir-

cumstance," trace their ancestry through their slave master and defend the *status* quo. Yet they are a part of the context of Caribbean theology whose task is to convict and convince,not only in terms of defining the enemy, but also in eliciting a reasonable response toward a sense of concern out of responsibility to the poor.

2. There are the struggling poor who never earn enough by which to gain upward mobility. Yet they know who their exploiters are and look forward to systems of liberation. These are people for whom Caribbean theology no doubt speaks.

3. Then there are those who are poor but have lost a sense of worth. As prior documentation shows, these are the people of whom Ashley Smith speaks as being so convinced of the unimportance of their status and country that their esteem depends solely on the "otherplaceness" in their reality. Other people are important, not they. Other countries are important, not theirs. And so they impose another kind of marginalization upon themselves, one which either results in a psychological exile or actual physical flight. But as long as they are a part of the context of Caribbean theology it bears the responsibility of providing the psycho-theological treatment their case deserves.

4. Finally, Caribbean theology comes upon a group which, despite its suffering, seems to wage a battle against itself and against its own liberation. It sees its destiny in foreign aid and ignores the glaring signals of exploitation. And the task of Caribbean theology, here, is to penetrate the numbness of a people who have suffered too long to be able to make and sustain the sharp distinctions between caring and paternalism, between the desire to assist and the desire to control.

The conclusion then, is that while Caribbean theology has recognized each of these groups in its social analysis it has to work out its theological praxis in reference to the inducement of creative change. On the other hand, it must be said with some amount of haste, that inasmuch as the process has identified the major contextual problem to be misevangelization on the part of the missionary church, has identified the consequences of this misevangelization, and has assumed responsibility for the task of finding the remedy, Caribbean theology has been faithful to its context. Needless to say there is some degree of difference between assuming the responsibility of the task and accomplishing the task.

Caribbean Theology as Liberation Theology
The category of Caribbean theology is established by an assessment of what it proposes its task to be, and how it approaches that task. The word "approaches" here is a deliberate choice over "accomplishes", since in contextualization this theology must leave an open space for change and for its own growth and development. Having said that, it may be wise to go on to say that even as the task is identified as re-evangelization of the Caribbean context, the scope of that definition must again be enucleated in terms of methodology. What makes this necessary is that addressing the problem as mere re-evangelization does not have sufficient conciseness to claim a category such as "liberation" for Caribbean theology. An assessment has to be made of how it does re-evangelization. In which case the verification may be made through a series of questions.

1. Does Caribbean theology find its point of departure in the concreteness of the human experience, or does it find it in the *a priori* categories of traditional theology, and therefore in the cogency of tradition itself? Harold Sitahal of Trinidad, when asked to assess the church's rethinking of mission in the Caribbean, had this to report:

> The responsibility of determining the mission of God for the churches in the Caribbean is no mere intellectual exercise for its own sake. It is a responsibility first and foremost, which means a response to a need or to a moral imperative, or to a theological imperative, meaning the responsibility to pronounce the word of God, in the prophetic sense, to the people of God in the Caribbean, and through the Caribbean, to the world. This responsibility is set by the worldly agenda of the church. Theology is the articulation of the response of the people of God to the cry to make human life more human. In fact theology is not an *a priori* but necessarily *a posteriori* in that it draws its agenda from the world.[6]

Furthermore what the church now sees, perhaps belatedly, as its theological mission is actually the "second moment" or "act" (as the Latin Americans call theirs) in the expressed insurgency against institutional oppression. This so-called second moment is a legacy of the Maroon determination, of the slave revolts, of the labor riots and organized rebellions, of James Beard's declaration that if God created Black apprenticeship God did Black people a grave injustice, [7] of Garveyism and political protests. The point is that it all begins with the historical experience which is an important ingredient for liberation theology.

2. Does it see itself as rising out of a situation of struggle, where the dominant viewpoints and systemic structures are antithetical to the rights and well being of the poor and powerless, and the powerless resist being overwhelmed by the structure?

Even Bartolome De Las Casas, who fought so gallantly for the Amerindians, was not immune to the European worldview which considered the African to be less than human, for he was persuaded to advise the Spanish on their enslavement in the New World. Much of modern day exploitation of the Caribbean is based on the perceived inferiority of non-Europeans. From the first moment a European set foot on Caribbean soil non-Europeans have had to struggle to affirm their self-hood. Caribbean theology rises out of that struggle. Having determined that God has confirmed humanity in those to whom it has been denied by worldview, it speaks for the affirmation of that humanity.

It is at this point that Caribbean theology must be drastically different from the missionary church's theology which Noel Erskine points out, was more interested in the souls of Black folk than their physical welfare, as the church avoided political conflict.[8] The missionary church, for example, felt the need to excuse itself by dissociation with the Black liberation uprising in Jamaica in 1865, known as the "Morant Bay Rebellion." It was led by a descendant of slaves, Paul Bogle. On the one hand, the colonial government never allowed the church to forget that Paul Bogle was a Baptist deacon. On the other, missionary history, looking disdainfully upon the total situation, suggests that proper evangelization would have prevented the rebellion:

It must be remembered that although missionary effort had been actively at work for generations it had not by any means reached the mass of the people. It was estimated at this time that only one third of the population were connected with places of worship, and that one-half were nominally heathen. The disturbance, it is significant to notice, occurred in St. Thomas in the East, a parish which had been sadly neglected by the missionaries, and where not a school worthy of the name could be found. Among the inhabitants also were a number of Africans who had been captured from Spanish "slavers" and established there, and who were almost as wild and ignorant as the tribes of Central Africa. In the centre of this district, October, 1865, an infuriated mob gathered in resistance to the local authorities, and, on blood being drawn by the latter, attacked them in ungovernable passion, killing eighteen persons and wounding twenty-one. [9]

It is probably a good thing that those Blacks had not been properly evangelized by the missionary church, because the conflict might have been avoided. Yet the new history in the Caribbean has vindicated Bogle and declared him a hero for the liberation of the people.

What is said of liberation theology and struggle and conflict, should not be misconstrued into meaning that liberation theology is the cause of conflict. Even missionary history makes sure to indicate that it is the oppressive structure that was first to shed blood. In any case without trying to side step the ethics of violence, it must be here said that liberation theology is not always involved in violence in its strictest sense. Yet in the Caribbean the struggle is real and the fact that babies die for lack of medication and proper nutrition is in itself a real kind of violence. Poverty is violent.

3. Does Caribbean theology see in its own task a responsibility to develop the praxis for change in this area of struggle? If so, has it developed an ideological perspective with regards to change for the good of society, and does it have a biblical mandate?

In a practical sense, as liberation theology must be, Caribbean theology understands that the worldview that tries to make its context inauthentic is wrong. At the basis of the rejection of that worldview there is a kind of egalitarian philosophy that impinges itself upon the consciousness of the struggle. It is an egalitarianism that is larger than Marxism, because it is an awareness that "God has made of one blood, all nations to dwell on the face of the earth." Hence Caribbean theology is much more than a social movement in that it seeks to understand and express the Christian faith in the Caribbean struggle for dignity, human freedom, and self-actualization.

Now, these are not criteria set from some superior position in some great hall somewhere where all theologies are judged by the "content of their character." They are simply the experience registered in other theologies which identify themselves in the liberation category. The point is that if Caribbean theology shares these experiences, it shares the right to be inducted into the "fraternity" that exists among these theologies.

Weakness Among Caribbean Perspectives

Edmund Davis once said that:

> Any attempt in the Caribbean to work out a new theological model must take into consideration its relevance to the needs and aspirations of the peculiar environment, a relevance which will lead to liberation, integration, and self-development of its people.[10]

He may not have expressed a greater truth. However, when he speaks of the designation "Caribbean theology" as being "emotive,"[11] he is using emotive to mean "emotional," and emotional as opposed to cerebral. Yet cerebral is exactly what liberation theology cannot be, because liberation theology is theology that is "done." This is what Bevis Byfield means when he says:

> Those...who articulate the real needs of society maintain that:(a) To come to grips with the local situation is a theological understanding.(b) To fight for the humanization of our societies is a theological exercise. (c) An understanding of the nature and depth of the struggle for power in the region requires theological skills. (d) The hope for social transformation is theological hope. (e) To understand the depth, the degree of which colonialism and slavery have made us dependent on metropolitan countries demands theological reflection. (f) To the extent that people participate in any of these exercises, to that extent they are theologians. Theology therefore should no longer be considered an elitist exercise.[12]

Concurrent with this definition of the theological task in the Caribbean is the significance of this stage of the process as the "second moment"; the second moment being the explication and the systematization of the "first moment." For the first moment did not end with James Beard's confronting the colonial magistrates, nor did it end with the Haitian Revolution for independence. The fact that Caribbean theological awakening followed upon the heels of the social protests of the late sixties and the early seventies is not an accident. The first moment in its active quest for liberation has set the standard for what Caribbean theology must be. Because of this very fact it has to be judged not so much by its intellectual appeal, as by its praxis. This final area will examine Caribbean theology to this end and suggest four of its weaker points. Caribbean theology may seek to develop far more intensely the following areas: Grass-roots Involvement, An Agency for Liberation Praxis, The Christian/Marxist Debate, and Paradigm Shifts from the Feminists' Perspective.

Grass-Roots Involvement
The suggestion has already been made that Caribbean theology needs to treat with more seriousness the non-European pre-Caribbean "leftovers." Specifically it needs to incorporate into its system some tenets of folk religion. It is a part of the people's roots and to get to real roots that count for "grass-roots" experience this is the practical and honest route. The problem between the missionary church and folk religion is that the church has taken no opportunity to understand it and has therefore treated it as heathenism. To believe in whatever the missionaries did not understand in this respect, was to be labeled superstitious. It has been by no means easy for those who have absorbed the sophistication of colonial religion to appreciate what they were so eager to leave behind, in an effort to escape charges of being "nominally heathen." However, it has been hard, because of the inferiority associated with that which is not blessed by the colonizing church.

One suspects that it would create sheer pandemonium if a priest were suddenly to introduce Cumina or Revivalist ritual into the calm collected atmosphere of cathedral worship. Yet the import of the critique here is hardly whether Anglicans can become Revivalists. The question is whether there are tenets in these or any other parts of folk religion capable of enhancing Caribbean liberation praxis. The possibility is not so distant when it is noted that Frances Henry made a study on the Shango religion in Trinidad and found that it had a fantastic resurgence in the mid-seventies. The reason for the resurgence was a tremendous reciprocity between the Shango religion and Black militancy which had its upsurge about the same time. The common denominator was the emphasis of both on the positives in the African past.[13]

Another apt example is indeed a case of personal experience. This writer's grandmother was an ardent Presbyterian. She was a member of the first Presbyterian Church to be built in Jamaica, a church which boasted a long history of missionary service in its ministry because it was a plantation church. On the first morning of each New Year she rose very early to perform a ritual which had nothing to do with Presbyterianism. She made a "punch" for the family and also the neighbors who cared to participate. However, before anyone partook of this most potent fare, she would take a container of it to be sprinkled all over the yard. The ritual had been handed down through her grandmother, and to her mother and then to her. It never went beyond her, because her descendants had tasted too much of European sophistication to care. However, when she explained each year why she did what she did, the ritual seemed a viable symbol to create a greater sympathy for the relationship among human spirits of the present and past, the earth and nature. She said that the ritual was one in recognition of ties between those who struggle now and those for whom the struggle is over. It was a ritual in respect of and thankfulness for the goodness of the earth to life itself. She said that the ritual was also a pledge to remember that since the earth belonged to none but was to be shared by all, it should be treated as a basis of unity. Those were the days when the whole neighborhood was an extended family and work on a farm plot was as much a shared experience as the reaped crops were shared according to need.

Perhaps if this grandmother knew how to explain in Presbyterian language the doctrine of the "Communion of Saints" the "invisible church" and the "visible church," she would then have been considered credible. For in her talk of relationships between the struggling past and present she was considered superstitious, but Article I of Chapter XXV of the Westminster Confession of Faith is vindicated for saying:

> The Catholic or universal Church, which is invisible, consists of the whole member of the elect, that have been, are, or shall be gathered into one, under Christ the head thereof;

This is undeniably a reference to those who have died, being yet in communion with the living members of the Church of Christ.

One admits quite freely the difficulty in unlearning even the learned prejudices against one's cultural experiences. One also admits that Article I of Chapter XXV of the Westminster Confession of Faith is necessary for emphasizing the universal character of the Christian Church. However, one admits just as freely that the African leftover in one's grandmother's experience does far more for one's understanding of what it takes to counteract the selfishness and greed which violates the earth and tempts nature's revenge, than does Article I of Chapter XXV of the Westminster Confession. Caribbean theology cannot continue to ignore its folk experience as the missionary church did. It must explore and utilize it to the enhancement of the liberation struggle.

Paridigm Shifts from the Feminists' Perspective

Dr. Sylvia Ross Talbot is right when she judges the church as often being the "tail light" instead of the "head light" for society.[14] Jesus had put it slightly differently when he said that "the children of this world show more ingenuity in their generation than the children of light" (Luke 16:8). She points out that even though the Bible is a book about men, it is time for the Caribbean church to bring a modern world view to its interpretation. The church's interpretation of the Bible in terms of women being in ministry is based on archaic positions on sexuality. In fact it causes this phobic reluctance on the part of the male to share power in the church.[15] While a few women in the Caribbean have been playing leading roles in government and commerce, the church has been slow to tackle its problem of sexism.

The Caribbean Church has been the inheritor of a religious system which is a sad commentary on dualism in every area of existence, beginning with the mind/body split. Of course for some unexplained reason when that split affects the male/female relationship it is the male who gets to be represented by the mind. Symptomatic of that miscalculation is the utterly sexist response Azariah McKenzie makes to Talbot's thoughtful presentation entitled "Contemporary Issues in Ordination of Women in the Caribbean."[16] There is absolutely no doubt that had it been a male person who made a similar presentation, McKenzie would not have taken the trouble to praise him for having managed to avoid emotionalism and plagiarism.[17]

Yet perhaps even this writer's attempt to raise the issue of sexism is out of step with the reality of the situation. The problem is that males cannot speak adequately for females, because the particularity of discrimination against women is unique. This must be true if McKenzie's case is any example of the insights men bring to the problem. Yet even from another male point of view, McKenzie's approach to the serious question of sexism leaves a lot to be desired. There are some points that McKenzie needs to be aware of.

1. It is just plain lack of insight to keep suggesting that the problem of sexism is a woman's problem because more women object to women's ordination than men. It is certainly not the truth to say that the denigration of women that is associated with Caribbean sexism is self-imposed.[18] The fact is that among the oppressed of the Caribbean, women are the oppressed of the oppressed.

2. It does not take a lot of imagination to assess that if indeed oppression seems acceptable to some oppressed people, it is not because they enjoy oppression and self-devaluation, it is because oppression has been so sustained that its accommodation has become a defense mechanism. It is not exclusively

limited to women among the oppressed to say: "A bin down so long dat down don't bother me none."

3. The fact that some women use male oriented exclusive language is no reason to condone its use universally.[19] Too many people have no sensitivity to exclusivity, but since others have been sensitized, history must move on with the employment of its corrective measures.

4. To deny that the Bible is, for the most part, a story about men[20] is to be ignorant of what patriarchy is. And to defend the denial by saying that "the Bible is essentially a record of God's dealings with people, men and women, human beings,"[21] is to underestimate totally the intricate positions in the debate on patriarchy in the Bible. Besides, that debate involves the idea of God being Father, Son and Holy Spirit(male).

5. To decide unilaterally as a male (a member of the oppressive gender) that it is better for women seeking liberation to choose options of the posture of "complementing" the male instead of the posture of "sharing power" with the male,[22] is most sexist in terms of its male-female evaluation. If it is the female who must complement the male, the secret regarding who is considered more important is out. It is also the exhibition of the sheer audacity of the oppressor to dictate the terms of the liberating process to the oppressed.

On the other hand attempting to raise the problem as male is important, not only for the solidarity in which all liberation perspectives ought to be with one another, but because the problem of sexism in the Caribbean is never "purely" sexism as that relates to ordination in church service. For example, in many parts of the Caribbean the family is headed by one parent who is female. This means that in many cases women and their children are the poorest and most powerless people in the region. This condition owes its existence to a legacy of slavery when women were workers and breeders and men were workers and mobile "studs." The imperatives of family responsibility were so negligible for so long that negligence on the part of the male became second nature in society. Hence the debate which, for the most part, has moved beyond the positions where churches may ordain one or two women and bask forever after in the glory of their accomplishment, is pertinent for the Caribbean situation.

The debate now emphasizes decisions to be made by the church regarding "paradigm shifts" which women have been advocating for theology and church liturgy. That debate is particularly relevant to the Caribbean because (a) the paradigm shifts have to do with how God is perceived, from one of domination to one of love and peace; and (b) the region is one which has suffered severe domination for some of the longest periods ever recorded.

The basic argument is posed in what Dr. Kathleen O'Connor of the Maryknoll School of Theology speaks of as implied analysis behind global economic analysis.[23] The implication is that the global economy will experience no change until it is realized that "patriarchy is at the basis of its planning as well as its process." This means that capitalism as judged by its most devastating effects upon the most powerless people, does not exist in a vacuum, but "exists as a tool of patriarchy." This economic trend, as it operates under the dictates of patriarchy, is influenced by the view of the world in "a fundamental dualism." The whole idea of "cut throat" competition and conflict through alienation between worker and employer is a result of this fundamental dualism. Furthermore this view is supported by a religion that tends to be dualistic in nature, "setting mind and body, male and female, master and slave splits."

Commensurate with the colonial domination, God has been conceived of in terms of a split which comes with the dominant and the dominated. Therefore as "Master" it is not difficult for God to become transferred into the slave-master role. As all powerful "Warrior" the images of violence are not far behind. As "King" images of exclusive and unreachable transcendence appear. Therefore the paradigm shifts present God in an image which seems less domineering and creates less exploitative situations for the powerless female and male. This is by no means encouragement to usurp the divinity of God, but to present a God who is not so alienating to the human being, a God who provides the influence against the dualisms which encourage classism, sexism and general powerlessness.

Agency for Liberation Praxis

Human nature being what it is, there may probably never be a time when liberation theology will become unnecessary. Yet there is every danger that liberation theology can be so formulated that it becomes a philosophy in deadlock between "Us" and "Them." At which point it becomes a "dead end" theology, saying nothing new and effecting no change. For this reason it is necessary to determine within its structure, agencies through which it may develop its praxis. Caribbean theology needs a strategy, so to speak, through which the rationale for liberation becomes its praxis.

It is necessary, at the outset, to determine the theological audience in this second moment of theology. It is not the first time that theology, even liberation theology, will have been asked to face up to this responsibility. And if within the audience there are poised two main liberation expectations to be fulfilled, namely integration and self-actualization, the audience has to be seen to comprise two sets of people. There are those who need to be self-actualized and there are those who ought to allow that self-actualization to happen.

In the case of the Latin Americans, when the theology began to be written the agency of liberation praxis was already in place. Given the claim that the writing was only the second moment, coming after the Base Christian Communities had already developed sound praxis, it is not difficult to see what is their agency of liberation praxis. Of course it has found it a taxing task to convince more than the "Iglesia Popular" that the preferencial option for the poor is the only viable option in certain states of oppression. But it is clear that at least the point at which praxis and theory meet is well defined for Latin American theology.

Some Caribbean theologians are perhaps too quick to point out that Caribbean theology has very little in common with Latin American theology. They come to this conclusion by means of many arguments. The two most prominent being that:

(1) Political dictatorship has not dominated Caribbean history. Of course such an argument may be true only when the Caribbean boundaries are defined a certain way, to the exclusion of those countries where this has been the experience.

(2) The revolutionary activity with which Latin American theology must struggle, is not a part of the Caribbean reality. That argument is also dependent upon the assumption that because of the revolutionary activity, liberation theology in the area must always interpret its praxis only through the Marxist analysis. The truth is that there are more shared principles between Latin American and Caribbean perspectives than axiomatic differences. Even if there are differences in some of the political realities the Caribbean cannot be said to have had only ballot box politics in peaceful power transfers in the climate of equal rights situations. There is slavery, the suppression of adult sufferage and absolutism of colonial and post colonial plantocracy to be taken into consideration. In fact, a mere cursory glance at slavery as one stage of the historical journey of the Caribbean, highlights one of the strongest contextual similarities between Latin America and the Caribbean.

In 1831, when the slave, Sam Sharpe organized the slave revolt in Jamaica, for which he paid the supreme price, it was not on a whim. The decision was made in a series of religious camp meetings. As a matter of fact, it is the same kind of diligent study of the Bible, as is done in the Base Christian Communities, that confirmed for the slaves the divine affirmation of equality among human persons despite color of skin or place of birth; hence their understanding of structural salvation. It provided the rationale for decision to withhold their labor even though they may have realized that it would lead to much violence. Which fact points to both the revolutionary aspect of liberation and the Biblical influence not only of faith but also of faith seeking justice.

Perhaps in these contemporary times, religious camp meetings on plantations may not provide the praxis for macro-structural changes in the Caribbean, but given their achievements in the past, the case may be made for the use of their basic design in some modern organizations for today's liberation praxis. The fact is that whatever organizations there may be, for this purpose they must form the link and drive between theory and "rank and file" participation in Caribbean theology. Here then are two ways in which an agency for praxis may be developed.

1. When the attempt at a West Indian Federation failed, there were those who concluded that the chief reason for the failure was that the Federation was a body that tried to come into being without a soul. Another interesting position on the contemporary efforts toward a Caribbean Common Market (CARICOM) is that the Caribbean Conference of Churches should function as the soul of CARICOM. Such a role is absolutely conceivable and ways and means to fulfill that role are too numerous. To take just one, the Caribbean Conference of Churches could organize the faith and praxis "think tanks" that could provide not only the sense of direction for the leadership of the Territories but also, education for the "grass roots" of society; education on what the leadership is doing, why, and whether there are alternatives; education on lifestyles and the conscious choices against the individualism that controls global interests today. That kind of education puts theory to practice and therefore provides Caribbean theology with its functional praxis.

2. Theological colleges, particularly the United Theological College of the West Indies, could develop a kind of strategy for education where Caribbean theology becomes the "leaven in the lump." Because the United Theological College of the West Indies serves so many areas of the wider Caribbean it stands to play a greater role in the area of leadership formation. Conscious of its importance in the self-actualization of the region, theological training should utilize Caribbean perspectives to the extent that ministers who are educated to their worth, instead of just being "pulpit stars" will become catalysts for the self-actualization process among the people they serve. Their understood role ought to be providing clear direction to the point at which the justice that God demands is transferred to the hurting, to repair the damage.

Notes

1 Barth, Karl, *The Word of God and the Word of Man*, New York, Harper and Row Publishers, 1957, pp 19-21.

2 Collins, Sheila D., "Feminist Theology at The Crossroads, "*Christianity and Crisis*, Vol. 41, No. 20, December 14, 1981.

3 Coe, Shoki, "Contextualizing Theology, "eds. Gerald H. Anderson and Thomas F. Stransky, C.S.P., *Mission Trends No. 3: Third World Theologies*, New York, Paulist Press, 1978, p. 20f.

4 Watty, William, *From Shore to Shore*, Kingston, Jamaica, West Indies, Cedar Press, 1981, p. 73.

5 Erskine, Noel Leo, *Decolonizing Theology: A Caribbean Perspective*, Maryknoll, New York, Orbis, 1981, p. 97.

6 Sitahal, Harold, "Re-Thinking Mission for the Caribbean," ed. Hamid, Idris, *Out of the Depths*, Trinidad, W.I., St. Andrew's Theological College, 1977, p. 29.

7 Erskine, Noel Leo, *Decolonizing Theology: A Caribbean Perspective*, Maryknoll, New York, Orbis, 1981, p. 71.

8 Ibid. p. 70ff.

9 McNeill, George, *The Story of our Mission in the West Indies*, Edinburgh, The Foreign Mission Committee of the United Free Church of Scotland, 1911, p. 43.

10 Davis, Edmund, *Roots and Blossoms*, Barbados, Cedar Press, 1977, p.111.

11 Ibid. p. 115.

12 Byfield, Bevis B. "Transformation and the Jamaican Society, "*Caribbean Journal of Religious Studies*, Vol. 5. No. 1, April 1983, p. 35.

13 Henry, Frances, "Religion and Ideology in Trinidad: The Resurgence of Shango Religion, "*Caribbean Quarterly*, Vol. 29. Nos. 3 & 4. Sept-Dec,1983, p. 63f.

14 Talbot, Sylvia Ross, "Contemporary Issues in the Ordination of Women in the Caribbean," *Caribbean Journal of Religious Studies*, Vol. 2, No. 2, September 1979, p. 17.

15 Ibid. p. 17.

16 Ibid. pp. 8-24.

17 McKenzie, Azariah, "Contemporary Issues in the Ordination of Women in the Caribbean: A Reaction," *Caribbean Journal of Religious Studies*, Vol. 1, No. 2, September 1979, p. 25.

18 Ibid. p. 26.

19 Ibid. p. 26.

20 Ibid. p. 27.

21 Ibid. p. 26.

22 Ibid. p. 27.

23 O'Connor, Kathleen, "Economic Options," an oral response to Ulrich Duchrow's lecture "East Asia and Economic Options," at the *Theology in Global Context Conference* 10/27/88, Princeton.

Epilogue

One of the more profound questions concerning indigenization in Caribbean theology is how the process is activated and executed. From the beginning there has to be a key to the understanding of the process of indigenization. The key in this case may be applied in the threefold hermeneutical principle of "the then," "the now" and "the always."

"The Then"

It is more than difficult to unlearn in a moment, centuries of colonial religiosity even if everything about the missionary church were bad. Indigenization in the broadest sense is re-interpretation of the Christian faith for and within the reality of the Caribbean situation. This means that the process must re-examine the legacy of centuries of religious and political domination.

It would seem an impossibility if all the zeal that went into the missionary venture did not carry some cultural baggage as it went from Europe to the West Indies. However, any perspective, including Christianity, that does not take seriously where people are, even if it calls itself Christian is guilty of imperialism. When it is suggested that theology has to be done anew for each generation, the statement addresses not only time but geography and situations. The gravity of the Caribbean situation is heightened when it is realized that the missionaries did not merely preach through their own culture, but took it as a matter of course that their culture was the norm. Thus they made local religious experiences insignificant and inauthentic.

Once the European culture became so interpreted as the norm the missionary process itself forced the judgment of inferiority upon the host culture. The host culture itself has not remained unaffected. In the interplay between culture and religion, evangelization in the Caribbean became synonymous with acculturation. Furthermore, with the protracted psychological pressure upon the host culture it transferred hatred toward itself and became its own worst enemy. Thus within colonialism there developed a type of neo-colonialism whereby those of the host culture who felt that they had experienced assimilation into the European cultural patterns became instruments of oppression against those who did not seem so assimilated.

Since religion and culture were already intermingled within the missionary venture, the missionary church in the Caribbean has always supported not only its cultural roots but also those who, because of their cultural and class assimilation, feel kinship toward the missionary venture itself. It goes without saying then that the missionary church has supported the colonial structures as it has been supported by them.

With all this in view it is not difficult to conclude that a primary part of the process of indigenization of theology in the Caribbean is both to demythologize the cultural impositions and to engage in a reinterpretation of indigenous cultural patterns.

"The Now"

For all the thoughtful Caribbean people who have understood the need for self-determination, the word "new" has become a most pregnant term. For example, when they make reference to a "new people" they mean people who are ready for new ways of thinking. They mean that the people of the Caribbean who have long been under colonial rule are rethinking their position as to the relevance of their heritage and self worth.

Theology itself must address the reality of "the now." However, Caribbean theology by its very delineation carries the connotation of "newness" which is both daring and suspect. It must therefore anticipate criticism by those who will label it untraditional provincialism.

In any case, no matter how difficult it may be to unlearn centuries of colonialism and missionary religiosity, indigenous theology has to be more than a "warmed over" European perspective. It must entail a radical transformation that is a new and different perspective, a completely Caribbean perspective.

"The Always"

The idea of the always has to be seen here in terms of the universal. However, the idea of the universal comes with its own problems because universal speaks of consensus. For the same reason that makes it difficult to determine the boundaries of the Caribbean, a single theological perspective for the Caribbean is equally difficult. The difficulty does not lie simply in the backgrounds of the territories, because regardless of the language in which each territory was colonized they share a common history of colonization and slavery. They also suffer the North/South division of neo-colonialist economics. The problem has to do with not only the authority of spokespersons, but also the uniformity of speech, given the diversity in socio-economic and political awareness in the Caribbean.

Cuba claims over 30 years experience and maturity in revolutionary politics for libera-tion. The Cayman Islands recently refused to have the United Nations ask for its independence from England. Puerto Rico is dead-locked in ambivalence between independence and United States statehood. Jamaica, spurning the radicalism of Michael Manley, under Seaga's leadership agreed with Dominica to join forces with the United States to eradicate Grenada's experiment with radical politics. Then it rejected Seaga's initiative for Manley's struggle with the I.M.F. to produce illusive capital. Yet there can be unity without uniformity. For example, there is a commonality at the base that makes it possible for the feminine, Black, Latin American, Asian, and African perspectives to relate to one another. That commonality is the fact of oppression. The same is true of the territories of the Caribbean. A part of the Caribbean consensus is the fact of oppression that is the unifying factor among the Caribbean voices. Hence some relevance of the Caribbean perspective must be viewed through the possibility of a commonality in liberation thoughts and struggles. In other words, Caribbean theology has to be liberation theology and the physical base at which that theology is interpreted is the Caribbean Conference of Churches.

The Caribbean Conference of Churches does not include every religious denomination within the Caribbean, but its relation to each territorial Council of Churches allows more unity of speech than is otherwise possible. Furthermore, it demonstrates more objectivity than the "pie in the sky" approach of the conservative bodies who stay opposed to it.

In the final analysis it is the task of indigenous theology to attempt the creation of a mindset in the local people toward liberation. Furthermore, the indigenous perspective is also responsible for addressing the system responsible for the plight of the Caribbean people, suggesting in unmistakable terms what the remedy ought to be. This means that it does not only identify the enemy but also declares to the enemy that it has been identified and demands that there be reform.

Bibliography

Alphonse, Ephraim S. *God on the Bridge.* Bridgetown, Barbados. W.I.: Cedar Press, 1975.

Arce, Sergio and Marichal, Oden. *Evangelization and Politics.* New York: Circus, Inc., 1982.

Arce-Martinez, Sergio. "Que es el Hombre?" in *The Caribbean Pulpit.* eds. C.H. Gayle and W.W. Watty: Kingston, 1983.

Arce, Sergio. *The Church and Socialism: Reflections From a Cuban Context.* New York: Circus Publications, 1985.

Augustus, Earl, Julian, Fr. Terry and Graham, Roland, eds. *Issues in Caribbean Theology.* Port of Spain, Trini-dad: Antilles Pastoral Institute. 1972.

Barrett, Leonard E. *Soul Force.* New York: Anchor Press/Doubleday, 1974.

Bisnauth, Dale A. "Religious Pluralism and Development in the Caribbean." *Caribbean Journal of Religious Studies,* vol.4. No. 2. September 1982.

Booth, Ernest. *The Cross in the Sugar Field.* Holborn Hall, E.C.I.: Cargara Press, n.d.

Byfield, Bevis B. "Transformation and the Jamaican Society." *Caribbean Journal of Religious* Studies. vol. 5. No. 1. April 1983.

CADEC. *Action for Community in the Caribbean.* (A Report on a Survey by Idris Hamid on the consultation held in St. Lucia, December 14-16,1972, on People's Participation in Rural Development in the Caribbean) Barbados: Island Press, 1972.

———. *Called to Be.* (Report of the Caribbean Ecumenical Consultation for Development, held in Trinidad, November 15-22, 1971.) Bridgetown: Barbados, 1972.

———. "Caribbean Unity: Christian Unity." (The Resolutions of the Caribbean Ecumenical Consultation for Development) Barbados. n.d.

———. "Caribbean Conference of Churches." *Peace: A Challenge to the Caribbean.* Barbados: Cedar Press, 1982.

———. "Caribbean Ecumenical Programme." *Towards A Caribbean Theology.* Trinidad: Vanguard Publishing Co., Ltd., 1981.

Carew, Jan. "The Origin of Racism in the Americas." ed. John Hearne. *Carifesta Forum: An Anthology of Twenty Caribbean Voices.* Jamaica, W.I. Institute of Jamaica and Jamaica Journal, 1976.

Chevannes, Barry. "Some Notes on African Religious Survivals in the Caribbean." *Caribbean Journal of Religious Studies.* vol. 5. No. 2. September 1983.

Chinula, Donald M. "Jamaican Exocentrism: Its Implications for a Pan-African Theology of National Redemption." *Caribbean Journal of Religious Studies.* vol. 6. No. 1. April 1985.

Cockburn, Michael. "Role of West Indian Schools of Theology." *Caribbean Contact.* vol 4. No. 8. November 1976.

Cracknell, Basil E. *The West Indians.* Kingston, Jamaica W.I.: Kingston Publishers, 1974.

Davis, Edmund. *Roots and Blossoms.* Bridgetown, Barbados: Cedar Press, 1977.

———. "Contextualization as a Dynamic Process of Theological Education." *Caribbean Journal of Religious Studies.* vol. 2. No. 2. September 1979.

———. "Social and Spiritual Implicatons of a Theology of Liberation." *Caribbean Journal of Religious Studies.* vol. 5. No. 1. April 1983.

Davis, Kortright. *Mission for Caribbean Change: Caribbean Development as Theological Enterprise.* Frankfurt. Main, Berlin. Verlag Lang GMBH, 1982.

———. ed. *Moving into Freedom.* "Working Together with Christ." Series No. 2. The Second C.C.C. Assembly, Guyana. 1977. Barbados" Cedar Press, 1977.

———. *Voices of Change from CADEC.* Antigua: CADEC,1973.

———. "Caribbean Basin Initiatives in Theology." *The Journal of Religious Thought.* vol. 40. No.2. 1983-84.

———. "Caribbean Emancipation and The Christian Gospel." *Caribbean Contact.* vol. 12. No. 3. August 1984.

———. *Foretastes of Emancipation in Third World Religion.* S.I. Caribbean Group for Social and Religious Studies, 1983. (CGSRS No.3)

De Las Casas, Bartolome. *The Devastation of the Indians: A Brief Account.* trans. Hermia Briffault. New York: Seabury Press, 1974.

de Pestre, Rene. "Problems of Identity for the Black Man in the Caribbean." ed. John Hearne. *Carifesta Forum: An Anthology of Twenty Caribbean Voices.* Jamaica, W.I.: Institute of Jamaica and Jamaica Journal, 1976.

Demas. William G. *Change and Renewal in the Caribbean.* No. 2 in the series "Challenges in the New Caribbean." ed. by David I. Mitchell. Barbados: Cedar Press, 1975.

————. *The Economics of Development in Small Countries with Special Reference to the Caribbean.* Montreal: McGill University Press, 1970.

————. *West Indian Nationhood and Caribbean Integration.* No. 1 in the Series "Challenges in the New Caribbean. ed. David Mitchell, Barbados: Cedar Press, 1975.

DeVerteuil, Michael. "A Spirituality for the Caribbean Today." *Caribbean Contact.* vol. 4. No. 10. January 1977.

Didier, Atherton. "What is the Mission of the Church?" *The Caribbean Pulpit.* eds. C.H. Gayle and W.W. Watty. Kingston, Jamaica. 1983.

Eaton, Wade. *Towards a Theological Understanding of Development: An Approach to Doing Theology.* Paper presented at the Caribbean Theology and Development Issues in Think Tank Consultation. Barbados: CADEC, 1981.

EPICA Task Force. *Grenada The Peaceful Revolution.* Washington, D.C.: Epica, 1982.

————. *Puerto Rico: A People Challenging Colonialism.* Washington, D.C.: Epica, 1976.

Erskine, Noel Leo. *Decolonizing Theology: A Caribbean Perspective.* Maryknoll, New York: Orbis, 1981.

Friday, Michael. "A Comparison of 'DHARMA' and 'DREAD' as Determinants of Ethical Standards." *Caribbean Journal of Religious Studies.* vol. 5. No. 2. September 1983.

Garvey, Ames Jacques. *Philosophy and Opinions of Marcus Garvey.* New York: Athenuem, 1974.

Gayle, Clement. "The Church in the West Indies: Bondage and Freedom." *Caribbean Journal of Religious Studies.* vol. 3. No. 1. April 1980.

Gomes, P.I. ed. *Come Let Us Reason.* Trinidad: Caribbean Conference of Churches, 1975.

Goodridge, Sehon. "How to Educate the Clergy." *Caribbean Contact.* vol. 8. No. 8. December 1984.

——. "Reasoning Together." *Caribbean Contact.* vol. 12. No. 1. June 1984.

——. "The Way of the Cross." *Caribbean Contact.* vol. 12. No. 2. September 1984.

——. *The Church Amidst Politics and Revolution.* Barbados: Cedar Press, 1977.

——. "The Domestication of Theology." *Caribbean Journal of Religious Studies.* vol. 1. No. 2. July 1976.

——. *Politics and the Caribbean Church: A Confesson of Guilt.* Barbados: CADEC, 1971.

Gordon, Ernle. "Christianity: A Religion of the Poor." *Caribbean Contact.* vol. 12. No. 4. September 1983.

——. "Evangelization and Politics: A British Caribbean Perspective," eds. Sergio Arce and Oden Marichal. *Evangelization and Politics.* New York: Circus Inc., 1982.

Goulet, Denis. *The New Moral Order.* New York, Orbis, 1974.

——, *The Cruel Choice.* New York: Atheneum, 1975.

Grenado, Gerrard. "Towards Caribbean Theology." *Caribbean Contact.* vol. 10. No. 12.

Guillen, Nicholas. "National Identity and Mestizaje." ed. John Hearne. *Carifesta Forum: An Anthology of Twenty Caribbean Voices.* Jamaica. W.I.: Institute of Jamaica and Jamaica Journal, 1976.

Hamid, Idris. *In Search of New Perspectives.* Paper presented at the Caribbean Ecumenical Consultation for Development, Trinidad. Nov. 15-20, 1971. Barbados: CADEC, 1971.

——. ed. *Troubling of the Waters.* San Fernando, Trinidad: Rahaman Printery, Ltd. 1973.

——, ed. *Out of the Depths.* San Fernando, Trinidad: St. Andrew's Theological College, Ltd., 1977.

——. "The Teaching of Theology." *Caribbean Contact.* vol. 7. No. 3. July 1979.

——. *Theological Options for Christianity.* By Idris Hamid, George Mulrain, Sehon Goodridge and Kortright Davis. S.I. Caribbean Group for Social and Religious Studies, 1983 (SGSRS No. 1, 1983).

——. *A History of the Presbyterian Church in Trinidad 1868-1968.* Trinidad, West Indies: Rahaman Printery, Ltd. 1980.

Hawkins, Irene. *The Changing Face of the Caribbean.* Barbados: Cedar Press, 1976.

——. "Education and its Imbalances." ed. David I. Mitchell. *New Mission for a New People: Voices From the Caribbean.* U.S.A.: Friendship Press, 1977.

Henry, Frances. "Religion and Ideology in Trinidad: The Resurgence of Shango Religion." *Caribbean Quarterly.* vol. 29. Nos. 3 & 4. Sept-Dec., 1983.

Holder, John. *Christian Commitment. A Collection of Devotional Bible Studies for Today's Christian.* Barbados. C.C.C. Church and Society Unit, 1985.

Jagan, Cheddi. *The West On Trial. The Fight for Guyana's Freedom.* Berlin: Seven Seas, 1966.

James, Michael. "Challenges to Caribbean Theology." *Caribbean Contact.* vol. II. No. II. April 1984.

Jellyman, David. "Protest, Pattern and Power: An Interpretation of Christian Faith and Action." *Caribbean Journal of Religious Studies.* vol. 1. No. 2. July 1976.

———. "To Caesar and to God—The Christian and the State." *Caribbean Journal of Religious Studies*. vol. 5. No. 1. April 1983.

Julien, Terry. "Christian Mission, Cultural Tradition and Environment." ed. Idris Hamid. *Out of the Depths*. Trinidad, West Indies: St. Andrews Theological College, 1977.

Kadless, Fr. Bernard. "Our Duty is to Help." *Caribbean Contact*. vol. 4. No. 4. July 1976.

King, Leo J. "Gegevens Betreffende Surinam." *With Eyes Wide Open*. ed. David I. Mitchell. Jamaica: CADEC, 1973.

Kirton, Allan. "An Option for Caribbean's Poor." *Caribbean Contact*. vol. II. No. 17. November 1984.

———. "From the General Secretary's Desk: Christianity and Popular Religion." *Caribbean Contact*. vol. II. No. 10. March 1984.

———. "From the General Secretary's Desk: Living the Easter Faith. Doing a Theology of Hope in the Caribbean." *Caribbean Contact*. vol. II. No. II. April 1984.

———. "From the General Secretary's Desk: Not to Speak is to Speak." *Caribbean Contact*. vol. II. No. II April 1984.

———. "From the General Secretary's Desk: A Theology to serve the Powerless." Caribbean Contact. vol. 12. No. 5. October 1984.

Lett, Leslie. "Church's Mission in Uniting Working People." *Caribbean Contact*. vol. 9. No. 4. August 1981.

———. "Development and Christian Liberation." *Caribbean Contact*. vol. II. No. 5. September 1983.

———. *Grenada: A Challenge to Caribbean Theology*. Barbados: Caribbean Conference of Churches, 1984.

——. "Third World Theology: Why it is Political." *Caribbean Contact*. vol. II. No. 10. March 1984.

——. "Theology of Development." *Caribbean Contact*. vol. 8. No. 8. December 1980.

——. "Theology and Politics: Part I." *Caribbean Contact*. vol. 8. No. 6. October 1980.

——. "Theology and Politics: Part II." *Caribbean Contact*. vol. 8. No. 8 December 1980.

——. *Social Experience as a New Hermeneutic of the Scriptures: Cultural Re-Interpretation of the Gospel.* Paper presented at the Conference on Missiology sponsored by the Caribbean Conference of Churches, Antigua. May 12-14, 1975.

Lewis, Gordon K. *Main Currents in Caribbean Thought*. Baltimore: The John's Hopkins University Press, 1983.

Lewis, Vaughn A. ed. *Size, Self Determination and Internationl Relations: The Caribbean*. Kingston, Jamaica: University of the West Indies,1976.

Manley, Michael. *The Politics of Change*. London: Andre Deutsch Ltd., 1975.

——. *The Search for Solutions*. Canada: Maple House Publishing Co., 1976.

——. *Jamaica: The Struggle in the Periphery*. London: Third World Media Ltd. in Association with Writers and Readers Publishing Coop. Society Ltd. n.d.

——, *Up the Down Escalator*. London: Andre Deutsch Limited, 1987.

McCormack, Michael. *Liberation or Development: The role of the Church in the New Caribbean*. Paper presented at the Caribbean Ecumenical Consultation for Development held in Trinidad. November 15-22, 1971. Barbados: CADEC, 1971 (Paper No. 5).

McKenzie, Azariah. "Contemporary Issues in the Ordination of Women in the Caribbean: A Reaction." *Caribbean Journal of Religious Studies.* vol. 1. No. 2. September 1979.

McNeill, George. *The Story of our Mission in the West Indies.* Edinburgh, Scotland: The Foreign Mission Committee of the Free Church of Scotland. 1911.

Mintz, Sidney W. *Caribbean Transformations.* Baltimore: The Johns Hopkins University Press, 1974.

Mitchell, David I. ed. *With Eyes Wide Open: A Collection of Papers by Caribbean Scholars on Caribbean Concerns.* Jamaica: CADEC, 1973.

——. "Haiti." ed. David I. Mitchell. *New Mission for a New People.* U.S.A.: Friendship Press, Inc., 1977.

——. *Some Elements in a Theology of Development.* Paper presented at the Caribbean Theology and Development Issues in the 1980 Think Tank Consultation. Barbados: CADEC, 1981.

——. "An Open Letter to Jose Miguez Bonino." eds. Gerald H. Anderson and Thomas F. Stransky, C.S.P. *Mission Trends No 4. Liberation Theologies.* New York: Paulist Press, 1979.

Moravian Church of the Redeemer, North Street, Kingston, Jamaica. *The Cross, the Sword and the Machete.* Kingston, Jamaica: Art Printery. n.d.

Mulrain, George MacDonald. *Theology in Folk Culture: the Theological Significance of Haitian Folk Religion.* Frankfurt: Verlag Peter Lang, 1984.

Neehall, Roy G. "Testimonio Y. Mision de la Iglesia Christiana En El Desarrollo del Caribe." in *With Eyes Wide Open.* ed. David I. Mitchell. Jamaica: CADEC, 1973.

——. "Christian Witness and Mission in the Caribbean Development." ed. David I. Mitchell. *With Eyes Wide Open.* Jamaica, W.I.: Christian Action and Development in the Caribbean (CADEC), 1973.

——. "Revolution with a Difference." *Caribbean Contact.* vol. 8. No. 12 April 1981.

Nettleford, Rex M. *Mirror Mirror.* Jamaica: William Collins and Sangster (Jamaica) Ltd., 1969.

——. *Caribbean Cultural Identity.* Kingston, Jamaica: Institute of Jamaica, 1978.

Niles, H. Clifton. "The Functions of the Ministry." *Caribbean Journal of Religious Studies.* vol. 4. No. 2. September 1982.

Owens, Joseph. *Dread: The Rastafarians of Jamaica.* Kingston, Jamaica: Sangster's Book Stores, Ltd., 1976.

Payne, Clifford F. "What Will A Caribbean Christ Look Like? A Preface to Caribbean Christology." ed. Idris Hamid. *Out of the Depths.* Trinidad, West Indies: St. Andrews Theological College, 1977.

Peenie Wallie, vol. 1 No. 1. Jamaica, 1973.

Reid, Alfred C. "Truth and Liberation." *Caribbean Journal of Religious Studies.* vol. 2. No. 1. April 1979.

Rivera, Luis N. "The Mission of the Church and the Development of a Caribbean Theology of Liberation." ed. Idris Hamid. *Out of the Depths.* Trinidad, West Indies: St. Andrews College, 1977.

Rocourt, Alain. "The Challenge of Development in Haiti." *With Eyes Wide Open.* ed. David I. Mitchell. Jamaica, West Indies: Christian Action for Development in the Caribbean (CADEC), 1973.

Russell, Horace. "The Emergence of the Christian Black Concept." *Caribbean Journal of Religious Studies*. vol. 2. No. 1. April 1979.

———. "The Challenge of Theological Reflection in the Caribbean Today." *Troubling of the Waters*. ed. Idris Hamid. Trinidad, W.I.: Rahaman Printery Limited, 1973.

Sitahal, Harold. *The Church and Agrarian Reform in the Caribbean*. Barbados: CADEC, 1972.

———. "Re-thinking Mission for the Caribbean." ed. Idris Hamid. *Out of the Depths*. Trinidad, W.I.: St. Andrews Theological College, 1977.

Sitomer, Curtis. "Scholars Differ on Vatican's Stand on Liberation Theology." *Caribbean Contact*. vol. 12. No. 7, December 1984.

Sklar, Holly. "Trilateralism: Managing Dependence and Democracy." ed. Holly Sklar. *Trilateralism*. Boston: South End Press, 1980.

Smith, Ashley and Deverteuil, Michael. *Renewal and Ecumenism in the Caribbean*. Barbados: CADEC, 1971.

Smith, Ashley. "Challenges of the Rural Church." *Caribbean Journal of Religious Studies*. vol. 2. No. 1. July 1976.

———. "The Christian Minister as a Political Activist." *Caribbean Journal of Religious Studies*. vol. 1. No. 1. April 1979.

———. *Real Roots and Potted Plants: Reflections on the Caribbean Church*. Mandeville, Jamaica: Mandeville Publishers, 1984.

Smith, M.G. *Culture, Race, and Class: In the Commonwealth Caribbean*. Kingston, Jamaica: University of the West Indies, 1984.

Sunshine, Catherine A. ed. *The Caribbean: Survival, Struggle and Sovereignty.* Washington, E.D.: EPICA, 1983.

Talbott, Sylvia Ross. "Contemporary Issues in the Ordination of Women in the Caribbean." *Caribbean Journal of Religious Studies.* vol. 2. No. 2. September 1979.

Taylor, Burchell K. "Caribbean Theology." *Caribbean Journal of Religious Studies.* vol. 3. No. 2. September 1980.

———. "Towards a Theology of Development. Part I. *"Caribbean Contact.* vol. 8. No. 7. November 1980.

———. "The Babylonish Captivity of the Church in the Caribbean." *Caribbean Journal of Religious Studies.* vol. 4. No. 1. April 1982.

Turner, Mary. *Slaves and Missionaries. The Disintegration of Jamaican Slave Society, 1787-1834.* Illinois: University of Illinois Press, 1982.

Vincent, Theodora G. *Black Power and the Garvey Movement.* San Francisco: Ramparts Press, 1972.

Watty William. *From Shore to Shore.* Kingston, Jamaica and Barbados: Cedar Press, 1981.

———. "The Gospel and the Crisis." *Caribbean Journal of Religious Studies.* vol. 3. No. 1. April 1980.

———. "Struggling to Be." David I. Mitchell. *New Mission for a New People.* U.S.A.: Friendship Press, 1977.

———. "Liberation-Popular as Calypso and Rumpunch but Caribbean People Less Free." *Caribbean Contact.* vol. 4. No. 6. September 1976.

———. "The De-Colonization of Theology." ed. Idris Hamid. *Troubling of the Waters.* Trinidad. W.I.: Rahaman Printery Limited, 1973.

——. "Christianity and Socialism—Socialists Swearing on the Bible." *Caribbean Contact*. vol. 4. No. 12. March 1971.

Watty, W.W. and Gayle, C.H.L. *The Caribbean Pulpit*. Kingston, Jamaica and Barbados: Cedar Press, 1983.

Williams, Eric. *Columbus to Castro*. London: Andre Deutsch, 1969.

Williams, Geoffrey B. S.J. "Classicism and the Caribbean Church." ed. Idris Hamid. *Out of the Depths*. Trinidad, W.I.: St. Andrews Theological College, 1977.

Research in Religion and Family
BLACK PERSPECTIVES

This series aims to provide a framework and opportunity for original research that explores both the ground and the goals of family and religion in the black tradition. Monographs in the series will examine the ways in which kinship networks were formed and maintained, how the community raised and socialized children, how they carved out a religion and fashioned a rich and expressive culture that reflected their uninhibited imagination and provided a means to articulate their hopes and hurts, their dreams and doubts.

Research will not only focus on the past and present, but will also look at the adequacy of current models of family and religion to take the black community into the twenty-first century.

The series editor is: Noel Leo Erskine
                               Candler School of Theology
                               Emory University
                               Atlanta, GA 30322

To order other books in this series, please contact our Customer Service Department:

                               (800) 770-LANG (within the U.S.)
                               (212) 647-7706 (outside the U.S.)
                               (212) 647-7707 FAX

Or browse online by series:

                               www.peterlangusa.com